Hél

D1610000

transitions

General Editor: Julian Wolfreys

Published titles
BATAILLE   Fred Botting and Scott Wilson
NEW HISTORICISM AND CULTURAL MATERIALISM   John Brannigan
HÉLÈNE CIXOUS   Abigail Bray
GENDER   Claire Colebrook
POSTMODERN NARRATIVE THEORY   Mark Currie
FORMALIST CRITICISM AND READER-RESPONSE THEORY   Todd F. Davis and Kenneth
    Womack
IDEOLOGY   James M. Decker
QUEER THEORIES   Donald E. Hall
MARXIST LITERARY AND CULTURAL THEORIES   Moyra Haslett
LOUIS ALTHUSSER   Warren Montag
RACE   Brian Niro
JACQUES LACAN   Jean-Michel Rabaté
LITERARY FEMINISMS   Ruth Robbins
DECONSTRUCTION • DERRIDA   Julian Wolfreys

ORWELL TO THE PRESENT: LITERATURE IN ENGLAND, 1945–2000   John Brannigan
CHAUCER TO SHAKESPEARE, 1337–1580   SunHee Kim Gertz
MODERNISM, 1910–1945   Jane Goldman
POPE TO BURNEY, 1714–1779   Moyra Haslett
PATER TO FORSTER, 1873–1924   Ruth Robbins
BURKE TO BYRON, BARBAULD TO BAILLIE, 1790–1830   Jane Stabler
MILTON TO POPE, 1650–1720   Kay Gilliland Stevenson
SIDNEY TO MILTON, 1580–1660   Marion Wynne-Davis

Forthcoming titles
TERRY EAGLETON   David Alderson
JULIA KRISTEVA AND LITERARY THEORY   Megan Becker-Leckrone
NATIONAL IDENTITY   John Brannigan
HOMI BHABHA   Eleanor Byrne
POSTMODERNISM • POSTMODERNITY   Martin McQuillan
ROLAND BARTHES   Martin McQuillan
MODERNITY   David Punter
PSYCHOANALYSIS AND LITERATURE   Nicholas Rand
SUBJECTIVITY   Ruth Robbins
POSTCOLONIAL THEORY   Malini Johan Schueller
TRANSGRESSION   Julian Wolfreys

DICKENS TO HARDY, 1837–1884   Julian Wolfreys

---

transitions Series
Series Standing Order
ISBN 0–333–73684–6
(outside North America only)

You can receive future titles in this series as they are published by placing a standing order.
Please contact your bookseller or, in case of difficulty, write to us at the address below with your
name and address, the title of the series and the ISBN quoted above.

Customer Services Department, Macmillan Distribution Ltd
Houndmills, Basingstoke, Hampshire RG21 6XS, England

---

transitions

Hélène Cixous
Writing and Sexual Difference

Abigail Bray

First published 2004 by
PALGRAVE MACMILLAN
Houndmills, Basingstoke, Hampshire RG21 6XS and
175 Fifth Avenue, New York, N.Y. 10010
Companies and representatives throughout the world

PALGRAVE MACMILLAN is the global academic imprint of the Palgrave Macmillan division of St. Martin's Press, LLC and of Palgrave Macmillan Ltd. Macmillan® is a registered trademark in the United States, United Kingdom and other countries. Palgrave is a registered trademark in the European Union and other countries.

ISBN 0–333–92239–5 hardback
ISBN 0–333–92238–7 paperback

This book is printed on paper suitable for recycling and made from fully managed and sustained forest sources.

A catalogue record for this book is available from the British Library.

Library of Congress Cataloging-in-Publication Data

Bray, Abigail, 1966–
      Hélène Cixous: writing and sexual difference/Abigail Bray.
          p. cm.—(Transitions)
      Includes bibliographical references and index.
      ISBN 0-333-92239-5
          1. Cixous, Hâlàne, 1937—Criticism and interpretation. 2. Feminism in literature. 3. Sex role in literature. 4. Feminism and literature—History—20th century. I. Title. II. Transitions (Palgrave Macmillan (Firm))
      PQ2663.I9Z53 2003
      848'.91409—dc22

                                                          2003053673

10   9   8   7   6   5   4   3   2   1
13   12   11   10   09   08   07   06   05   04

Typeset by Cambrian Typesetters, Frimley, Camberley, Surrey
Printed and bound in Great Britain by Creative Print and Design (Wales), Ebbw Vale

For Dylan
for your golden laughter

Contents

General Editor's Preface

Transitions: *transition*—, n. of action. 1. A passing or passage from one condition, action or (rarely) place, to another. 2. Passage in thought, speech, or writing, from one subject to another. 3. **a**. The passing from one note to another. **b**. The passing from one key to another, modulation. 4. The passage from an earlier to a later stage of development or formation . . . change from an earlier style to a later; a style of intermediate or mixed character . . . the historical passage of language from one well-defined stage to another.

The aim of *Transitions* is to explore passages, movements and the development of significant voices in critical thought, as these voices determine and are mediated by acts of literary and cultural interpretation. This series also seeks to examine the possibilities for reading, analysis and other critical engagements which the very idea of transition – such as the transition effected by the reception of a thinker's *oeuvre* and the heritage entailed – makes possible. The writers in this series unfold the movements and modulations of critical thinking over the last generation, from the first emergences of what is now recognized as literary theory. They examine as well how the transitional nature of theoretical and critical thinking is still very much in operation, guaranteed by the hybridity and heterogeneity of the field of literary studies. The authors in the series share the common understanding that, now more than ever, critical thought is both in a state of transition and can best be defined by developing for the student reader an understanding of this protean quality. As this *tranche* of the series, dealing with particular critical voices, addresses, it is of great significance, if not urgency, that the texts of particular figures be reconsidered anew.

This series desires, then, to enable the reader to transform her/his own reading and writing transactions by comprehending past developments as well as the internal transitions worked through by particular literary and cultural critics, analysts, and philosophers. Each book in the series offers a guide to the poetics and politics of such thinkers, as well as interpretative paradigms, schools, bodies of thought, historical and cultural periods, the genealogy of particular concepts, while transforming these, if not into tools or methodologies, then into conduits for directing and channelling thought. As well as transforming the critical past by interpreting it from the perspective of the present day, each study enacts transitional reading of critical voices and well-known literary texts, which are themselves conceivable as having been transitional and influential at the moments of their first appearance. The readings offered in these books seek, through close critical reading and theoretical engagement, to demonstrate certain possibilities in critical thinking to the student reader.

It is hoped that the student will find this series liberating because rigid methodologies are not being put into place. As all the dictionary definitions of the idea of transition above suggest, what is important is the action, the passage: of thought, of analysis, of critical response, such as are to be found, for example, in the texts of critics whose work has irrevocably transformed the critical landscape. Rather than seeking to help you locate yourself in relation to any particular school or discipline, this series aims to put you into action, as readers and writers, travellers between positions, where the movement between poles comes to be seen as of more importance than the locations themselves.

Julian Wolfreys

Acknowledgements

I owe a gratefully acknowledged debt to the kindness, patience and intelligence of my editor Julian Wolfreys.

I am grateful to the Centre for Research on Women for providing me with a publishing grant, and to Peta Bowden of Murdoch University for her support during my position as an Honorary Research Fellow in the School of Arts.

Anth Ginn's energy and integrity will always be a source of inspiration. I am grateful I know him. Tess Williams encouraged me with her courageous affirmation of female creativity in the face of illness.

I want to thank the friends who encouraged me to write through the depths: Elizabeth Reid Boyd, Carol D'Cruz, Erica Freeman, Charity Haynes, Belinda Morrissey, Gordana Nesicsimic and Felicity Walker.

And lastly, I want to thank my scattered but loving family in France, England and Australia: Jody Chettoe, Hugh Chettoe, Ivan Bray, Mischa Bray, Chris Bray, Carla Reid, Luke Reid, Jessica Bray and Grace Bray.

Introduction

> Fortunately, when someone says 'woman,' we still don't know what that means, even if we know what we want to mean. . . . In any case, she is not *a* woman. She is plural. Like all living beings, who are sometimes invaded, drawing life from others, giving life. Who do not know themselves.
>
> Hélène Cixous, 'Tancredi Continues' (1991c)

> The relationship to pleasure and the law, and the individual's response to this strange, antagonistic relationship, inscribe – whether we are men or women – different paths through life. It is not anatomical sex or essence that determines us in anything; it is, on the contrary, the affable from which we never escape, individual and collective history, the cultural schema, and the way the individual negotiates with these structures, with these data, adapts to them and reproduces them, or else gets around them, overcomes them, goes beyond them, gets through them – there are a thousand formulas – and connects or never connects with a universe 'without fear and without reproach'.
>
> Hélène Cixous, 'The Author in Truth' (1991f)

Hélène Cixous is a key thinker within feminist literary theory, politics and philosophy: her work has shaped the cutting-edge questions of post-structuralist literary theory and philosophy and her writing continues to be an important reference for the issues which Western intellectuals have been interrogating since the revolutionary 1960s. Cixous's refusal to conform to the traditional boundaries of academic writing, her championing of a profoundly 'feminine' style of thinking which is both rigorous and intimate, intellectual and defiantly personal, has opened up many creative possibilities for how we think and write about sexual difference, philosophy and literature. Throughout her writing, Cixous challenges the exclusions which inform dominant systems of representation in an attempt to make language circulate more freely, less destructively, more democratically. Cixous's work continually comes back to the importance of grounding knowledge in a humble recognition of the power of the quotidian forces in our lives. In effect this means recognizing the possibility of subverting larger power structures through a revolutionary change on an embodied everyday level.

Cixous was born in 1937 in Algeria to a mother of Austro-German origins and a father of French-colonial and Jewish origins. Like many of us, then, she was born into a mixed and fragile cultural heritage with competing loyalties and affiliations, and complex histories. And like many of us she felt she did not belong, that her place in the world was fragile, on the borders, condemned to an exile never quite understood. This cultural background made her sensitive to the physical dynamics of exclusion and throughout her work the idea of exile, and of the border between the proper and the improper, continue to drive her championing of freedom from oppressive and exclusive forms of naming.

Another gift from her childhood (and it must be understood as a gift) is her early intimacy with death. Her father died when she was a little girl. This early death touched her deeply and it is a death which continues to weep through her writing. The loss of her father was also an initiation into depth and it is through the process of mourning his loss that Cixous has sought a poetic and philosophical intimacy with loss in general. Her writing is preoccupied with death, loss and lack not because she is bound by a fear of the abyss but because through mourning this formative loss she was able to fall through it into a life-affirming writing. Death for her became an initiation into living deeply and thinking down through the depths of the unspoken. Negativity in all its myriad forms, the destruction of others, the dynamics of self-destruction, everything which uses death as an excuse for loss of love, passion, freedom and justice is fought against in Cixous's writing as a limit which must be passed through in order to reach life. Through death, then, Cixous found her will to write and live.

Lacking a home, she sought one in the limitless country of writing, which knows no borders, which welcomes all exiles. One of her first passions was for myth and the works of German Romanticism, which was followed by her interest in English literature. Shakespeare, now so unfashionable, caught her imagination and she continues to find his writing profoundly inspiring. *Antony and*

Cleopatra is one of her favourite plays. This avant-garde writer, then, has her inspiration in the classics. She began her career as an academic when she was twenty-two, then married and bore two children. She divorced in 1965 and moved to Paris, where she entered the intellectual scene with some energy, soon establishing herself as a leading activist and intellectual. She was vocal during the events of May 1968 and afterwards she established the radical and experimental (anti)institution the Université de Paris VIII–Vincennes, which was designed as an alternative to what was thought of by many as the oppressively hierarchical structure of French education. Sometime later, in 1974, she founded the Centre de Recherches en Études féminines. With Tzvetan Todorov and Gerard Genette, around this time she also founded the influential experimental revue *Poetique*, which gained critical recognition in American intellectual circles. Her publications also began in the late 1960s with her doctoral dissertation on James Joyce, and her first novel, *Dedans*, in 1969, which won a prestigious French literary award.

Since then she has written and published an impressive range of writing within many genres. However, she perhaps still remains best known in America and England for her relatively early work in the 1970s on her controversial yet influential concept of *écriture féminine*, or 'writing in the feminine'. Cixous can be understood not simply as the founder of *écriture féminine* but as an 'organic' intellectual, in the sense that she can genuinely think and write in a range of genres about a range of issues. She is also a very avant-garde writer, who can be difficult to read because her poetico-philosophical writing interrogates itself just as much as it interrogates dominant systems of representation. However, what might be perceived to be a rather lofty disdain for the everyday in her writing is strongly undermined once one recognizes that most of her work is about the quotidian, the extraordinary within the ordinary, and the importance of grounding thinking in an attention to the minute and often overlooked gestures embodied in everyday life. Despite what may be read as her rather elite status as a difficult French avant-garde writer, a darling of the exclusive Parisian salons, she writes with an often very raw openness about concerns which touch us all.

Cixous's passion for freedom inspires all of her work; it motivated her initial interest in psychoanalysis and the repression of female sexuality, guided her feminist writing, inspired her writings on the plight of the Third World, and motivated her writing on the Russian and German death camps. Such passions have guided her interest in Clarice Lispector, Nelson Mandela, Paul Celan, Marina Tsvetaeva and Ossip Mandelstam to name a few. On a biographical level, her continuing friendship with Jacques Derrida, and her close relationships with the well-known feminist activist and founder of the Des Femmes publishing house, Antoinette Fouque, and the founder of the experimental Théâtre du Soleil, Ariane Mnouchkine, have all had a profound influence on her life and work. Cixous is clearly an energetic force within the French intellectual scene, her writing has had a major impact on feminist thought in the last three decades and she remains one of the most respected French feminist intellectuals living today. This is reason enough to read her work. To read Cixous is to read one of the most important thinkers of our time and to engage in some of the more important ideas that have shaped intellectual life in recent history. To read Cixous is also to enter into the challenge of thinking through sexual difference not just on a grand poetico-philosophical level but on the level of the everyday, for how we think of ourselves as women and men and how we assume, enact and subvert the roles and languages of sexual difference affects us on that level. For Cixous, change and freedom comes into being at this very intimate everyday level, by unmasking and interrogating the language we use to speak through sexual difference.

One of the most powerful and provocative categories of analysis to have emerged within critical thinking in the last few decades is sexual difference. The question of sexual difference, largely circulated by feminism, has haunted a diverse range of discourses and critical practices, from cultural studies to philosophy, from literary theory to sociology, producing a plethora of popular and specialized debates. That the question of sexual difference has generated such a diverse range of writing on the subject, that sexual difference is largely understood to be integral to all cultural practices and all forms of knowledge production, indicates the importance of continuing to think through the relationship between it and writing. How we perform or write sexual difference affects us on a personal and a political level. Neo-evolutionary discourses about the genetic destiny of men and women, as well as government policies which affect families, are all ways of writing about sexual difference which impact on the way we perform our sexual identity in the world. In other words, sexual difference is not simply a rarefied, disembodied term which circulates within theory or philosophy, for how one's sexuality is read by the world and how one writes one's sexuality impacts on the way one lives, works and thinks. How we understand sexual difference affects the choices we make in life and the choices which are made available to us.

Cixous's contribution to the question of sexual difference is, perhaps quite simply, that it must remain a question – that answering finally and forever just what sexual difference is, is to limit our democratic freedom. By calling attention to the importance of keeping alive the question of sexual difference she is not advocating hedonism, a lawless libertarian indulgence, or an ethical relativism. Rather, Cixous argues that if we define what it means to be a man or a woman we risk a fundamentalist orthodoxy about sexual difference which limits rather than liberates our understanding of what it means to be human. As history has shown, definitions of what female sexual identity is has often led to a reduction in women's democratic rights. To argue that we have now escaped the clutches of an oppressive past, that somehow we are more democratic and more enlightened simply because time has passed, is to retain a rather naïve faith in a linear narrative of historical progress. New limitations of what it means to be a sexed being are now facing new subjects, while some of the older limitations are still very much in place.

While Cixous does not directly deal with the socio-economic problems associated with fixed definitions of what it means to be a sexed being, she offers a way of opening up the question of sexual difference to thought, so that such problems can be challenged. By this I do not mean that Cixous is offering a blueprint for social change or a prescriptive politics – she has no global answers because such answers are for her the very problem she seeks to overcome in her writing. (In this respect her work should be distinguished from Luce Irigaray's later work, which has tended to formulate rather dogmatic cultural and political interventions.) Instead of searching in Cixous's writing for a consistent politics of intervention or an easily applicable theory of sexual difference, it is more productive to approach her writing as a guide to thinking. For Cixous, the question of sexual difference is inseparable from thought itself, from the process of cognition, consciousness or the creation of meaning. To think through the question of sexual difference is also, therefore, to enter into the process of thinking. This does not mean that Cixous is arguing that thinking about sexual difference is the only way of thinking, but rather that sexual difference presents us with an opening up into thinking because thought is a process through which we explore the relationship between self and other, identity and difference, and that relationship is primarily one which is represented as sexual difference.

However, if sexual difference is recognized as a primary difference it does not mean that all other differences are read as an effect of sexual difference. Cixous would not argue, for example, that sexual inequality is the grounds for all other racial or economic inequalities – she is not a radical feminist. Rather, she would argue that the violence which results in a devaluing of a particular sexed being is part of a larger violence in which difference is ordered and valued. It is this larger violence which Cixous writes against, for while she obviously writes a great deal about sexual difference, she does so in order to explore the force of violence in general, in order to move towards a more democratic, less destructive thinking.

On one level Cixous is a writer of simple wisdom, she argues that it is fear which endows power with the ability to oppress, that the spectre of our own death prevents us from living, that hatred tortures the one who hates, that love is infinitely mysterious. She is also an intimate writer, or a writer of intimacies, and some have found this close, slow attention to detail, this elaborate exploration of subjectivity, to be a mannered posturing before the altar of the Self. And yet, her attention to intimacy with the other, and the other within the self, the not-self, is not so much a weak narcissistic retreat but a courageous confrontation with the writing, the textuality, of subjectivity. Self-serving piety towards the other, gratuitous sentiments, indulgent retreats into the already written, the already known, a passive acceptance of sexual destiny, fear before the Law, are all ways of thinking and relating which Cixous fiercely challenges as practices which support oppression. In this respect she is a hard thinker to follow because she is relentless, in the sense that Nietzsche is relentless, in her affirmation of life over death, of courage over fear. To think is to think creatively, argues Cixous, and to think creatively is to have a courageous relationship to difference.

What do we mean by this? To have a courageous relationship to difference, to the other, is to master the fear of the unknown which nourishes destructive thinking. Such a relationship is also a movement towards, a crossing over. As Cixous writes in 'Tancredi Continues': 'Is the crossing vertiginous? Like every crossing. Useless to contemplate or fathom what separates: the abyss is always invented by our fear. We leap and there is grace. Acrobats know: do not look at the separation. Have eyes, have bodies, only for there, for the other' (Cixous 1991c: 79). To enter into a courageous relationship with difference is to take a leap of faith in life and discover grace, to meet the other's body through a fearless movement which recognizes the abyss as merely a spectre. Creative thought is a courageous movement, an acrobatic leap across the vertiginous shadow cast by fear.

This movement occurs within 'writing', which for Cixous is a word that encompasses signification, or the process of making meaning, thinking in general. Dismissing the power of a Cartesian separation between mind and body as a phallocentric fiction, Cixous understands embodied thinking as a form of writing in order to emphasize the productive force of such a thinking. To think is also to write, to create meaning, and that process of production is embodied. The writing which, Cixous argues, performs a creative movement towards difference, which is capable of mastering a fear of the abyss, is feminine because it is productive, generative, radiant with affirmation. Masculine or phallocentric writing is caught up in a reactionary relationship to fear, difference and the other, and remains locked into a destructive repetition of hierarchies. Such a writing remains petrified before the abyss, rigid with fear, and so cannot enter into the acrobatic flight of thinking. In other words, phallocentric writing is a type of *anti-thinking*. Such a thinking would manifest as fundamentalism, as homophobia, economic oppression, sexism, racism, anthropomorphism, all forms of thinking which rest upon a fear-based relationship to difference and the other. Such a writing would lack the necessary courage to challenge the authority of what Cixous terms the 'Logic of Destruction', or a reactionary relationship to fear of the other, and therefore becomes a form of violence. In an ironic sense then, it is phallocentric writing or thinking which *lacks* the necessary strength of courage to overcome fear: rigid strength is revealed to be petrified fear. If the feminine has been associated with lack within psychoanalytic discourses, with absence, the abyss, and endowed with all that is less than the masculine by a plethora of other discourses, Cixous suggests, rather wickedly and with some humour, that yes, the feminine does lack, but what 'she' lacks is the fear of lack. Lacking a fear of lack or the abyss, feminine writing is able to perform an acrobatic flight into thinking, to cross over to difference and the other.

It is important to recognize that masculine and feminine writing are not tied to biological sexed bodies. Cixous circulates the feminine as a metaphor in her writing and not as a literal reference to a biological sex. In this respect she would not argue that phallocentric thinking or writing is limited to men or that feminine thinking or writing is limited to women. Women too can fear lack, indeed have been often encouraged to assume that they lack, and have become petrified with fear in the face of the abyss. Men can form a non-reactionary relationship to fear, difference and the other. If Cixous encourages women to write their bodies in the *écriture féminine* manifesto 'The Laugh of the Medusa' (1980a), it is because she is a feminist who is urging women to enter into the flight of thinking by rewriting female lack. The essentialist charges made against Cixous often neglect the metaphoric content of her writing.

Cixous is a prolific writer, having authored dozens of novels, plays, philosophical, critical and autobiographical texts. Here we will not be attempting a comprehensive and final overview of work which is still in progress, still being written. Instead, we will be focusing on the subject of writing and sexual difference in her work in order to clarify how she approaches these subjects. The first part of the book examines her intellectual roots, setting the scene for her writing by exploring the context in which she thinks. Various debates about the intellectual and political merit of her writing will also be considered. I will also be identifying some of the major concepts in her writing so that readers who are not familiar with her work have a better understanding of Cixous's major concerns. The second part will offer a series of Cixousian readings of a number of writers. The texts of James Joyce, Virginia Woolf, Clarice Lispector and Angela Carter are all opened up to Cixousian readings. The purpose of this section is to continue to elaborate Cixous's ideas and also to enter into the acrobatic flight of thinking which she names 'feminine'. Hopefully, what is achieved is a demonstration of the creative possibilities available to a Cixousian reading of texts. While she has written extensively on both Joyce and Lispector, the chapters on those writers take her readings further, engaging in the challenge of her thinking rather than merely repeating what she has already written. The last and third section offers a critical summary of her work, her impact on post-structuralist feminist thought in particular, and her contribution towards an ethics of sexual difference.

Cixousian readings need not be limited to literary texts, however. Potentially, her approach to thinking can be used to think through any number of issues in any number of different texts. Because she describes an approach to thinking in general and not a narrowly prescriptive critical paradigm, the potential applications of Cixous's thought are limitless. If we are to understand her as an avant-garde philosopher who works within different genres and not simply as a literary critic, playwright, novelist or poet, we have, I would argue, a deeper understanding of her work. Cixous is an avant-garde philosopher because she does not think or write within traditional philosophical parameters, because she understands the practice of philosophy as a creative activity which is capable of engaging in any number of subjects and genres. If we are open to it, her writing offers us lessons in thinking. It is not insignificant that Derrida has claimed she is the greatest living French writer and poet-thinker.

Part I
Writing and Sexual Difference

1   Poetry and Politics: Cixous and her Critics

Poets are the hierophants of an unapprehended inspiration; the mirrors of the gigantic shadows which futurity casts upon the present; the words which express what they understand not; the trumpets which sing to battle, and feel not what they inspire; the influence which is moved not, but moves. Poets are the unacknowledged legislators of the world.

Percy Shelley, 'A Defense of Poetry' [1821] (1977), p. 542

I would lie if I said that I am a political woman, not at all. In fact, I have to assemble the two words, political and poetic. Not to lie to you, I must confess that I put the accent on the poetic. I do it so that the political does not repress, because the political is something cruel and hard and so rigorously real that sometimes I feel like consoling myself by crying and shedding poetic tears.

Hélène Cixous, 'An Exchange with Hélène Cixous', in Conley (1984)

Such provocative confessions from Cixous have tended to alienate many feminist critics, who dismiss her as something of a pampered middle-class dilettante who irresponsibly side-steps the real and hard political questions. Indeed, it might appear here that Cixous is retreating into the comfort zone of the poetic and that her response to the question of the political is irresponsible. In *Sexual/Textual Politics: Feminist Literary Theory* (1985) Toril Moi finds Cixous's position 'disturbing' (124) and argues that 'the distance posited here between the political and the poetic is surely one that feminist criticism has consistently sought to undo' (123–4). What Moi means by this is that feminist criticism has on the whole attempted to politicize the poetic, to bring the aesthetic domain under political scrutiny, to analyse the operation of power

at every level of representation. No text is innocent of an investment in power and thus no text is devoid of political significance.
It seems, at first glance at least, that Cixous is claiming for the
poetic a type of political innocence and that her position is wilfully
naïve and at odds with a broader feminist project of uncovering
and dissecting the operation of patriarchal power. By avoiding the
political it appears that Cixous is taking up an apolitical stance.
Such a stance, it might be argued, actually reinforces the problematic distinction between the poetic as the domain of femininity and
the political as the domain of masculinity.

And yet if we read her more carefully we find that Cixous is in
fact making a statement about the operation of power. 'The political' is understood as repressive, and not simply that which guaran-
tees liberation, and moreover, 'the poetic' is framed as that which
can resist the repressive effects of 'the political'. What does Cixous
mean by this? The relationship between the political and the poetic
is central to Cixous's writing and her reception within feminist
circles. I shall spend most of this chapter teasing out the distinctions between the two realms and indeed asking whether or not a
separation between the poetic and the political is useful or if such
a separation tends to reduce our understanding of the complexity
of both Cixous's work and larger cultural forces.

In order to begin to make sense of Cixous's understanding of
'the political' it is worth reading her within the context of the
history of ideas from which her position emerges. It is important to
recall that a radical shift in consciousness among French intellectuals intensified around the time of the failed revolution of May
1968. Faced with the failure of Marxism to capture the imagination
of the people, the Left had a crisis of faith in many of the political
and philosophical tenets they had invested in. A radical disen-
chantment with the political and theoretical orthodoxy of social-
ism led to a critical re-evaluation of the founding concepts of the
Left. In particular, the concept of the rational Cartesian subject
came under intense scrutiny by many who argued that philosophical and political structures were founded upon the sovereignty of
the rational subject. In effect, this critical re-evaluation of the
Cartesian subject represented a crisis of faith in reason as a guiding
political tool.[1] A growing avant-garde interest in psychoanalysis
also contributed to this crisis. During the events of May a group of
post-surrealist activists called the Situationists wrote slogans on

the walls of the besieged city of Paris affirming the unconscious and the power of individual desire. The high modernist critique of the rational subject which had been expressed since the early decades of the century influenced the Situationists.

While the events of May 1968 were significant and rippled across the world in the form of student protests and new socio-political organizations, it would be naïve to argue that this particular moment in history was responsible for a radical critique of reason. Nietzsche's critique of metaphysics and Freud's critique of self-presence certainly paved the way for a general disruption, a decentring and putting into question of the founding dichotomies which structured Western thought.

The faith the Left had placed in the economic science of Marxism and its Hegelianism had been largely predicated upon the concept of a rational subject operating within the rational political domain. When the concept of rationality became unveiled as a repressive fiction, and not as a self-evident truth, then so too did the idea of the rational political subject. The whole idea of 'the political' came under scrutiny as a repressive fiction which inevitably leads us to opposition, violence, conflict. Gradually, then, an interest in socio-economic oppression was replaced (or at least enhanced) by an interest in sexual repression and the role the unconscious plays in political life. To put it very simplistically for our purposes here, psychic repression was thought to lead to political oppression: the unconscious operation of power was tied to sexuality. For many feminists who participated in the events of May 1968 this had a particular relevance as they were dismayed to discover that their male comrades were as patriarchal as the bourgeois enemy.[2] Cixous was among these women who realized that the rational (political) subject was masculine.

This briefly sketched history is merely an introduction to a more complex context which can help us understand why it is that Cixous can make such controversial statements about the repressive nature of the political. For Cixous it is perhaps more important to 'put the accent on the poetic', for 'the poetic' is precisely that which rationality attempts to repress and it is the very repression of 'the poetic' which is thought to lead to violence. The poetic is the domain of excess, the unconscious, the body, sexuality, creativity, the feminine, all that the political attempts to limit and contain through the application of 'hard' and 'cruel' reason. To align oneself with the poetic is, then, for Cixous, to commit oneself to working against the repressive forces which bring about political oppression. It is a rather round-about way of doing things but makes perfect sense once we recognize that the very concept of the rational political subject is understood to be an oppressive fiction. As Ruth Robbins puts it in *Literary Feminisms* (2000), materialist feminists argue that Cixous fails to provide us with any political solutions to the problems she describes: 'Marxist/Socialist feminisms might object to the idealism and impracticality of a political agenda based on language without action. Cixous's response to this kind of criticism is to seek a rewriting of the terms of politics and activism' (174).

While we might not want to adopt Cixous's response to the cruelty of the political and shed poetic tears, we are at least closer to an understanding of where she is 'coming' from when she confesses to what appears at first glance to be an apolitical and irresponsible position. For Moi though, Cixous remains out of touch with pressing political realities and she invokes Catherine Clement in order to make this clearer. In *The Newly Born Woman* (Cixous and Clement 1991), Clement observes that for her Cixous's 'sentences are devoid of reality', that Cixous's 'description is one where I don't recognize any of the things I think in political terms', and that the subjects Cixous describes are 'not subjects existing in reality' (124). Cixous is simply too poetic and not political enough. Behind these judgements, though, there are several assumptions which need to be examined further. First, we can argue that there is what we might term a realist (and thus pre-modernist) assumption that writing should offer a transparent reflection of social reality. In this sense Clement might be asking of Cixous that she assume the didactic genre of a political realist such as Dickens or Godwin and not the mythic poetic genre of a high modernist such as H.D. or Gertrude Stein, to use some very loose examples. My point here is that there might be an expectation of Cixous's work which fails to account for a difference in genre and writing and that an inappropriate judgement has been made of her work because of this. Secondly, it is assumed that by failing to represent 'reality' Cixous fails to offer political insight and solutions.

Behind this judgement lies an assumption about the correct form for writing or communicating about feminism. On one level we might argue that an expectation that a feminist text conform to a realist/political agenda is limiting. One of the issues at stake in the debate about the value of Cixous's work and the whole distinction between the political and the poetic which this debate so often pivots on, is the very nature of feminist criticism and feminist writing. What counts as useful feminist writing and criticism? Where does our assumption about what is and is not useful come from? What is the purpose of feminist writing and criticism? Where does that concept of purposeful writing come from? These are philosophical and political questions and they will remain with us throughout our examination of Cixous's writing about sexual difference. For now though it is worth continuing to think through the whole question of the political, especially in its impact on our expectations of what a text should and should not be communicating.

In some respects, the accusation that Cixous is apolitical can be compared to the criticisms which have been directed at the work of Derrida, a philosopher with whom, as we shall see, she has many intellectual affinities. In *Debating Derrida* (1995) Niall Lucy makes the provocative point that directing many of the criticisms of deconstruction work is a concept of the 'political imperative' (74). By this Lucy means that within the humanities, texts are now made accountable to particular political agendas. Lucy is careful to point out that it would be a mistake to argue that there was ever a moment when humanities pedagogy was not innocent of politics. Rather, it is now the case that pedagogic politics are more sophisticated, more identifiable and have various critical and political traditions and methodologies. Questions about the way a text represents class, race and gender, for example, have emerged as important pedagogic issues within the humanities, and for very sound reasons too. Unlike Harold Bloom's argument in *The Western Canon* (1994), which decries the corruption of the humanities by 'academic pseudo-Marxists, mock French philosophers, and multicultural opponents of all intellectual standards whatsoever' (439), Lucy is not expressing a nostalgia for a mythic past when everybody simply appreciated Great Works of Literature. Rather his point is that we need to continually interrogate the political grounds upon which we make evaluations about the worth of various texts. In other words, it is important to continue a self-reflexive critical practice which is able to question the grounds of its own political and theoretical base in order to ward off prescriptive reading. By prescriptive readings I mean a type of criticism which prescribes what is and is not appropriate according to a more or less fixed political idea of what counts as useful. Such readings can, at the worst, ask of a poetic text the same questions it would put to a text produced in parliament. To put it another way, to criticize Cixous for failing to offer clear, pragmatic strategies for overcoming patriarchal oppression is almost to accuse a poet of not being a politician. However, it is not just a question of genre.

Perhaps all this can be made clearer by thinking of some of the pedagogic problems which feminist criticism encountered in the seventies and eighties, for this will lead us back into a discussion of Cixous and the whole distinction between the political and the poetic. In 'Pedagogies of the Feminine' (1999), Charlotte Brunsdon argues that a feature of some feminist discourse of this era was an assumption that the pedagogic aim of feminist analysis was to transform various aspects of feminine identity into a feminist identity. 'Feminist identity was, in some ways, understood as an identity for women which transcended – and by implication, put an end to – traditional femininity' (1999: 359). This led, argues Brunsdon, to a dismissal of feminine desire as inauthentic. A recruitist pedagogy emerged which sought to transform ordinary, feminine women into feminists. The drawback of such a position is that it fails to take into account the resistant power of femininity while also remaining invested in reproducing what is often a singular and rather prescriptive feminist identity. In this context, texts were judged according to whether or not they represented the preferred aspects of feminist identity.

With this in mind it is possible to argue that for Moi and Clements (and many others) the value of Cixous's work hinges on whether or not she has represented empowering images of feminist identity, or offered useful strategies for the formation of a feminist identity. Moi argues that there is a libertarian individualism running throughout her work which fails to take into account the complex political realities women face. Commenting on Verena Andermatt Conley's (rather florid) description of Cixous's lecturers at the University of Paris at Vincennes, at which Cixous wore an ermine coat, Moi writes: 'Ermine as emancipation: it is odd that the women of the Third World have been so ludicrously slow to take up Cixous's sartorial strategy' (1985: 126). Here wearing an ermine coat comes to signify a lack of political consciousness, a self-interested aestheticism, an indulgent sensuality, and a failure to provide useful strategies for forming feminist identities. And that, in a nutshell, is the core of the problem of Cixous's investment in the poetic: it is simply too feminine. It is now appropriate that we turn to an appreciation of Cixous's intellectual heritage in order to more fully explore how the poetic and the feminine function in her work. As we have seen they are not straightforward categories and they will become further complicated once we recognize the range of inter-textual sources she draws upon in her writing. I shall return to the subject of Cixous's critical relationship to feminism in the section 'Writing the body: *écriture féminine*', but for now it is worth providing her with a more comprehensive intellectual heritage.

Setting the scene

Cixous's intellectual heritage is very broad and she has often described herself as a 'thief' who poaches ideas. As she writes, in 'Sorties: Out and Out: Attacks/Ways Out/Forays': 'To fly/steal is woman's gesture, to steal into language to make it fly. . . . I have always practiced flight/theft, and as a thief/who-flies, I got away, flew away, moved away from lands and seas (I never crawled, burrowed, dug, trudged; but I swam a lot). And as a thief, for a long time, I inhabited Jean Genet' (Cixous and Clement 1991: 96, 99). (The novelist Jean Genet is one of the writers, Cixous argues, who offers a feminine textuality.) Stealing and re-creating language is a woman's gesture because language has so often been the property of men. While any text is woven with references to broader ideas, because Cixous's writing moves beyond a traditional academic model, her references and influences can be hard to trace at times. In terms of her literary influences the following are the more important, all of whom for Cixous display a certain femininity in their writing, or an awareness of the fluidity of subjectivity. Among her influences are, along with Jean Genet, the German dramatist Heinrich von Kleist, Shakespeare, Kafka, Clarice Lispector, James Joyce, Poe and Hoffman. Her relationship to these writers is complex and she at times works with them to show how they engage in the process of feminine writing or how they confront a limit and struggle against the feminine. In the lengthy poetic essay 'Sorties: Out and Out: Attacks/Ways Out/Forays', for example, Cixous refers to Derrida, Mallarmé, the story of Sleeping Beauty, Pygmalion, Joyce's *Ulysses*, Freud, Nietzsche, the myth of Medusa, Euripides, Plutarch, Virgil, William Blake, Hegel, Bataille, Ernest Jones, the Swiss historian of 'gynocracy' J. J. Bachofen, Jean Genet, Ovid, Valéry, Kleist, Hoffman, Shakespeare, Kafka and Engels. With regard to her philosophical heritage Derrida is perhaps the philosopher she works with most closely but her work is also influenced by Nietzsche. Cixous also challenges some of the central assumptions behind Freudian psychoanalysis, stealing some of Lacan's concepts; and her critique of Hegel is important to her attempt to rethink the antithetical relationship between self and other.

More broadly, Cixous shares many intellectual affinities with a group of post-structuralist feminist theorists who have been influenced by the work of Jacques Lacan and Jacques Derrida. I deliberately avoid placing Cixous as a 'French feminist' because such a move risks collapsing national identity with philosophical and political positions. Intellectual movements are not restricted by parochial borders. Moreover, there are many feminist theorists in America and Australia whose theoretical and political positions are aligned with Cixous just as there are many feminist theorists in France who are intellectually aligned with English-speaking feminists. Too often Cixous has been lumped together with Julia Kristeva and Luce Irigaray as though this powerful triad represents the essence of French feminist thought. While the anti-representationalism of all theorists has many overlaps, this has more to do with a shared intellectual tradition than with a shared or united feminist politics. Instead of thinking of Cixous as a 'French feminist' then, I am approaching her here as a post-structuralist feminist of difference. An important distinction to keep in mind is that between the different philosophical traditions which inform various feminist paradigms: in the case of Cixous and feminist theorists of difference they often draw upon a *continental* tradition of speculative philosophy, while for materialist feminists it is an Anglo-American tradition of *analytic* philosophy which often informs their work.

Post-structuralist feminist theorists of difference argue that sexual difference is an effect of representation and, as such, capable of being subverted and remade. Some prominent English-speaking theorists within this group include Luce Irigaray, Julia Kristeva, Moira Gatens, Jane Gallop, Elizabeth Grosz, Rosi Braidotti and Drucilla Cornell. In contrast to egalitarian feminisms which seek justice for women through the achievement of equal rights in the political domain, difference feminism argues that the achievement of equal rights remains caught up within phallocentric representational systems. In this context, equality depends upon the erasure of the specificity of female difference and the consumption of women into masculine models of power. Instead, difference feminism argues that it is vital that we develop autonomous definitions of woman and femininity for it is only then that the phallocentric dialectic of man/not-man, self/other can be challenged. To this end, difference feminism is committed to an exploration of the aesthetics of femininity and to the creation of new ways of thinking through sexual difference. This is a radical project, one which challenges the very foundations of Western metaphysics, which is thought to rest upon an unacknowledged debt to the fecund materiality of the female body.

In this context the feminine comes to stand as Otherness and alterity. As Moira Gatens puts it in *Feminism and Philosophy: Perspectives on Difference and Equality* (1991):

> Otherness, or alterity, is here linked positively to the issue of sexual difference. However, the aim is not the simple reversal of the hierarchy between man and woman, masculine and feminine . . . but rather involves challenging and unsettling the coherence of the opposition itself. This aim is achieved by showing the ways in which woman, the feminine and female sexuality exceed the complementary role they have been assigned in the oppositions man/woman, masculine/feminine, phallic sexuality/castrated sexuality. (113)

Gatens's point is important, for often Cixous and other theorists of sexual difference are accused of privileging the female body, of merely re-ordering a phallocentric binary so that the feminine is valorized over the masculine. As Gatens makes clear, it is the unsettling of the binary itself which is the aim of such theorists.

To summarize, the main philosophical and political insights of a post-structural feminism of difference are as follows:

1. The Western representational system is governed by a phallocentric libidinal economy.
2. Inherent within this system is a hierarchical *Cartesian
   dichotomy* which privileges mind and masculinity over body
   and femininity.
3. Within this representational economy (sexual) *difference* is
   represented as (sexual) *opposition.*
4. Phallocentrism excludes and colonizes (feminine sexual) difference as *Other.*
5. It follows that feminine sexual difference has no real autonomy
   but rather is submerged into a masculine *economy of the Same.*
6. The *feminine* as the corporeal or the body offers a libidinal
   economy which exceeds the logics of this (Hegelian) opposition.
7. It is vital that a *feminine representational economy* is articulated
   so that the repression of the body is undone.

The project of post-structuralist feminists of difference is a radical
and far-ranging one, for they seek to rewrite the very grounds of
representation in order to create a more ethical (feminine)
culture.[3] In this respect, in *Je, Tu, Nous: Towards a Culture of
Difference* (1993c) Irigaray has called for the radical transformation
of a wide range of disciplines and knowledge in order to undo the
violence associated with a phallocentric repression of the (feminine) body. Likewise, in *Volatile Bodies: Towards a Corporeal
Feminism* (1994), Grosz has argued that phallocentric representational systems are disembodied: Western concepts of space and
time, for example, are argued to be isomorphic reflections of a
disembodied masculinity – her goal is to enflesh such systems so
that they represent a more fluid corporeality. All in all, it is about
challenging the denial of the body within Western culture through
a detailed rewriting of the relationship between representation and
the body. However, in order to do this without falling prey to the
very Hegelian logic of opposition in which *A* exists because of its
relation to not-*A*, it is necessary to move beyond the logics of sameness so that not-*A* (as feminine difference, for example) is able to
be represented without being dependent on a negative relationship to *A*. In order to make this rather complex logic clearer, and in
order, too, to investigate Cixous's relationship to one of her more
important philosophers, it is necessary to consider the work of
Derrida.

Derrida

> Insofar as philosophy is concerned, if I refer myself especially to
> Derrida, it is because he, of course, works on excess. How to
> exceed, how not to exit from, how to go out of, and exceed with-
> out forgetting or retracting.
>
> Hélène Cixous, 'An Exchange with Hélène Cixous', in Conley
> (1984: 150)

One of the best known of Cixous's contributions to a post-structural analysis of difference is the set of binary oppositions she
offers in 'Sorties: Out and Out: Attacks/Ways Out/Forays'.

Where is she?
Activity/Passivity
Sun/Moon
Culture/Nature
Day/Night
Father/Mother
Head/Heart
Intelligible/Palpable
Logos/Pathos
Form, convex, step, advance, semen, progress.
Matter, concave, ground – where steps are taken, holding- and
dumping-ground.
Man
Woman
   Always the same metaphor: we follow it, it carries us, beneath
all its figures, wherever discourse is organized. If we read or
speak, the same thread or double braid is leading us throughout
literature, philosophy, criticism, centuries of representation and
reflection.
   Thought has always worked through opposition,
Speaking/Writing
Parole/Ecriture
High/Low
   Through dual, hierarchical oppositions. Superior/Inferior.
Myths, legends, books. Philosophical systems. Everywhere
(where) ordering intervenes, where a law organizes what is
thinkable by oppositions (dual, irreconcilable; or sublatable,

dialectical). And all these pairs of oppositions are couples. Does that mean something? Is the fact that Logocentrism subjects thought – all concepts, codes and values – to a binary system, related to 'the' couple, man/woman?   (Cixous and Clement 1991: 63–4)

Here Cixous is clearly indebted to a deconstructive critique of Western metaphysics as a system of oppositions. For Cixous and for post-structuralist feminists of difference, the system of oppositions is also, and importantly, gendered. Within this system an autonomous representation of woman or femininity does not have a place. Rather, the feminine is that which exceeds being totally captured by logic.

A rigorous deconstructive attention to the underside of representation, the repressed materiality of writing, has provided feminism with a method for destabilizing phallocentric discourses. For Derrida, Western metaphysics is logocentric, or based on the purity of a singular self-present truth as word or Logos. Within this system, meaning is presented as unmediated, uncontaminated, immediate, given. However, as Derrida shows, the presence of reason, truth and meaning depends upon a series of exclusions. To use our example, *A* only comes into being through the exclusion of not-*A*. *A* renders its negative invisible, as no-thing. Another way of understanding this is to think of identity as something which only comes into being through an unacknowledged debt to difference. It is this careful attention to the dichotomous logics of exclusion which can be said to inform a deconstructive ethics of reading. The textual remains of this exclusion, the traces, excesses, supplements of the disavowed debt to difference (or not-*A*), are the focus of deconstructive readings. Like Lacan, Derrida acknowledges that it is impossible to escape the logics of the text of identity and difference, self and other, *A* and not-*A*, to arrive at a point outside representation – rather, deconstruction subverts from within by calling attention to the fragile logic of identity. However, deconstruction is not simply a negative practice which seeks to undo or tear down truth or meaning through a nagging attention to the complex hypocrisies which support truth or identity. Rather, recognizing that meaning is continually in the process of becoming, that identity is not fixed, means that by calling attention to the exclusions which enable identity to take up a position of truth or meaning, identity is opened up to a more ethical, positive relationship with difference.

For Derrida, and for Cixous as we shall later see, writing has a particular significance. Writing, in the sense that Derrida understands it, is not simply words written on a page. In *Of Grammatology* (1979) Derrida argues that, with the Western philosophical tradition since Plato, truth has always been associated with the spoken word while writing has been associated with the falsification, or corruption, of truth or the spoken word. The traditional Platonic dislike of representation as an invitation to deceit is traced through Western philosophy as a guiding narrative. Within this tradition the spoken word, or Logos, is assumed to communicate a direct, self-present truth while writing or representation, on the other hand, is understood to be a corrupt copy of the truth. Writing stands in for the spoken word, or Logos. Arguing that Western metaphysics is structured around this division, Derrida goes on to argue that the division has its foundation in the privileging of presence over absence. Logocentrism is thus a system which assumes that presence is the foundation of truth and identity while absence represents a fall from truth, a corruption, a lack. In other words, Western metaphysics is structured by a dichotomous hierarchical logic which attempts to order meaning by privileging (or bringing into presence) one side of the binary. Thus a series of binaries such as man/woman, nature/culture, mind/body will work to assert the first term as the property of truth or Logos and the second term as a defective copy of the first, as incomplete. It is in this way that woman, for example, comes to signify Adam's spare rib, a corrupt version of a perfect model – man. As Derrida puts it in 'Limited Inc.' (1988):

> All metaphysicians have proceeded thus, from Plato to Rousseau, from Descartes to Husserl: good before evil, the positive before the negative, the pure before the impure, the simple before the complex, the essential before the accidental, the imitated before the imitation. etc. This is not just one metaphysical gesture among others; it is the metaphysical exigency, the most constant, profound, and potent procedure.   (236)

Writing, however, resists and troubles this calling into presence of truth (as the good, the positive, the pure, the simple etc.) because writing, being a system which is founded on absence, continually defers the arrival of presence. Deconstruction attempts to show that the arrival of self-present truth in writing is achieved only by placing a limit on the process of signification. For example, the statement 'man is rational' is a self-present truth only because it denies otherwise, or closes off the ability of 'man' to signify something else (and irrationality is only one possible other signification). However, the statement 'man is rational' occurs within writing, or is connected to a broader signifying context which exceeds the self-present logic of the truth of the statement. This signifying context is potentially limitless such that an infinity of different meanings might come into play within the truth statement. For example, what is meant by 'man', what is meant by 'rational'? There are many different sociological, biological, historical, psychological, political definitions of man just as there are many definitions of 'rational'. Each attempt to define the truth of 'man' or 'rational' is itself made within a potentially limitless signifying system so that in effect the truth of the statement 'man is rational' leaks into a vast and complex chain of signifiers, like an infinite Chinese box.

Of course, one would not necessarily want to spend one's entire life deconstructing 'man is rational' and there are moments when, for pragmatic or political or ethical reasons, an end to signification is attempted. But Derrida is careful to point out that any attempt to arrive at the truth is provisional. Why a text calls for a limit to meaning is both arbitrary (in the sense that meaning can never be arrived at) and also invested with political significance.

It is this understanding of signification as a potentially endless process which informs Cixous's assertions that the female body and unconscious is the source of an infinite writing, a writing that is capable of exceeding the logics of the limit, the logic of a phallocentrism which seeks to limit the female body within an order of signification that places the feminine below the masculine.

Lacan

Given Cixous's engagement with psychoanalysis, in particular her use of the term *jouissance,* it is worth discussing Lacan briefly. Lacan argues that sexual identity is caught up in a relationship between the Self and the Other. Within the Symbolic Order the

Other comes to function as the source of truth about the subject or Self, but this certainty or truth is an illusionary effect, a misrecognition of the power of the Phallus. The search for meaning or certainty within the Symbolic Order, or the realm of representation, is always thwarted by the Other's absence: the truth of the Other is spectral, haunted by absence. The subject moves toward meaning within language but only ever arrives at meaning through the repression of the unthought, the unsaid. Yet this repression is never complete or total for the repressed continually leaks through language, subverting meaning, disrupting identity.

It is in this context that Lacan's concept of *jouissance* is important.[4] *Jouissance* is a moment of libidinal intensity which erupts into the Symbolic from the Imaginary, transgressing the Law of the Father. Associated with the pre-oedipal body of the Imaginary and thus the domain of the mother and the feminine, *jouissance* is not just a physical experience, it is also the representation of that experience. On a literary level, it is Antoine Artaud's screams in his Theatre of Cruelty, James Joyce's narrative disruptions, the experiments of the avant-garde, those moments of excess within language when meaning slides into non-meaning, when thought is opened up to the unthought. *Jouissance*, or the explosion of sexual energy, is a revolutionary moment capable of rupturing the coherence of the Symbolic. In particular, Lacan's suggestion that there is a 'jouissance of the body which is . . . beyond the phallus' (1982: 145) has been taken up by feminists such as Cixous who are interested in the possibilities of a feminine libidinality which is capable of transgressing and subverting the Law of the Father and reinscribing sexual identity in non-phallic terms.

For Lacan, feminine *jouissance* is supplementary, it is the residue, the remainder, that which is left over from the phallic dialectic woman is subjected to. She is the Other of the (phallic) Other. However, such a position tends to mystify femininity as primordial, something which is pre-discursive, outside the Law. In such a way, the feminine comes to represent the impossible, the unthought. For Lacan, however, all of this is caught up in a paradox: 'How to return, other than by means of a special discourse, to a pre-discursive reality?' (1975: 33). For Cixous, that special discourse is *écriture féminine*, or writing in the feminine, writing feminine *jouissance*. Acutely aware of the paradoxical relationship between language and the feminine, Cixous none the less moves her writing toward an unfolding of the feminine. By refusing the psychoanalytic myths of female sexuality as the unknowable 'dark continent', the great lack, Cixous affirms the positive specificity of feminine desire.

Writing the body: *écriture féminine*

> This is how I would define a feminine textual body: as a female libidinal economy, a regime, energies, a system of spending not necessarily carved out by culture. A feminine textual body is recognized by the fact that it is always endless, without ending: there is no closure. ... There's *tactility* in the feminine text, there's touch, and this touch passes through the ear. Writing in the feminine is passing on what is cut out by the Symbolic, the voice of the mother, passing on what is most archaic.
>
> Hélène Cixous (1981: 53–4)

In the first section of this chapter we discussed some of the issues surrounding the critical reception of Cixous's work among feminists and argued that most of the debates centred around whether or not she was perceived to be political. It is now time to turn our attention to these debates again and to discuss the spectre of biological essentialism which has also played a central role in the debates around her work. One way of reading the above quotation from Cixous would be to understand *écriture féminine* as an essentialist practice which relies upon a type of biologism. If *écriture féminine* is about recuperating the lost voice of the archaic mother then surely, suggest many of Cixous's critics, this is a form of mystical biological essentialism. Pamela McCollum, for example, suggests that the stress on the mother's voice is a 'textually fervent biological mysticism' (1985: 131). Haven't we had enough of mystifying the female body as Other – isn't this a regressive move?

Biological essentialism is basically the idea that biology determines being – for example, that one is born and not made a woman. Feminists have remained wary of such essentialism because it has provided patriarchy with an excuse for framing women as the weaker, more febrile sex. As the Editorial Collective's *Questions Féministes* put it, the biological is *'an ideology which rationalizes the political'* (1980: 227). For example, a scientifically sanctioned form of biological essentialism enabled educationalists in the nineteenth century to argue that women should not be admitted to universities because their wombs would atrophy in direct proportion to the stimulation of their brains. Ideological bias masquerades as a neutral, impartial biological truth. Indeed, many feminists argue that biological essentialism is the cornerstone of patriarchal oppression. By invoking a specifically feminine language and writing practice, feminist critics understand Cixous to be merely playing the oppressor's game, that is, simply reinforcing the idea that women are other and that the otherness of women is located in their sexual or biological difference from men. While philosophers such as Gatens might defend Cixous's position and argue that the valorization of the (m)other is a strategic move in the deconstruction of phallocentrism, many others remain unconvinced. It is time to consider these other voices.

Much of the criticism directed against Cixous is caught up in the assumption that she is an essentialist, that the whole issue of sexual difference which preoccupies her work is in fact a rather glamorous form of biological essentialism. One of the first and most unreserved critiques of Cixous came from the *Questions Féministes* of the Editorial Collective, who argued that the assumption that women are radically different from men and must therefore invent a new language of the body in order to undo the oppressive effects of phallocentric representation is romantic and regressive. 'We are only playing the oppressor's game if we deprive ourselves of knowledge and conceptual tools because he has used them before us. . . . When we claim that we are different, and outsiders in the world of men, we are only parroting them' (1981: 221). The Collective also questions the idea that 'women's language is closer to the body' and that such a language of the body is inherently subversive (219). They point out that there is no direct 'natural' relation to the body for we are all social beings and so it follows that our relationship to our bodies is mediated through a plethora of cultural texts. By invoking a timeless, natural and even mystical sense of the feminine as a space which exists outside the confines of patriarchal culture, feminists who celebrate the subversive energies of *écriture féminine* are not only indulging in a futile celebration of the essentialist myths which have been used to prohibit women from gaining power within a male-dominated culture, but they are also returning to the 'enemy an effective weapon' (ibid.). 'There is no essence. There is no

woman, no femininity, no eternal feminine', writes the Collective,
only a complex social group which has experienced systematic
oppression over a period of time (1981: 230). What is needed is a
detailed socio-historical analysis of women's oppression, not a
whimsical celebration of the subversive feminine. As socialists,
they find Cixous's position a dangerous impediment to the more
pragmatic task of transforming the inequitable social structures
that so deform women's lives.

Most of the criticisms directed against Cixous rest upon what is
perceived to be the essentialism of *écriture féminine*. For example,
the literary critic Mary Jacobus (1986) has dismissed *écriture féminine* as an essentialist practice. To argue that there exists a specifically feminine textuality which directly expresses a subversive
feminine sexuality is problematic on two counts. First, many of the
texts which Cixous draws upon for her definition of a feminine
textuality are written by a male avant-garde. Secondly, the idea
that a feminine textuality offers a direct relationship to feminine
sexuality ignores the powerful effects of complex socio-historical
narratives which women embody.

The Marxist feminist Teresa Ebert writes that *écriture féminine*
'risks re-essentialising the feminine and constructing a new identity anchored in a reified notion of the body and language' (1996:
166). Elsewhere Alice Jardine (1985: 62–3) suggests that *écriture
féminine* is limiting for feminism because by privileging a particular style as more authentically connected to femininity, women
writers and feminist theoreticians who do not write in the feminine
are open to being rejected on the grounds that they think and write
within a phallocentric framework. The irony here is that rather
than opening up new creative ways of expressing a repressed
female body, *écriture féminine* restricts the expression of the
female body within the constraints of what is read by Jardine and
others as a formulaic and normative style. In other words, the liberation of the female body is limited to a particular style of avant-
garde writing. The risk here is that an experimental disruption of
generic constraints and linear logic can congeal into a new norm, a
new orthodox definition of the feminine. As Janet Wolff suggests,
'[i]t is likely that any new definition of "femininity" would equally
provide the basis for control and self-surveillance' (1990: 127).

As some of the critics above have noted, Cixous's understanding
of femininity is hardly new. For Rita Felski, 'The celebration of

"feminine" desire as plural, spontaneous, chaotic, and mysteriously "other" itself reiterates and is easily assimilated into a longstanding cultural symbolization of woman in Western society' (1989: 37). There is nothing subversive or oppositional about Cixous's 'femininity' – rather than going against the grain of patriarchal definitions of feminine desire, it is argued that Cixous is merely repeating entrenched assumptions about women. While those assumptions have been used to discredit women for being irrational it does not necessarily follow that a celebration of irrational feminine desire will transform inequitable social structures. Discussing a post-structuralist feminist approach to women's language, Andrea Nye argues that:

> Neither 'a maternal semiotics', nor a 'feminine operation', nor 'écriture féminine' returned speech to its concrete human situation. These strategies of French feminism either disrupted conceptual order or supplemented the ahistoricity of structure with an ahistoricity of pure bodily and emotional expression. In neither case are meanings seen as a function of historically grounded intentions. (1988: 213)

The idealization of the female body, in other words, produces an image of the body which is divorced from the complex historical and social contexts in which women live their bodies. Cixous's female body is a poetic fiction and has little bearing on the political reality of lived bodies.

In this context, the idealization of the liberatory potential of feminine desire is understood to be problematic. As Ann Rosalind Jones states in her comprehensive overview of *écriture féminine*: 'The French feminists make of the female body too unproblematically pleasurable and totalized an entity' (1981: 254). Claiming that the female body is the source of a radically different and subversive libidinality which when released will somehow destabilize entrenched phallocentric structures is seen as politically naive. Indeed, Cixous is often dismissed as a revolutionary phrase-maker, someone who is able to craft spirited revolutionary texts but who cannot offer useful pragmatic solutions. Moreover, by privileging feminine desire as a revolutionary force *par excellence*, other aspects of women's experiences are marginalized. Cixous's celebration of feminine desire is read as a counterproductive reiteration of conservative masculine myths about femininity and not, therefore, a radical position. For many of Cixous's critics the focus on the female body invariably leads back to the problem of essentialism.

Another issue which critics have focused on has to do with the historical connections between high modernist claims about the subversive effects of art and the radical potential Cixous accords *écriture féminine*. As Felski points out, an assumption that a subversive experimental writing is capable of transforming society is itself the hallmark of an earlier utopian strain within modernism which heralded the revolutionary potential of art. In this sense, Cixous's celebration of *écriture féminine* carries with it a number of conceptual and political problems associated with a Utopian avant-garde idealization of the relationship between art and society, the poetic and the political. In this context, the avant-garde over-estimates the liberatory effects of its own productions through a rather naive faith in the transformative power of art. Artistic innovations are often only accessible to an educated elite and thus hardly capable of effecting larger social changes, if indeed the avant-garde effects any real change at all. As Andreas Huyssen (1986) has pointed out, postmodern culture has a canny ability to incorporate and to mass market radical aesthetics, neutralizing their subversive impact by redeploying them as witty adverts and so on. Moreover, Cixous's celebration of what she argues is a specifically feminine style of writing is largely derived from male avant-garde writers. How is it, ask many feminist literary critics, that one can say that such a style offers a special expression of the female body and feminine sexuality when it is a style of writing largely indebted to men? Tina Chanter observes that Cixous's assertion that writers such as Genet offer a feminine textuality is often read by wary feminists as 'an indicator of a post-feminist sensibility' (1995: 29). While Cixous's concept of feminine sexuality reiterates patriarchal myths, her concept of feminine textuality relies upon male writers. What appears to be radical is revealed to be a form of conservatism.

The strange twists which lead a radical politics or poetics into a form of conservatism are also the subject of Pauline Johnson's (1994) critique of Cixous. Johnson suggests that many post-structuralist feminist theorists of difference such as Cixous can be understood as reproducing a Romantic opposition to modernity, logic, reason and established cultural roles. Romanticism grew out of a frustration with what were perceived to be the alienating and corrupting effects of scientific rationalism, industrialization and the mechanization of humanity. Broadly speaking the Romantics offered one of the earliest idealizations of the revolutionary potential of poetry and art. Irrationality, nature, an edenic past, mysticism, sensuality, the sublime and the exotic were all valorized against the alienating effects of modernity. In effect, Romanticism was an anti-Enlightenment movement in so far as it questioned a belief in the ability of a sovereign reason to bring about social progress. A mistrust in the culture of the Enlightenment also led to the celebration of the anti-hero, an oppositional figure whose cultural exile communicated a profound truth about the limits of modernity. For Johnson, feminists of difference such as Cixous have taken up the position of the anti-hero, idealized women's exile from a phallocentric culture, and offer a feminism of the anti-role. In effect a feminist anti-role would be a continual rebellion against phallocentric definitions of femininity, an ironic and parodic subversion of the very roles (or identities) that have been ascribed to the feminine by masculine reason. In this sense, we can argue that Cixous's 'femininity' is self-consciously resisting any particular role, for all roles are masks which phallocentrism has imposed on women.

There are, however, some limits to this Romantic rebellion against feminine roles and identities. If phallocentrism is understood to permeate culture and impose numerous feminine roles which must be continually rebelled against, there must be a concept of self and agency which enables this very opposition. Johnson points out that 'the strategic evocation of a feminist anti-role inevitably hosts a positive description of a particular type of feminine subjectivity' (1994: 61). This self, suggests Johnson, runs the risk of becoming a normative and limited image of feminine identity as pure opposition. Moreover, by emphasizing, re-creating and rewriting the female body/self, Cixous also runs the risk of being seen to espouse a private–aestheticist creed, a sort of dandyesque self-fashioning which has more to do with satisfying individual desires than with bringing about social change. Again, this is seen as a retreat into an essentialist poetics of the body and an inability to deal pragmatically with the multiple sociohistorical constraints facing women. Such an attitude, identity or politics runs the risk of simplifying the relationship between centre and margin and producing blanket rejections of language, for example, as simply phallocentric. Indeed, such a stance has been argued to be a form of anti-intellectualism. Identifying what she terms 'the logic of a psycho-politics' in specific feminist work, Marion Tapper argues that one of the pedagogic effects of a feminist rejection of phallocentric representations is that it risks repressing the very autonomy of the subjects it seeks to liberate (1993: 141–2). In other words, it is important to avoid an uncritical uptake of theories of subjectivity which appear to be self-evidently liberatory.

The major points made in the criticism of Cixous's work can be summarized as follows:

1. She relies upon a concept of phallocentrism which is *ahistorical* and thus unable to account for complex social change.
2. *Écriture féminine* is *utopian* and so potentially reactionary and unable to offer pragmatic, situated interventions.
3. Sexual difference becomes a *meta-narrative* which erases all other (racial, class, etc.) differences and so risks a simplistic, even reactive, account of social and political reality.
4. Cixous *idealizes* the revolutionary potential of language and confuses linguistic change with social change
5. The feminine is *romanticized* as oppositional.
6. Her position is based on a form of *biological essentialism.*

Having dealt with some of the more pertinent issues at stake in the critiques of Cixous's work we can now consider more positive responses. This is not to say that the critiques of Cixous are negative, indeed they are highly productive and enhance our understanding of the context in which her work is situated. The majority of the defences of Cixous's work depend upon what is perceived to be a misunderstanding of her essentialism. Important to this misunderstanding of Cixous's essentialism is a distinction between anatomy and *morphology*. Anatomy basically describes the physical, biological body. It is through reference to women's anatomical difference that biological essentialism gains ideological currency. As Freud once said of women's sexual difference, 'anatomy is destiny'. Women are hysterical because they have wombs, and so on. What this amounts to is an understanding of cultural (and other) differences as simply a reflection of natural differences.

Such an ideology is not particular to Freud though and has in fact supported multiple forms of sexism and racism. The Nazi classification of the subtle and sometimes imaginary anatomical differences between the Aryan and non-Aryan body, for example, was based on a racist ideology which confused anatomical differences with moral differences: Aryan culture was morally superior because Aryan anatomy was biologically superior. As Gatens succinctly puts it: 'It is not *anatomy* which decides cultural value or status but rather the way in which that anatomy is represented and lived' (1991: 106).

Morphology, on the other hand, refers to the cultural representations of anatomical differences. The concept of morphology achieves two strategically important moves. First, morphology challenges the ideological 'purity' of scientific truths about anatomical difference by calling attention to the fact that such 'truths' are historically and socially situated representations of 'natural' differences. Secondly, an emphasis on the morphological construction of the body refuses the 'anatomy is destiny' model (and thus the idea that culture is merely a blueprint of nature), and so opens up the possibility of producing more empowering representations of the body. For Gatens, when Cixous writes about a woman's body she is referring to 'the way in which the shape or form of the female body is represented in culture. Morphology is not given, it is interpretation, which is not to say that it has nothing to do with our understandings of biology' (1991: 115). Indeed, the discourse of biology can be understood as culturally privileged representation of anatomy. If we recognize that biologists in the late nineteenth century asserted that women's wombs atrophied when they studied we can clearly see that it was a morphological body which was being represented in these discourses. This is not to say that biology is merely a system of ideologically polluted representations or that bodies do not bleed, get sick and die, but rather that the ways in which bodies are represented are not immune to ideological contamination. It is how we interpret and give meaning to the anatomical body which is the issue.

Once we recognize the distinction between anatomy and morphology the issue of Cixous's essentialism becomes more complicated. For Gatens, it is precisely at this point that Moi's reading of Cixous falters. 'Cixous's writing', Moi claims, 'is about the *female* body. This is to apply categories to Cixous's writing that

are inappropriate. . . . This is certainly not to say that French feminists do not make a distinction between biological and social
aspects of sexual difference. However, the distinction is not made in
terms of another binary polarity, like sex and gender, but rather in
terms of a middle term, a term which is *reducible* to neither
anatomy nor socialization: that term is *morphology'* (1991: 115).
Here Gatens makes clear that the term 'morphology' attempts to
move beyond a sex/nature/body and gender/social/mind binary.
This is in keeping with the critique of the dichotomous metaphysics
which underpin phallocentrism. The body understood as morphology is not reducible to either nature or culture but is, rather, the
scene of a dynamic writing which exceeds the limits of either category. The body as morphology also opens up the possibility of a
radical rewriting of the place of the body within the nature/culture,
mind/body by exploring the relationship in between. This is why
Cixous states that *écriture féminine* is capable of transforming
previous definitions of the female body and opening up new horizons for rewriting the body. As Cixous writes in 'The Laugh of the
Medusa': 'The future must no longer be determined by the past. I do
not deny that the effects of the past are still with us. But I refuse to
strengthen them by repeating them, to confer upon them an irre-
movability the equivalent of destiny, to confuse the biological and
the cultural. Anticipation is imperative' (1980a: 245).

A related point about the confusion between anatomy and
morphology is made by Pamela Banting (1992), whose focus is on
the body of the hysteric in Cixous's work, which she reads as a
model for resistance. As Banting puts it:

> For Cixous, the hysterical or 'poetic' body inscribes the outlines of a
> signifying practice that is neither logocentric nor strictly Derridean.
> The poetic body, the body as pictogram, allows her to hypothesize
> women's writing as, in part, translation between language and
> corporeality.   (231)

In effect, Banting reads *écriture féminine* as a process of translation, not simply representation, of the female body. 'Feminists
such as Cixous', writes Banting, 'are trying to unname the
Cartesian body. Not back to a natural or maternal source or to a
body prior to Descartes or prior to language but toward a new
conception of the body' (239).

Banting also argues that many of the anti-essentialist criticisms remain invested in a model of the body as a passive tabula rasa, or blank page, upon which culture inscribes itself. In contrast to this negative image of the female body as a passive surface onto which phallocentric texts are written, Cixous's 'body' writes and speaks back – 'biting the tongue [of phallocentric language] with her very own teeth to invent for herself a language to get inside of' (257) – and in doing so creates a language which moves beyond a phallocentric separation between mind and body. Banting is careful to point out that Cixous is not advocating a language of the body which is composed of grunts, wails, screams or nonsense, and if we find it absurd that Cixous might be accused of this we only have to recall that the Editorial Collective's *Questions Féministes* implied just that. Rather, Cixous is suggesting a language which is capable of translating those moments when language fails us and the body attempts to speak. Quite simply, Cixous is attempting to forge a new language which communicates the space between language and the body, a space of the (m)other. When one is lost for words and overwhelmed by experiences of pain or pleasure those moments call attention to the limits of language in expressing the injustices and joys which render us speechless. *Écriture féminine* is not simply about speaking out instead of remaining silent or crying, or communicating those silences or cries as symptoms of women's lack (which is precisely how Freud read the body of the hysteric); rather it is about producing a language which is able to move beyond the very phallocentric Cartesian duality which renders the body speechless. For Cixous, the hysterical body is profound because the hysteric calls attention to a language which is in the difficult process of being born through the body. As Cixous writes: 'Language is a translation. It speaks through the body. Each time we translate what we are in the process of thinking, it necessarily passes through our bodies' (1988: 151–2).

An avant-garde feminist?

One way of avoiding the conceptual deadlock which can ensue when Cixous's work is judged according to whether or not she is political or an essentialist, is to situate her work within the tradition of the avant-garde. This is not to avoid the question of the political but rather to understand Cixous's work within the historical and literary context of a movement of ideas which she works within and against. It has already been noted above that Cixous's work is indebted to the avant-garde and it is now appropriate that we explore this debt more critically. By situating Cixous within the avant-garde I have in mind her close affinities with Surrealism, which have been touched upon by Susan Rubin Suleiman in *Subversive Intent: Gender, Politics and the Avant-garde* (1990).

First though, some background information on Surrealism. The Surrealist movement was most active in the 1920s and 1930s in France and western Europe and some of the more prominent members of that group included André Breton, Louis Aragon, Paul Eluard and Salvador Dali. The aim of the Surrealists was to create a perpetual revolution against order, which, for them, signified the oppression of freedom. As Maurice Nadeau comments, 'If surrealism rests on a dogma, it is indeed on that of "absolute revolt, of total insubmission, of formal sabotage" ' (1973: 175). For Breton, 'The immediate reality of the surrealist revolution is not so much to change anything in the physical and apparent order of things as to create a movement in men's minds. The idea of any surrealist revolution aims at the profound substance and order of thought' (Nadeau 1973: 114). To this end, the surrealists revolted against culture, logic, reason and society, stressing instead the primacy of desire, the liberating power of free love, the unconscious and the imagination. Madness was celebrated against reason, as a state which offered a special insight into repressed creativity. Significantly, Breton and Aragon celebrated hysteria as 'the greatest poetic discovery of the nineteenth century' (Nadeau 1973: 158). Refusing pathological explanations for hysteria, they claimed it as a densely poetic expression. Mummified in the shrouds of logic, the desiring body withers and with it the creative spirit. The Surrealists aimed to create a new body, a new creative spirit, which would move beyond the bourgeois constraints of reason and logic and bring about a joyful and radical poetic revolution. 'The true revolution, for the surrealists, was the victory of desire' (Nadeau 1973: 207). Desire was thought to constitute the essence of man: I desire therefore I am. Or as the post-Surrealist group the Situationists put it, on the walls of Paris in May 1968, 'I take my desires for reality because I believe in the reality of my desires.' Libertarianism

was politicized, and it is no coincidence that the surrealists idol-
ized the Marquis de Sade as a revolutionary.

Cixous also celebrates the hysteric as an anti-hero, as a figure
who speaks from the edges of rational discourse, hinting at new
understandings of desire, new poetic ways of imagining the relationship between the body and desire. Moreover, for Cixous love
and desire are also revolutionary forces capable of undoing the
repressive constraints of reason and logic. Poetry too plays a
central part in Cixous's radical vision and we might compare *écriture féminine*, with its challenge to create a new language of the
body, with the Surrealists' espousal of automatic writing as something which was thought capable of releasing the unconscious and
unlocking desire. They drew upon Rimbaud who, in 'The Alchemy
of the Word' (1873), writes, 'I boasted of inventing, with rhythms
from within me, a kind of poetry that all the senses, sooner or later,
would recognize. And I alone would be its translator. . . . What was
unutterable, I wrote down' (1976: 204). In brief, automatic writing
involved going into a trance state in which free-association and the
inhibition of literary constraints produced a long, flowing
discourse which was thought to uncover repressed meanings.
Automatic writing was also a means for achieving self-awareness.
As Suleiman comments: 'Like automatic writing, H.C.'s practice is
"at once a vocation and a technique," "a practice of the greatest
passivity" which is actually "an active way – of getting to know
things by letting ourselves be known by them". Cagey H.C., to
rewrite the avant-garde by feminizing it!' (1994: 80).

For Cixous, every woman has access to a revolutionary unconscious, every woman is capable of becoming a liberated and liberating writer – 'Her libido is cosmic, just as her unconscious is
worldwide' writes Cixous in 'The Laugh of the Medusa' (1980a:
259). The unconscious is thought to be the wellspring of creativity
and thus every woman is capable of nourishing herself with her
(specifically feminine) unconscious. A similar notion informs a
Surrealist refusal to create a hierarchy of talent and genius –
'Surrealism is within the compass of every unconscious' (Nadeau
1973: 97). The Surrealists mocked the realist representationalism of
the novel and argued that the literary canon was an undemocratic
and repressive system which limited thought. The novel was mechanistic, logical, a slave to repressive reason (ibid.: 95). Similarly,
Cixous writes in 'The Laugh of the Medusa' that 'Nearly the entire

history of writing is confounded with the history of reason, of which it is at once the effect, the support, and one of the privileged alibis' (1980a: 249). It is only the poets who have escaped reason, 'not the novelists, allies of representationalism' (250).

Central to both Surrealism and Cixous are the following fundamental assumptions: a revolution in language will bring about a social revolution; poetry and experimental writing is the favoured method of revolution; the repression of desire by reason and logic must be undone; the hysteric is an anti-hero who communicates a radical language; laughter, irony and parody are subversive forces; the unconscious is the source of a revolutionary creativity. Of course, having put it like that one can understand why it is that both Surrealism and Cixous have been dismissed as hopelessly romantic. I have risked a vulgar reduction here of the overlaps I perceive between Surrealism and Cixous because there is not enough space to fully elaborate the more subtle connections. However, we shall return to the question of Surrealism and Cixous in the chapter on Angela Carter. Carter offers a decisive critique of the Surrealist imagination in *The War of Dreams* (1972) and by applying Cixous's own work to Carter we will be able to test the limits of both Surrealism and Cixous. For now though, it is important to discuss the ways in which Cixous can be read as appropriating the central tenets of Surrealism in order to theorize writing and sexual difference.

The central difference between Cixous and Surrealism is of course to do with sexuality and in particular Cixous's figuring of the maternal. In her insightful work on the avant-garde, Suleiman explores the ways in which many male avant-garde texts reveal a pathological repudiation of the maternal and argues that this betrays a deep-seated patriarchal fear of an engulfing maternal body. One example she cites is the Surrealist document *Hands off Love!* (1927), which was a vitriolic diatribe against Mrs Charlie Chaplin who was at the time suing her husband for divorce. Signed by Ernst and another thirty-one male Surrealists, it is a savage attack on the bourgeois repression of free love, poetry and the creative life. It is directed at 'those bitches who become, in every country, the *good* mothers, *good* sisters, *good* wives, those plagues, those parasites of every sentiment and every love' (Nadeau 1973: 265). And there is Paul Eluard's and Benjamin Peret's infamous Surrealist 'proverb': 'You must beat your mother while she's young' (Nadeau 1973: 156). The 'rejection' of motherhood (for want of a better way of describing it) was not just a proto-punk sniggering at 'good girls', for the Surrealists, as Suleiman points out, read the mother in particular as a representative of the very values they were fighting against. As Suleiman argues, the mother was despised by the Surrealists for embodying a self-righteous and stifling morality and supporting the repressive and hypocritical beliefs of the bourgeoisie. Mother represents the weight of tradition, appropriate conduct, limited social roles.

In contrast to this pervasive avant-garde rejection of motherhood (and Suleiman is careful to note that this attitude towards the mother is not particular to male surrealists but also informs the work of many women of the avant-garde), Cixous offers a different story. For Cixous, the mother is an ironic and creative figure who shows no alliance to paternal authority, whose energies are not husbanded by male power. Rather, the mother is a radical innovator and a slightly threatening one too. Cixous invokes the Medusa as mother. In Greek mythology Medusa turned men into stone because she was so hideous. Later, in Freud, Medusa is appropriated as a symbol of the mother's castrated genitals and thus, for the men who gaze at her, a representation of the possibility of their own castration and symbolic annihilation. And for Cixous? 'Too bad if they fall apart upon discovering that women aren't men, or that the mother doesn't have one. . . . You only have to look at the Medusa straight on to see her. And she's not deadly. She's beautiful and she's laughing' (1980a: 255). The mother as Medusa, as castrated female genitals, as women's lack (of symbolic and sexual power), is transformed here into a positive figure of Convulsive Beauty (to borrow a term from Surrealism) through a typical Surrealist use of parody and reversal. The Medusa's laughter is rebellious for she not only mocks the fragility of patriarchal myths about the mother's lack but she also opens up the possibility that it is the mother's sexual/symbolic power which is feared – 'Wouldn't the worst be, isn't the worst, in truth, that women aren't castrated' (ibid.). The psychoanalytic presumption that the mother lacks is revealed here as a defence against the recognition of woman's creative power. Cixous's rewriting of the mother through a rebellious and humorous parody of the myth of Medusa is just one example of the ways in which she subverts an avant-garde poetics. More broadly, she can be said to take up many of the strategies of

Surrealism – Suleiman notes her use of parody, reversal, humour –
and reframe them as feminine. In effect we can read 'The Laugh of
the Medusa' as a post-surrealist feminist manifesto.

   While Cixous is still most widely known for her theorization of
écriture féminine, in her Medusa text her work is much more
complex and wide-ranging than that. In the next chapter we turn to
a consideration of Cixous's major concepts in some order. This will
allow us to become familiar with her overall work before applying
it to a number of writers.

2   The Major Concepts

> Writing is precisely the very possibility of change, the space that can serve as a springboard for subversive thought, the precursory movement, of a transformation of social and cultural structures.
>
> Hélène Cixous, 'The Laugh of the Medusa' (1980a)

> Writing is the delicate, difficult, and dangerous means of succeeding in avowing the unavowable.
>
> Hélène Cixous, 'The School of the Dead', *Three Steps in the Ladder of Writing* (1993b)

First, it is important to recognize that an ordering of Cixousian concepts, while pedagogically important in so far as it allows us to distinguish her major ideas, forces a separation between concepts which often overlap and support each other in vital ways. For example, a definition of Cixous's concept of the feminine libidinal economy cannot avoid drawing upon her notion of the gift, of fidelity and the unthinkable, and so on. Expect then, in the following definitions of concepts, some leaks and flows, some border crossings. It should also be noted that some of the concepts discussed here are not particular to Cixous and are, in fact, part of a wider post-structuralist vocabulary. The Other and the Law are two such examples. However, while Cixous works with a post-structuralist vocabulary she provides her own interventions, enriching rather hackneyed concepts in subversive and interesting ways.

Throughout Cixous's writing there is a rhetoric of movement often suggested by metaphors of flight, passages, forays and so on. This sense of movement is typical of much post-structuralist writing, which seeks to emphasize the subject as a process, as a form of becoming, rather than fixed by various social structures or political and philosophical categories. Writing, for Cixous, is an attempt to move the subject away from the stagnant confines of phallocentric thought. In order to grasp some of her ideas it is necessary to enter into that movement within her writing, to think with the writing creatively rather than fixing it with, or making it accountable to, a dichotomous logic. This is not an easy process and Cixous is acutely aware of the difficulty. However, the attempt to 'think otherwise' or to 'think the other' is not peculiar to Cixous alone so it would be a mistake to dismiss Cixous on the grounds that her writing is particularly complex. Philosophical writing is difficult because it challenges us to think.

Despite the originality of Cixous's thought she has not coined many new words, or neologisms, in the way that Derrida or Deleuze and Guattari have. Early on in her writing she might have made reference to the 'Phallocentric Performance Theatre' or the 'Empire of the Selfsame' but this was done in the spirit of a subversive and sometimes humorous manifesto against phallocentrism and these words cannot properly be called concepts. What then is a concept? If we explore this question we must ask: What is thinking? and then, What is philosophy? and so, finally, What is writing? For Deleuze and Guattari, following Nietzsche, philosophy is the creation of concepts. The concept is 'an act of thought, it is thought operating at infinite (although greater or lesser) speed' (Deleuze and Guattari 1994: 21). In other words, the concept is thinking in action, a movement of thought. Perhaps one of the reasons that Cixous has not produced a large conceptual terminology in the sense that, say, Deleuze and Guattari create the concept of the 'plateau' or a 'minor literature' is that she seeks to work within language in order to subvert and transform.[1] She might produce the occasional 'original' concept such as '*écriture féminine*', 'the other bisexuality' or the 'third body' but this is, by and large, a rarity. Rather, she works with existing concepts such as the Other and 'woman' and re-conceptualizes, rewrites them. And she also turns subjects like femininity and the maternal into philosophical concepts. It is important to recognize that the creation of a concept does not necessarily involve the production of a new term. Cixous works like a virus within language in order to decode and recode existing meanings. More radically, I would suggest that for Cixous, reading the sign 'woman' opens up thought itself.

To make this claim clearer it is worth drawing upon Heidegger's essay 'What Calls for Thinking?' (1954), which resonates with Cixous's approach. In this essay Heidegger offers a careful meditation on the process of thinking and quotes a line from the poet

Holderlin – 'We are a sign which is not read.' For Heidegger, 'man' is that which has yet to be interpreted, as a 'sign' man is that which points towards a horizon of thought which is continually withdrawing. Here is what Heidegger means by the sign 'man'. 'Something which in itself, by its essential being, is pointing, we call a sign. As he draws toward what withdraws, man is a sign. But since this sign points toward what draws *away*, it points not so much at what draws away as into the withdrawal. The sign remains without interpretation' (Heidegger 1977c: 351). And if that sign were 'woman'? Perhaps, we can imagine a 'feminine' withdrawal which is also a pulling into abundance, into a horizon of thinking otherwise in which the sign 'woman' points toward thought.

Heidegger notes that one of the titles for Holderlin's hymn was 'Memory' and he writes:

> Memory, Mother of the Muses – the thinking back to what is to be thought – is the source and ground of poesy. That is why poesy is the water that at times flows backward toward the source, toward thinking as a thinking back, a recollection. Surely, as long as we take the view that logic gives us insight into what thinking is, we shall never be able to think how much poesy rests upon thinking back, recollection. Poetry wells up only from devoted thought thinking back, recollecting. (Heidegger 1977c: 352)

Cixous's own emphasis in her writing on a thinking back through the body of woman to a new poetics of thought bears many uncanny similarities with Heidegger here. Moreover, Cixous argues that when we begin to read/write the sign 'woman' (which she argues has not yet been 'read' by phallocentrism) then we enter into thought. If 'woman' is a sign which has not yet been read, 'woman' calls on us to think. 'What calls for thinking?' asks Heidegger, and Cixous might reply 'the sign woman does'. However, it is not the sign 'woman' in relation to the sign 'man' which calls us into thinking (that relation has already been thought), but rather the autonomous and not yet interpreted sign 'woman' which calls us into thought. The autonomous specificity of the sign (woman) is therefore the threshold to a thinking otherwise.

For Cixous, to think through the sign 'woman' is to enter into another economy of thinking, one that isn't determined by a phallocentric logic which depends upon the sacrifice of the other. This economy of thinking is similar to the one Heidegger describes. In the same essay he writes: 'What calls on us to think gives us food for thought. . . . And what it gives us to think about, the gift it gives to us, is nothing less than itself – itself which calls on us to enter thought' (1977c: 367). We could argue that Heidegger is describing a feminine economy of thinking which offers a gift that does not demand a narcissistic return but rather gives in order to open up a space for an unlimited thinking, a thinking which is not restricted by the logic of exchange but rather is poetic, maternal in its abundance, its generosity, its giving of the self. And strangely this itself is thought. So Heidegger imagines a type of thinking which moves beyond logic, which is fecund, poetic, maternal, in which the gift (of the other as thought) is given freely.

I have chosen to discuss Heidegger here in the context of Cixous's work because I think it is important to highlight that Cixous works on a philosophical level. If Heidegger (who is arguably the most influential Western philosopher of the last century), suggests that the poetic is the maternal source of thought we can understand and respect more fully Cixous's emphasis on the poetic. Hers is not simply a dilettante's indulgence with pretty words or a romantic mystification of the maternal, but a serious ethical and philosophical investigation into the grounds of thought.

The stress Cixous places on the importance of a creative metaphysics and not a sterile repetition of previous thought also resonates with Nietzsche. In a section from *Beyond Good and Evil* (1886), Nietzsche offers a passionate critique of what he perceives to be the dominance of scientific objectivity within philosophy. Such a philosophy is uncreative, it is 'an instrument, let us say a *mirror*' (1973: 115). 'The objective man', he goes on to argue, 'is an instrument, a precious, easily damaged and tarnished measuring instrument and reflecting apparatus' (116). We might argue, with a nod towards the previous chapter, that such thinkers belong to the tradition of analytic realism, in the sense that this form of philosophy is grounded upon a type of empiricism and is about how to most accurately reflect reality. For Nietzsche, the philosophers of the future must embrace their own subjectivity and forge an experimental ethics in order to 'create values' (123). In this Nietzschean sense, we can understand Cixous as a philosopher of the future – she embraces her own subjectivity as a thinker and forges new values, creates new future possibilities for thought. Her autobiographical reflections are not so much a feminist confessional narrative but a meditation on the metaphysics and the materiality of her own subjectivity which provides a passage into thinking through subjectivity in general. Like Nietzsche and his philosophers of the future, Cixous recognizes the importance of testing concepts against the self.

We might also approach Cixous as a dissident. In an insightful essay, 'A New Type of Intellectual: The Dissident', Julia Kristeva offers the following definition of dissidence.

> For true dissidence today is perhaps simply what it has always been: *thought*. . . . Torn between being the guardian of the law and that instance which disavows the law, hasn't philosophy turned away from thought? . . . But through the efforts of thought in language, or precisely through the excesses of the language whose very multitude is the only sign of life, one can attempt to bring about multiple sublations of the unnameable, the unrepresentable, the void. This is the real cutting edge of dissidence. (Kristeva 1986c: 299–300)

And this is, precisely, Cixous's project – to restore to language or writing thought itself, to 'avow the unavowable', to think through a writing of the metaphysics of sexual difference in order to represent the unrepresentable, those pools of significant silence which nourish thought. As a Heideggerian thinker, as a Nietzschean philosopher of the future, and an intellectual dissident, but most of all and foremost, as a writer, Cixous calls upon us to think creatively. Her challenge is a powerful one. Are we capable of meeting it?

Sexual difference

When Cixous discusses a concept of sexual difference she is referring not to the anatomical differences between men and women but rather to the morphological differences. In her essays in *The Newly Born Woman* (Cixous and Clement 1991), Cixous is careful to stress that when she discusses sexual difference she is not reinforcing phallocentric biologism. 'I make a point of using the qualifiers of sexual difference here to avoid the confusion. . . . We have to be careful not to lapse smugly or blindly into an essentialist ideological interpretation' (Cixous and Clement 1991: 81). As Gatens (1991) points out, morphology is a representation of anatomy, so it follows that sexual difference and its representations are inseparable. This is not simply to say that sexual difference is a matter of writing but it is to insist that writing, or representation, complicates a transparent relationship to a pure, naturally given, anatomically different body.

In a lecture on Cixous and sexual difference called 'Fourmis', Derrida writes the following:

> [H]ere is my hypothesis, as soon as there is sexual difference, there are words or rather traces *to read*. It begins *in this way*. There can be traces without sexual difference, for example, with asexual living things, but there cannot be sexual difference without trace, and this holds not only for 'us', for the living things we call human. But from here on, sexual difference is to be interpreted, to be deciphered, to be decoded, to be read and not to be seen. Readable, thus invisible, the object of testimony and not of proof – and in the same stroke problematic, mobile, not assured – it passes by, it is in passage, it passes from one to the other, by the one and the other (from l'*une* to the other like *un fourmi, un fourmi* of a dream).   (Derrida 1997, 121)

The idea that sexual difference is not stable and is somehow invisible might seem absurd, for surely men and women are visibly different and this difference is by and large stable. However, this apparent absurdity is on one level merely a recognition that how sexual difference signifies is not fixed within language. If we recognize the plasticity of sexual difference then we also recognize that it is possible to create positive reinscriptions.

In the section 'The School of the Dead' from *Three Steps on the Ladder of Writing* (1993b), Cixous argues against a simplistic theorization of sexual difference:

> This is why the man–woman conflict is insufficient for me, in my time, in my place. It is a question of sexual difference, only sexual difference isn't what we think it is. It's both tortuous and complicated. There is sexual difference, and there is what it becomes in its appearance and distribution in each one of us.   (50)

In this sense, sexual difference is as infinitely complex as every social being is. To offer an orthodox definition of sexual difference is to limit an understanding of this complexity. Nevertheless, Cixous acknowledges that in order to argue against the injustices committed against women it is necessary to limit this complexity. We might call this limit a form of strategic essentialism.

In the same text Cixous returns to this subject:

> as women we are at the obligatory mercy of simplification. In order to defend women we are obliged to speak in the feminist terms of 'man' and 'woman'. If we start to say that such and such a woman is not entirely a woman or not a woman at all, that this 'father' is not a father, we can no longer fight since we no longer know who is in front of us. It's so destructive, so destabilizing that those of us who are conscious of what is at stake are often pushed toward a form of interdict.   (201)

Here Cixous addresses one of the central problems that confront a feminism which is sensitive to the multiple and shifting complexities of sexual difference. In order to fight against oppression on a political level it is necessary to limit a thinking through sexual difference, to arrive at a point of meaning or closure in order to strategically oppose political violence even while the closing off of signification even for strategic purposes is itself a form of violence. The only resolution of this ethical dilemma lies in the future re-significations of sexual difference and an increased political awareness of their complexity. For Cixous this can only be achieved by thinking through sexual difference, through a writing that moves beyond the limits of phallocentrism, for it is this very phallocentrism which calls for an interdict, a restriction of meaning. Perhaps this is another reason why Cixous is wary of the political for it is inherently combative and thus not open to the Other. In this sense the political remains antithetical to the opening up of thought.

Sexual difference, then, is an infinitely complex process of signification and yet also, paradoxically, this very process of signification must be restricted if feminism is able to hold claim to a speaking position. Such an awareness does not have to lead to political apathy or pessimism but rather to an increased understanding of the instability of political truths which recognizes that fundamentalist claims are capable of being deconstructed. To ground women's sexual difference in an identity or definition is, for Cixous, to fail to recognize that this very foundation is continually shifting, and yet this 'failure' is essential if feminism itself is to have any political grounds. However, a 'poetic' or philosophical appreciation of the instability of meaning does not close off the possibility for political action. Rather, a Cixousian feminist politics of sexual difference would acknowledge that this very foundation or ground is not an empirical foundation, which can be anchored in the *anatomical* body, but rather it is a *morphological* foundation, which is therefore open to writing, to a subversive reinscription. In effect, Cixous's emphasis on the fluidity of sexual difference is made against the solidity of any fundamentalist politics which is grounded on an equation between biology and ideology.

The other bisexuality

For Cixous, heterosexuality is part and parcel of the phallocentric writing machine which has inscribed subjectivity into a restrictive masculine libidinal economy. The heterosexual male and female couple are central to the hierarchical dualism of phallogocentrism. Such a relationship can only ever be repressive and constricting, argues Cixous, because it limits an experience of love and desire by imposing rigid roles and prefixed sexual identities onto men and women. Moreover, what we might term the metaphysics of heterosexuality, the sense that this sexed couple is the foundation of binary thought, also restricts creative thought. And yet the idea of bisexuality, while apparently more fluid and open than heterosexuality, is, argues Cixous, just as restricting because it so often just repeats the central male/female dichotomy.

Instead, Cixous proposes what she calls 'the other bisexuality', that is, a sexuality which is more than female or male, a sexuality that can move beyond, exceed the very limits of what counts as female desire or male desire. 'To this bisexuality that melts together and effaces, wishing to avert castration, I oppose the *other bisexuality*, the one with which every subject, who is not shut up inside spurious Phallocentric Performing Theatre, sets up his or her erotic universe' (Cixous and Clement 1991: 84–5). Cixous wants to move beyond singular and separate definitions of masculine and feminine desire. 'To say that woman is somehow bisexual is an apparently paradoxical way of disciplining and reviving the question of difference. And therefore of writing as "feminine" or "masculine" ' (85).

This concept of the 'other bisexuality' is also another passage through the limits of the binary opposition of masculinity and femininity for it introduces a third sex which is not reducible to either masculine or feminine but exceeds both. Bisexuality, suggests Cixous, has been understood through a Hegelian logic in which the differences between femininity and masculinity are resolved in a synthesis. (For example, masculinity would be the thesis, femininity would be the antithesis, bisexuality would be the synthesis.) Her argument about bisexuality echoes some of the criticism directed against Virginia Woolf's celebration of androgyny. For Woolf, androgyny represented a third type of sexual being who was free from the constraints of both masculinity and femininity. As several critics pointed out, this amounted to the erasure of the positive specificities of female subjectivity while also celebrating the sexually neutral subject, which has historically been the ex-nominated space of the masculine subject in the sense that this subject has historically been masked by ideologies of impartial reason and so on.[2]

Cixous's concept of the 'other' bisexuality also feeds into her intervention into masculinity. This new third subjectivity challenges the (masculine) subject's phobic disavowal of the feminine as that lack which calls the subject into death, loss of self, castration. Instead of oppressing women because they are projected as the source of a threatening castration and lack, men who are able to inhabit the feminine through the passage of the 'other' bisexuality will enter into a less violent relationship with the feminine. She also asserts that this type of bisexuality is caught up in the writing process. 'I will say: today, writing is women's. That is not a provocation, it means that woman admits there is an other. In her becoming-woman, she has not erased the bisexuality latent in the girl as in the boy. Femininity and bisexuality go together. . . It is much harder for men to let the other come through him. Writing is the passageway, the entrance, the exit, the dwelling place of the other in me – the other that I am and am not' (85–6). In this sense, the other bisexuality is about an ethical opening to the Other: it is the sexuality of the Other.

The feminine libidinal economy

Cixous's concept of a feminine libidinal economy is central to an understanding of her work. Her basic premise, like that of Lyotard in *Libidinal Economy* (1974), is that the operations of desire or the libido underpin and support socio-political exchanges of any kind. She can also be said to draw upon Lacan's brief theorization of *jouissance*, and more strongly on Georges Bataille's notions of expenditure and his critique of 'closed economies' such as the Hegelian dialectic in which difference is contained and colonized in a grand unifying synthesis.[3]

For Cixous and for many theorists, sexuality lies at the heart of freedom and social change. Much of her work can be understood as a poetic invocation of the feminine libidinal economy, an economy of desire which is open, productive, creative. As we have seen, in 'Sorties: Out and Out: Attacks/Ways Out/Forays', Cixous begins by establishing that 'thought has always worked through opposition' and that this structure of opposition or hierarchical dualisms is phallogocentric. Within phallogocentric thought woman is positioned as passive, 'Either woman is passive or she does not exist. What is left of her is unthinkable or unthought' (Cixous and Clement 1991: 64). For Cixous the masculine structure of phallogocentrism has 'passed itself off as eternal–natural' when in fact it is a type of writing machine which artificially orders reality, social structures, everyday lives, our very history, our very philosophy. She asks us to imagine another way, another economy if you like.

Phallogocentrism is predicated upon the exclusion of female desire. 'And each story, each myth says to her: There is no place for your desire in our affairs of State' (1991: 67). She is the absence that enables his presence. 'Night to his day – that has forever been the fantasy, Black to his white. Shut out of his system's space, she is the repressed that ensures the system's functioning' (1991: 67). The repressed, that which does not fit into the neat equations, possesses a potency which must be liberated.

The feminine libidinal economy is about liberating a repressed female desire, about circulating that desire within language, but it is also about recognizing and encouraging an economy which moves beyond the strictures of phallocentric law.[4] In this context, the feminine libidinal economy describes the fluidity of female desire on a material, corporeal level and also a more conceptual, metaphysical level. The feminine libidinal economy encompasses both an understanding of the sexual specificity of female desire and a different metaphysical economy. Such an economy is 'meta' physical in the original Greek sense of *meta* as 'with, across, or after' and the original Greek definition of physic as 'knowledge of nature': it is not an abstraction of nature or materiality, an impartial, distant scientific ordering, but rather an intimate knowledge 'with' materiality. It is a knowledge of materiality which moves with, across, through bodies. Usually it is the sense that *meta* means 'after', a type of temporal reflecting back on what is, a type of conceptual distance or separation from materiality which is attributed to metaphysics. Here I would argue that the feminine libidinal economy is not a metaphysics of the presence or immediacy of the materiality of desire, but rather describes a movement in the same direction as materiality. This paradoxical relationship between the sensible or empirical and the transcendental is itself a deconstruction of the body/mind dichotomy which underpins Western metaphysics.

The gift

A concept of the gift is also central to Cixous's work and is closely connected to her understanding of the feminine libidinal economy. Within this economy there is a giving which does not expect a return, an openness to the other which is not a veiled demand for the other to provide something which the subject can appropriate. Indeed, in this sense the subject gives to the other without experiencing the gift as a loss of the self, something which will reduce the self's worth. Rather, giving is about opening up a space in which the other can exist autonomously and not on the condition that the other reciprocate by giving back an equivalent of that which was given. This is also to acknowledge that the other has gifts which exceed the subject's own understanding of economy. To put it another way and to make this a little more comprehensible perhaps, if one were to give away something, for example a family heirloom or even precious time, there would be an implicit expectation that a gift would be returned in a manner which acknowledges the nature of the gift given. If this did not happen then one would feel affronted. The gift now becomes a loss. Or as Cixous puts it: 'loss and expense are stuck in the commercial deal that always turns the gift into a gift-that-takes. The gift brings in a return' (Cixous and Clement 1991: 87). However, this is to assume that the other I have given to is able to recognize the language game, if you will, that we are engaged in, that the other possesses an equivalent gift and that this should be exchanged. I expect a return by giving.

What if the giving itself was the return? What if I was able to give to the other without expecting a return out of a fear that if a return was not forthcoming I would be diminished in some way? What if there was a giving which moved beyond a narcissistic exchange? What sort of economy, language, metaphysics, writing, sexuality, thought would this look like? Cixous poses this question when she discusses the gift. And she calls this economy 'feminine' and relates it to the maternal body which is the body in our culture which gives of itself (the mother gives life itself) and does not demand a return (another life, or even a death). In simple terms, the phallocentric libidinal economy is death-driven while the feminine libidinal economy is life-affirming. In 'First Names of No One' Cixous poses the (feminine) gift against the limits of death, of repression, totalitarianism, that which seeks authority over the self and other. Writing opens up the possibility of this limitless economy in which the subject is 'no one' and yet innumerable, multiple. 'In every place that it passes through, structures burst open, the affective or social economy changes form, unknown possibilities for desire and life surge out; exchange loses its privileged position, and the *gift* takes it away' (in Sellers 1997: 29).

In 'Coming to Writing' Cixous also discusses the exchange of negativity through the concept of the gift:

> Mystery of hatred, of spite: isn't the one who hates devoured alive by hatred? Whoever keeps wealth and nourishment for himself is poisoned alive. Mystery of the gift: the poison-gift: if you give you receive. What you don't give, the anti-gift, turns back against you and rots you. The more you give, the more you take pleasure. (Cixous 1991a: 49)

Here Cixous seems to be advocating a type of passivity, a refusal to circulate hatred and aggression. The more you give pleasure, the more pleasure you receive. The more you give hatred (the anti-gift, or poison-gift), the more hatred you receive. And yet, how would one translate this into a political pragmatics? How does one name oppression or abuse without participating in a bad economy? How does one name the debt an abuser owes without becoming caught up in an abusive economy or exchange of hatred? In one sense, Cixous's description of the gift evokes the following, rather paradoxical, question: how does giving to, or receiving from, an abuser achieve justice? This question is not fully explained or dealt with by Cixous when she discusses the gift.

In an essay on 'Clarice Lispector: the Approach', Cixous goes on to develop this notion of the gift, arguing that 'we no longer know how to receive. Receiving is a science. Knowing how to receive is the best of gifts. Clarice gives us an example: it is a matter of receiving the lesson of things' (1991b: 62). Again, to play devil's advocate here, we might argue that there are some lessons which one would not want to receive. If a true receptivity entails an active awareness of the gift as a lesson, doesn't this assume that the lesson is somehow positive? Would one want to be receptive to a gift which contains a lesson about one's inferiority? Can one call this lesson a gift? How does one distinguish a poison-gift or an anti-gift when one is just being receptive to the gift as lesson? How does one circulate that lesson if it is an abusive one? Even if one would argue that the lesson is really a reflection of the giver, how would one circulate this lesson in such a way that the abusive gift re-educates the abuser?

These sorts of questions are perhaps inappropriate in the context of Cixous's argument about the gift and yet they also touch upon what we might call the idealization of the Other within poststructuralist thought. To put it simply, if the other is abusive should one remain open to him? How does one create a pragmatic ethics and a politics if one is continually attempting an opening to and a receptivity to the other when this other is violent? At what point should we distinguish between the Other as an ontological category and the other as an empirical subject in the world? Isn't such a distinction necessary to a politics of sexual difference which is grounded upon an ethical commitment to the limitation of abuse? It seems that Cixous is saying 'don't fight fire with fire', and yet it is not clear what her other strategy is. Putting a flower in the end of a rifle is all very well until a bullet comes shooting out.

Ultimately perhaps, Cixous's concept of the gift is part of a utopian strand of thinking within her work. The gift is part of a sensitive meditation on the nature of things, on being, on the complex exchanges which occur between the sexes within a capitalist culture. It is a critique both of the phallocentric politics of capitalism and of the metaphysics which support this. Perhaps it is up to us to be receptive to the lesson her concept of the gift bestows and to circulate it in other ways.

The feminine

Within Cixous's work the feminine signifies the social repression of female autonomy and desire and also a subversive *élan vital* or vital creative force. The feminine can also be understood as a description of a type of ethics which affirms women's vitality and creativity against the deathly constraints of a social order which has historically denied women the free expression of their desire, and their liberty as fellow human beings. The feminine is thus an affirmation of the vital body which is akin to Nietzsche's earlier celebration of corporeality. Throughout *Thus Spake Zarathustra* (1885) Nietzsche invokes a return to the earth, to the body, for it is only when the body is affirmed joyfully that the superman as creator will be born and a new, healthier, vital morality will come into being. In 'The Despisers of the Body' Nietzsche argues that the body is a great intelligence and a multiplicity. To deny the body is to also deny creativity. 'Your Self wants to perish, and that is why you have become despisers of the body! For no longer are you able to create beyond yourselves' (Nietzsche 1969: 63). Against this reactive alienation Nietzsche affirms the positivity of the body as a source of creativity.

Femininity for Cixous, then, is both a description of a range of social and historical narratives which have been mapped onto women's bodies and also a subversive, dissident energy which is capable of transforming metaphysics, language, social relations. Femininity is thus, for Cixous, both a socio-political entity as well as a linguistic and philosophical movement. The two senses of this definition of the feminine are captured in her essay 'La – "The" (Feminine)'. The first passage from 'La' is a densely poetic invocation of the feminine as a potent life-affirming force and of feminine writing as the joyful destruction of death-bound negativity. Here the feminine overcomes alienation.

> Her affirmations. Her scene of wild writings forever escapes vigi-
> lance, armed reason, force, jealousy, death wish, *Schadenfreude*, the

traps and bites of life's enemies'. . . . She will become so robust during her lives that it will be easy for her to make sickness sick, to find in injuries the healing virtue that resides there, to thwart the threat of death of which the mask covers nothing. She will laugh heartily. (Cixous, in Sellers 1997: 59, 61)

Elsewhere in this same essay Cixous offers a humorous but challenging description of women's desire for a shelter. Her attitude towards women's freedom is similar to Simone de Beauvoir's here, who in *The Second Sex* [1953] urged women not to relinquish their freedom by hiding in a relationship with a man. Like de Beauvoir, Cixous calls upon women to embrace their freedom, to refuse to romanticize or mythologize a dependency upon men. There is strength in being alone, without a man to take care of her. 'It's as well if you are frightened of your solitude. It's a sign that you have come to the moment of your birth,' writes Cixous (in Sellers 1997: 61). Instead of understanding herself as nothing without a man, the Cixousian woman refuses to give herself away to 'these diabolical leftover mothers, always there to protect you from seeing . . . from life!' and cherishes her autonomy (in Sellers 1997: 64). Rather than experiencing her self as no-thing, as alienated and castrated without a man, the Cixousian woman understands that she must nourish herself, give birth to herself in freedom.

I would also argue that for Cixous femininity is caught up in a theorization of female alienation. To submit to the classic social and psychoanalytic narratives of what it means to be a feminine woman is to enter into an alienated relationship with one's own desires. However, unlike many feminists such as Betty Friedan and Naomi Wolf, who have simply equated femininity with alienation, Cixous also offers up femininity as an antidote to alienation and as a passage to freedom.[5] This is another case, I think, in which she subverts the negative connotations which have surrounded a concept like femininity and moves on to a radical philosophical reinterpretation of femininity and alienation.

In order to make my claims clearer it is worth considering what I mean by alienation. In a concise essay on 'Existentialism and the Alienation of Man', Albert William Levi provides a useful summary of the philosophical history of alienation:

In every case the use of the term implies an axiological dualism, a valuational contrariety, and the essential pairs in this case are, I

> think, three: (1) the unified or the integrated versus the divided or
> fragmented; (2) the organic, the sexual, the human, versus the
> mechanical, and (3) the feelingful versus the impersonal and the
> distant. *Fragmentation, mechanization, distantiation, are the three
> dimensions of alienation, and every usage, however remote, will in
> some sense presuppose, or explicate, or explore one or more of these
> crucial aspects.*   (Levi 1967: 254)

From at least Freud onwards, femininity has been typically associated with these three characteristics. In the context of Cixous's
work, she achieves a radical reinterpretation of alienation. She
critiques the unity Hegel seeks as an antidote to alienation – framing this whole as a phallocentric, cannibalistic consumption of the
alterity of the feminine and the Freudian theory of female castration as a fear of female abundance; the organicity which Marx
seeks is for Cixous anchored in the infinite materiality of
consciousness, the morphology of the body itself becomes a
theatre of inscription in which the poetics (and not, importantly, a
pseudo-science) of thought are remade. Moreover, instead of
stressing the immediacy of the personal as an antidote to alienation, for Cixous distance becomes loaded with an ethical relationship to the other. She argues that it is necessary to achieve a certain
distance before the other, within us and without (see the next
section, Fidelity). In these ways we can argue that Cixous radically
reinscribes phallocentric concepts of alienation, and specifically,
of femininity as alienation.

   Women, she argues, are already separate from themselves.
Women give birth, their very bodies separate. For women this is
not a form of alienation but love, a form of giving of the self not a
loss of self. Moreover, fragmentation can also be understood as
jouissance, and as a form of writing which celebrates the pleasures
of marginality, exile, being a stranger to oneself. To lose one's Self
is not necessarily to lose oneself. Loss of self does not necessarily
have to lead to death, alienation, fear, hostility, but there can be a
loss of self which is a giving to a new self, to others. The feminine
gives without return, it is a form of fragmentation which does not
describe a turning against the self by an internationalized oppressive other.

   In a sense Cixous argues that one must move through the
passage of alienation to reach the other side – leap over the abyss,
confront fragmentation, risk loss in order to gain not an organic

whole self (that is a phallic myth which is used to pathologize the fragmented feminine) but a self which has the courage to play with fragmentation, schisms, distance, without experiencing annihilation. It takes a certain courage and strength of spirit and mind to accept death, alienation, fragmentation and transform these intimate, close experiences into a life-affirming writing. The feminine moves against death by passing through loss.

Fidelity

Fidelity is something that Cixous often meditates upon in her writing. Fidelity is a noun which means 'continued loyalty to a person, cause, or belief', and 'the degree of exactness with which something is copied or reproduced' (*OED*). The word comes from the Latin *fides*, for 'faith'. For Cixous, feminine writing is an attempt to demonstrate a loving fidelity to the other, to let the other come into being within writing by remaining faithful to the essence of the other, knowing all the while that this essence cannot ever be captured or totally reproduced within writing. Fidelity, then, describes a particular relationship to the other, or to the object or thing which is written about. Fidelity is also another way of describing a feminine libidinal economy in which the appropriation of the other is avoided. In 'Extreme Fidelity', Cixous writes that 'One might say that the work of Clarice Lispector is an immense *book of respect, a book of the right distance*' (in Sellers 1997: 136). In 'Clarice Lispector: The Approach' (1991b), Cixous discusses how Lispector's writing in particular is able to accomplish this fidelity toward the other, an approach which moves towards the other without attempting to erase difference or 'strangeness'. A loyalty or fidelity to the difference of the other is about refusing to appropriate the other into sameness, or recognizing the importance of distance.

Central to Cixous's theorization of writing with fidelity is also a metaphysical relationship to the thing or the materiality of existence. Commenting on *Illa*, the feminist philosopher Andrea Nye writes that here Cixous offers an 'experience of things, an experience which does not attempt to master or to classify, but listens, looks, feels, hears. To speak a rational language is to kill the things, to refuse to hear them or look at them' (Nye 1988: 199). Indeed,

much of Cixous's writing is an attempt to comprehend the materiality of the world without imposing what she perceives to be the
death-bound, colonizing language of phallocentrism. In her essay
on Lispector, Heidegger's thought infuses Cixous's careful invocation of the unique poetry of this writer.[6] Lispector 'makes us hear
things calling. The call there is in things: she gathers it back. The
clarice voice gathers. And offers us the orange. Gives us back the
thing' (Cixous 1991b: 61). Calling, gathering and a metaphysical
mediation on the thing are of course Heideggerian preoccupations
and indeed she quotes from Heidegger's 'What Calls for Thinking'
(1968).

It is worth pausing for a moment and recognizing a significant
difference between Cixous's attempt to open up thought to the
mysterious materiality of the 'thing' and more sombre existential
theories of alienation and the objectification of the self and world.
In Jean-Paul Sartre's first novel *Nausea* (1938) the protagonist's
alienation is expressed as a nausea with the objects or things in the
world.

> Objects ought not to touch, since they are not alive. . . . But they
> touch me, it's unbearable. . . . How unpleasant it was! And it came
> from the pebble, I'm sure of that, it passed from the pebble into my
> hands. Yes, that's it, that's exactly it: a sort of nausea in the hands.
> (Sartre 1975: 22)

Eventually the unhappy protagonist's own body is contaminated
by this nauseous objectification and he himself, his very flesh and
thoughts, become objects, the source of nausea. In contrast to this
sickening attention to the materiality of the world, Cixous offers
wonder, an openness and proximity to the other (be it orange,
flower, cockroach or human) which is driven by love rather than
the Sartreian disgust. If Sartre's protagonist is alienated precisely
because he experiences his own passivity as an opening up to the
other, Cixous has a very different reading of passivity. 'As for
passivity, in excess, it is partly bound up with death. But there is a
non-closure that is not submission but confidence and comprehension; that is not an opportunity for destruction but for wonderful expansion' (Cixous and Clement 1991: 42).

One of the reasons for this loving attention (or fidelity) to the
materiality of the other is a sense of connection to the substance of

the world as mat(t)er, an ability to embrace the difference outside and within ourselves without experiencing this contact with difference as alienation, passivity, objectification or loss of self. For a feminine approach to the other is not made with fear: castration, loss of self, fear of engulfment by the (m)other, and the cannibalizing, destructive defence mechanisms which this fear produces are not part of the libidinal economy of feminine writing. For Cixous it is only an insecure death-driven phallic subjectivity which perceives the 'touch' of things in the world as a nauseous alienation. Sartre's protagonist is unable to receive the pebble because he is 'afraid of entering into contact with [things] just as if they were living animals' (Sartre 1975: 22). Commenting on Lispector, Cixous writes: 'We must save the approach that opens and leaves space for the other. . . . And we no longer know how to receive. . . . Knowing how to receive is the best of gifts' (1991b: 62). Instead of closing off thought and turning thought towards death, a feminine approach to the 'thing' opens up thought, receives the 'thing' as a gift for thinking. In 'Extreme Fidelity' (in Sellers 1997), Cixous locates this approach as the feminine libidinal economy.

At this point it might also be fruitful to contrast Sartre's 'nausea' with Luce Irigaray's concept of 'wonder'. Like Cixous, Irigaray is committed to rethinking a metaphysics of sexual difference in order to open up thought to an ethical relationship to the other. In 'Wonder: a Reading of Descartes' *The Passions of the Soul*', Irigaray argues that we must preserve a sense of wonder towards the strangeness or difference of objects and things in the world if we are to revitalize thought itself. She quotes Descartes, who writes that 'wonder is the first of all the passions' and that '[w]onder is a sudden surprise of the soul which causes it to apply itself to consider with attention the objects which seem to it rare and extraordinary'.[7] It is important, argues Irigaray, to keep a sense that all objects are rare and extraordinary, including each other, men and women too. Wonder, for Irigaray, 'is the passion of the first encounter. . . . The passion that inaugurates love and art. And thought. . . . Wonder would be the passion of the encounter between the most material and the most metaphysical, of their possible conception and fecundation one by the other' (Irigaray 1993a: 82).

In this context Sartre's pebble would not be a threat to subjectivity, it would be caressed, touched, smelt, weighed in the hand, contemplated. The relationship between the pebble, the beach, the sea and the body which holds it would open up thought, and not close thought off into a contemplation of death and negativity. The materiality of the body which holds the materiality of the pebble would not be threatened but rather open up to the strangeness and wonder of the pebble. Obviously I am not suggesting that to think we must meditate on the difference of a pebble (although William Blake saw the universe in a grain of sand). The pebble is a metaphor for the materiality of the other as well as the thing. How we approach the other, argues Cixous, is of profound ethical importance. In order to approach the other we must not confuse passivity with alienation and death but rather understand that within the slow stillness of an open contemplation of the other there is the movement of thinking.

To summarize: fidelity is a form of keeping alive the passion of wonder towards the materiality of the world in order to receive the gift of Otherness by being faithful to its continual strangeness. This approach is thoughtful, careful, slow, it does not rapidly colonize the other with language, imposing an already sterile conceptual map onto the materiality of the other, but rather transforms an encounter with the other into an opening up of thought, '*to allow a thing to enter into its strangeness*' (Cixous 1991b, 66). As such, fidelity is about a certain distance and respect. In the essay on fidelity Cixous also discusses the biblical narrative about Eve and the apple. 'Every entry to life finds itself *before the Apple*' (in Sellers 1997: 132). The Law tells us that if we eat the apple we will die. The Law is, for Cixous, 'pure anti-pleasure' (135). What is prohibited by the Law is the passion of wonder towards the other, for it is this wonder which leads to a subversive thinking beyond the Law, which calls into question the phallocentric ordering of things in the world. To refuse the gift of the apple, the other, is to refuse the gift of knowledge and thought. In this sense the Law itself is an attempt to ward of the pleasure of thought.

The third body

Le Troisième corps [The Third Body] is the title of a book Cixous originally published in French in 1970. Translated and published in English in 1999 it is a complex autobiographical meditation on the relationship between the narrator and her lover. The text is a sur-realistic examination of the complexities of love, the theme of incorporation and appropriation of the desired other, which weaves through intimate descriptions of family relationships, liter-ary tales and mythic characters. The third body, like the 'other bisexuality', is a concept which calls attention to the in between, the liminal, that which passes through one and the other. She gives textual 'flesh' to this uncanny third term and with typical Cixousian attention she renders it poetically as the source of some-thing which can open up love and writing to a more ethical rela-tionship between the sexes. Perhaps this is romantic, but then for Cixous the poetry of love and desire are metaphysical properties which are deserving of careful thought.

Cixous also briefly discusses the third body in 'Coming to Writing'. Here she describes writing as the meeting of masculine and feminine, as an ecstatic engagement with another's body which rather than resulting in an erasure of difference, a cancelling out of the other, offers the gift of alterity, producing rather than reducing difference. Again this is linked to Cixous's deconstruction of phallocentric binary thought and her emphasis on the creation of other ways of being. Writing becomes a type of rapture, an ecstasy in which the subject stands outside herself and becomes aware that she is other.

> I sense that I am loved by writing. How could I help loving it? I am woman, I make love. Love makes me, a Third Body (Troisième Corps) comes to us, a third sense of sight, and our other ears – between our two bodies our third body surges forth, and flies up to see the summit of things, and at the summit rises and soars toward the highest things: dives, swims in our waters, descends, explores the depths of the bodies, discovers and consecrates every organ, comes to know the minute and the invisible – but in order for the third body to be written, the exterior must enter and the interior must open out.   (Cixous 1991a: 53–4)

The third body is 'that which is projected outside me and covers over me, this body foreign to my body that rises from my body and shrouds it' (Cixous 1999: 34). Here this body opens up another way of thinking through corporeality as something which is not simply anchored in the presence of the flesh but which is nomadic, moves beyond the body and yet is part of the body. The third body is that which is created through the exchange, the flow, of desire: 'At the intersection of our tongues there came to us a third body, at a place where there is no law' (70). Instead of writing about an intense and intimate meeting between the sexes as the death of the self or other, Cixous conjures up the uncanny image of a third entity: contact with the other creates a third term, a third body which exists outside the confines of the law and so gestures toward a sense of the limitless. A sense of this is evoked when she describes this entity in the following way.

> We have already fashioned the place of our immortality: it is located at the intersection of both our desires stretched straight out, sprung from the same side of our silent united tongues, and, having fathers and mothers, origins and infinity, it appears all at once on the other side, in the form of a third body which is the mirror of my eyes in his image which in the mirror of his eyes is in my image – in this body we are exchanged up to the highest degree of resemblance; in this body we translate each other. What will be born of my desire? The unique and unknown body of our silence: we must find that word-less, limitless language that will perpetuate us without error and without weakening.   (153)

The third body is a space in which a type of translation occurs, a form of writing which exchanges representations of the other (the mirror, the image, the resemblance) and creates a 'limitless language' which will 'perpetuate us'. This language is paradoxically also 'wordless', the third body is a form of 'silence', perhaps a type of gestation.

Another way of understanding what Cixous means by the third body is to link her concept to other ways of trying to re-imagine the body within post-structuralist thought. In 'The Fecundity of the Caress', Irigaray also writes poetically about an intimacy which continually unfolds itself into an alterity that exceeds the corporeal limits of those who touch:

> Thus a new birth comes about, a new dawn for the beloved. And the lover. The openness of a face which has not yet been sculptured. . . . Not a mask given or attributed once and for all, but an efflorescence that detaches itself from its immersion and absorption in the night's most secret place.   (Irigaray 1993b: 189)

Here Irigaray also calls attention to the birth of an alterity which goes beyond representations ('a mask given or attributed once and for all') and moves, flows outwards.

Cixous also describes the third body as polymorphously loquacious: 'We have mouths all over our body. Words come out of our hands, our underarms, our belly, our eyes, our neck' (1999, 79). This body has endless possibilities for speaking. Speaking is not organized around the mouth. Cixous's disorganization of the body through her description of the third body can also be compared to Deleuze and Guattari's concept of the Body without Organs (BwO). The BwO is imagined against the organized, regulated and calculated morphology of Freudian narratives about loss and castration which limit libidinality to a phallocentric Oedipal economy. Rather, the BwO continually undergoes a process of experimental becoming, it is a 'connection of desires, conjunctions of flows, continuums of intensities' (Deleuze and Guattari 1987: 161).[8] 'The BwO is desire; it is that which one desires and by which one desires' (1991: 165). As Michel Foucault puts it in his by now famous introduction to *Anti-Oedipus*, Deleuze and Guattari ask 'How does one introduce desire into thought, into discourse, into action?' (Foucault 1992, xii). This quest resonates with Cixous's project and like Cixous we might argue that their concept of the BwO is an attempt to think the body in and through desire, against the negativity of the Law.

Laughter

Could laughter ever be a philosophical concept? Isn't it rather frivolous to include laughter here within the categories of philosophical thought? Seriously though, the act of laughter does have an important place in Cixous's work. If we recall her affinity with Surrealism we recognize that laughter is a subversive act which is capable of undoing the intimidating sobriety of the Law. The very title of her manifesto 'The Laugh of the Medusa' highlights the moment in the text when the maternal figure laughs at the absurdity of phallocentric assumptions that women lack.

> They riveted us between two horrifying myths: between the Medusa and the abyss. That would be enough to set half the world laughing, except that it's still going on. . . . They haven't changed a thing:

they've theorized their desire for reality! Let the priests tremble,
we're going to show them our sexts! . . . You only have to look at the
Medusa straight on to see her. And she's not deadly. She's beautiful
and she's laughing.   (Cixous 1980a: 255)

Here phallocentric power is reduced to a cowering confusion
before the voluptuous figure of the maternal body. She hasn't got
one! She finds their bewildered terror hilarious. Phallocentric
power is revealed as a terrified defence mechanism against the
imagined spectre of phallic loss. Such is the investment in the phallus as the locus of power that the only way masculine subjectivity
can imagine the (m)other is to figure her as she who does not have
one. This absence is so feared it is imagined as a type of death.

Laughter marks the crossing of a boundary between the proper
and the improper, it signifies a movement of transgression. The
pleasure obtained in transgressing the law is immediately invested
in the production of the new. In the case of Cixous's Medusa,
laughter transforms the absence attached to the female sex into an
image of the maternal as the source of a subversive plenitude and
jouissance. In an exchange with Mireille Calle-Gruber, Cixous
writes:

I think that laughter is set off when we are not afraid. When we see
that the immense is not overwhelming; and also, perhaps, when the
maternal in us can manifest itself: as the imaginary possibility of
taking a mountain in one's arms. That is to say, knowing that one
can always give life, protection, care, even to the biggest. And that
the biggest also needs that care. And that we escape or we have
escaped death.   (Cixous and Calle-Gruber 1997: 21–2)

Death, the fear of the immense, those forces which can so easily
overwhelm, are reduced by a laughter which recognizes that all
things need maternal care. On one level this laughter is about
seeing the frustrated and needy child behind the threats and
posturings of phallocentric power. Cixousian laughter recognizes
not only the fragility of the immense but also the ability of the
maternal to bestow life to that which is seemingly death-bound.

Unlike Kristeva's concept of apocalyptic laughter which arises
from a confrontation with abjection from within horror, and
merely signals the expenditure of the excess which is confronted
and experienced, Cixous's laughter passes through death and

abjection into life and *jouissance*. Cixousian laughter is therefore far more positive and productive than the apocalyptic laughter Kristeva analyses in avant-garde writers such as Celine. A relationship toward the maternal is crucial here: Kristeva's apocalyptic laughter springs from a horror of maternal abjection while for Cixous the figuring of the maternal as abject (i.e. the Medusa) is itself a source of laughter.[9] In 'La – "The" (Feminine)' Cixous offers a description of the feminine writer who is capable of 'crossing unscathed the foul economies, in a spirited stroke, from her inexhaustible source of humour' (in Sellers 1997: 59). Instead of being contaminated by death, alienation and abjection, the feminine writer's laughter opens up a passage through these 'foul economies' towards a joyful and abundant affirmation of life.

In *Rootprints*, Cixous also provides an example from her own life to illustrate the connection between death and laughter.

> It is the jubilation we feel to be still living, the excitement without pity of the narrow escape. When I was little, I was told about the death of a cousin of my father, which happened shortly after that of my father and in the same way: I burst out laughing. Death went through me and I laughed. I became frightened until I understood. The phenomenon of great nervous hilarity was this: I was alive! Exactly that meritless victory which makes us giddy – and which can manifest itself, by the way, otherwise than in bursts of laughter – when we have been brushed with death.   (Cixous 1997: 26)

Here laughter is an affirmation of life and overcoming of the power of death. Laughter affirms existence, overcomes the spectre of death present both in the death of someone close and in those threats from all sources of negativity which attempt to annihilate and reduce the subject.

Death

Cixous is preoccupied with death throughout her writing. She frequently describes the impact her father's death had on her as a young girl and states that it was this early death which brought her to writing. For Cixous, writing is caught up in the process of mourning but it is also a way of reconstructing a damaged self after and through death. Writing becomes the passage to and away from death, towards a new self, a new body. In *Three Steps on the Ladder of Writing* (1993b), Cixous offers an initiation into writing which is also a type of shamanistic journey toward the experience of writing, composed of 'moments' of the 'apprenticeship'. The first of these is the School of the Dead, the second, the School of Dreams, and the third, the School of Roots.

> To begin (writing, living) we must have death. . . . Writing is learning to die. It's learning not to be afraid, in other words to live at the extremity of life, which is what the dead, death, gives us. . . . We need to lose the world, to lose a world, and to discover that there is more than one world and that the world isn't what we think it is.   (1993b: 7, 10)

Death, then, is a gift, a gift because it destroys old conceptions of the self and the world and makes room for new life, new ways of being. Death is the loss of an inauthentic, singular, narrow self and the birth of a multiplicity of new selves.

Death is both a negative and a positive force in Cixous. Death signifies the limits of the Law, all that attempts to stifle the writing self in life-denying definitions. The death of death itself is, in a sense, what Cixous means by a positive death, a death or loss of that which denies vital energies and that which limits becoming. In 'The School of Roots' Cixous speaks of writing the *imund*, the profane, that which is disavowed. Writing, in this sense, is about calling back in to being the forbidden, the exiled, the taboo: it is 'an exercise in that delicate and respectful form of life we call dying' (1993b: 156). In *Three Steps on the Ladder of Writing* Cixous writes, 'Only the ones who love us can kill us. Those who love us kill us. And we kill those we love' (93). She discusses writing and the axe, wandering through a series of narratives and dreams in which an axe is present, and she links this to Kafka's assertion 'A book must be the axe for the frozen sea inside us' (17). One must, she urges, write by the 'light of the axe', that is one must produce a writing which destroys the structures which keep us frozen, stagnant, which prevent movement and becoming. To write by the light of the axe is to destroy limits.

Death is also, for Cixous, another term for the *limit*. In 'First Names of No One', she writes of texts which hunt down the limit:

All of them speak of the search for the limit, the regret of the limit (a
limit to be defined doubly, as:
– the limits imposed in the real on life, on freedom, on individual
  possibilities, by the institutions and their go-betweens: laws, etc.;
– the limits imposed on writing by the literary establishment).
     This limit has several 'sites' and names: on the near side of its
limiting face, its name would be death, and all the figures of death
which are given to death by psychoanalysis or projected fantasies.
Hunters of death, these texts pursue it and drive it out in the same
impulse.
     But the limit is also a vertiginous peak, from which elsewhere, the
other, and what is to come, can be seen.   (Sellers 1997: 28)

To write by the light of the axe is to have the courage to resist death
not just by avoiding it but by confronting it and relentlessly pursu-
ing it as the limit from which new horizons of thought open up.
Significantly (and this is a contentious point, as the criticism
directed against Cixous which we discussed in the last chapter
demonstrates), there is a problematic collapse between a textual
movement beyond limits, in the form perhaps of avant-garde literary experiments, and a political transgression of limiting social
structures and laws. Such a collapse is problematic because it
assumes that a writing which breaks the limits of 'the literary establishment' is also politically transgressive. There is no such guaran-
tee though, for experimental writing can also contain a
conservative and even reactionary content.
     There is a type of bravado in Cixous's refusal to let death have
any power over her writing. In 'First Names of No One' she writes:
'Death is nothing. It is not something. It is a hole. I can fill it with
fantasies, and give it a name, freely. I can also think castration.
But nothing human, nothing real, obliges me to. Nothing can
stop me from thinking otherwise, without accounting or death'
(in Sellers 1997: 27). To write against death is to continuously
pursue and challenge the limits of identity, not from some anar-
chic desire for the lawless, but from a desire to overcome the
oppressive and self-destructive constraints which limit our ability to connect compassionately and creatively with others. To
write against death, with the light of the axe, is not simply a ther-
apeutic exercise designed to ward of existential anxieties, it is to
write against the barriers erected by negativity which prevent the
opening up of the self through writing. Writing, in this sense, is

not just about composing words upon a page, it is a mode of living in the world.

Death is also linked to the Hegelian dialectic, to the 'Empire of the Selfsame', to phallocentrism in 'Sorties': 'History, history of phallocentrism, history of propriation: a single history. History of an identity: that of man's becoming recognized by the other (son or woman), reminding him that as Hegel says, death is his master' (Cixous and Clement 1991: 79). Cixous's work echoes that of Georges Bataille who provided a seminal discussion of Hegel in 'The Critique of the Foundations of the Hegelian Dialectic' (1985b) and throughout his writing challenges the notion of a Hegelian 'closed economy' by avowing the profane power of the outside or that which cannot be consumed by culture. This excess or remainder offers us another way of thinking through the tightly bound logic of the Hegelian dialectic. Cixous wonders, rhetorically, if Bataille engages in 'pushing Hegel to the edge of the abyss that a civilized man keeps himself from falling into? This abyss that functions as a metaphor both of death and of the feminine sex?' (Cixous and Clement 1991: 80). There appears to be a confusion here between death as the phallic master and death as the feminine. If we recall Cixous's use of the Medusa myth we have a clearer understanding of what she means though: death is the master of the limit only in so far as the absence of the phallus (singular, fixed identity) is confused with the feminine as abyss (the castrated one, the lack, absence). A feminine writing (and perhaps this is the key to her understanding of death), sees abundance and plenitude in the limit of death for this limit is a spectre produced by a subjectivity which has no other way of thinking otherwise. If death is the limit, the Law, the spectre of castration (the feminine abyss, no-thing), a feminine writing moves through this spectral limit knowing that it is a representation produced by phallocentrism. In this sense death or the limit is a 'mind forged manacle' which feminine writing throws off in the pursuit of thought.

L'écriture féminine – writing the body

Much has already been mentioned of l'écriture féminine in the previous chapter; however, a clearer definition of it is still needed. Writing in the feminine is a deconstructive avant-garde textual practice which challenges and moves beyond the constraints of phallocentric thought: it demonstrates a textual economy which is open, and thus it is in some ways inseparable from the feminine libidinal economy. For Cixous, writing in the feminine is, above all, an attempt to let the other exist without imposing a definition of the self, the writer. *Écriture féminine* is about providing a space for the material and ontological specificity and autonomy of the other to exist, be, shine forth. Indeed as Susan Sellers puts it in *Hélène Cixous: Authorship, Autobiography and Love*, 'I shall argue that this "I", which refuses the glorification available to the self in writing and which seeks, instead, to encounter and inscribe the other, is the hallmark of an *écriture féminine*' (Sellers 1996: xv). In this context the self in writing becomes 'the site, the occasion of the other' (Cixous, in Sellers 1996: 25).

However, *l'écriture féminine* is not just a writing practice, it is a mode of thinking otherwise. It describes a path towards thought through the body. I would also argue that *écriture féminine* is not just about 'writing the body'. It is not just about putting the (female) body back into discourse, inscribing a repressed female sexuality, playing with metaphors and images of femininity, subverting existing narratives about the inferiority of sex over the mind and so on. As Judith Butler puts it: 'there is no reference to a pure body which is not at the same time a further formation of that body' (1993: 10). This is another way of recognizing that when we communicate about our bodies, ourselves, we are entering into language, into the arena of representation. Once again it is a question of the morphology of the body and not an essence. All bodies come into being through language.

While a great deal of attention has been given to *écriture féminine* as a discourse which translates and rewrites the body, relatively little attention has been paid to the philosophical, even existential, grounds of *écriture féminine*. *Écriture féminine* is also about creating a philosophical and political ethics, a continual calling into question of the foundations of thinking. Sellers suggests, with reference to Cixous's 'To Live the Orange', that:

> Cixous' account of feminine writing can be fruitfully compared with the work of Martin Heidegger. In an essay entitled "The Thing," Heidegger describes how thought has laid claim to things with the result that "the thing as thing remains prescribed, nil, and in that

sense annihilated." The alternative, that "the thing's thingness would have become manifest and would have laid claim to thought" has, consequently, become unthinkable [sic]. Heidegger concludes that progress involves a "step back from the thinking that merely represents – that is, explains – to the thinking that responds and recalls.   (Sellers 1997: 83)

Here we return to the question of writing as a path towards thought, of Cixous's radical reinscription of the feminine as an antidote to alienation, and of the issue of fidelity as a means by which the materiality of things in the world, including sexed bodies, is contemplated with a wonder which allows the thing to 'speak' anew. For Cixous, *écriture féminine* is part of 'the work of un-forgetting, of un-silencing, of unearthing, of un-blinding oneself, and of un-deafening oneself' (Sellers 1997: 83). In other words, *écriture féminine* is not simply about recapturing an imme-diate connection to a body which has been colonized by phallo-centric language, it is about contemplating the material process of thought itself. Writing, in this sense, is inseparable from the mate-riality of thought.

    Heidegger concludes 'The End of Philosophy and the Task of Thinking' with the following words: 'The task of thinking would then be the surrender of previous thinking to the determination of the matter for thinking' (Heidegger 1977d: 392). We might argue that Cixous understands the task of thinking as the surrender of previous phallocentric thinking to the determination of the matter for thinking. Matter is the substance of the world, our bodies, the bodies of others. Mater, or mother, is for Cixous also a metaphor for that substance, that which lies beneath, the hidden substratum which nourishes thought. As Cixous writes of Clarice Lispector, 'she returns the ability not to forget *matter*, which we don't notice: which we live, which we are. Clarice descends the ladder to the point of returning to think over matter. To think is to reach down below and contemplate the matter of the world' (Cixous 1993b: 130). Cixous goes on to say that '[m]atter for her is not abstract but intelligent, alive, and powerful' (150). In 'The School of Roots' she describes this as reaching down into the 'nether realms'. 'This risky country is situated somewhere near the unconscious: to reach it you have to go through the back door of thought' (1993b: 114). Such a process is by it's very nature slow, thinking requires time, one needs to respect the time it takes to think and not rush into imposing already established conceptual maps of the world. 'Slowness', writes Cixous in 'To Live the Orange', 'is the essence of tenderness' (in Sellers 1997: 88).

On a phenomenological level, 'writing the body' is also the contemplation of matter. In *The Poetics of Reverie*, Gaston Bachelard writes that 'We believe that our reveries can be the best school for the "psychology of the depths"' (1971: 58). For Bachelard 'the poetics of reverie' is a poetics of the *anima*', or the feminine (62). He attempts 'an *anima* philosophy, a philosophy of the psychology of the deep feminine' (67). Cixous's *écriture féminine* resonates with such an attempt. It is, broadly speaking, a phenomenological exploration of the materiality of the feminine as thinking itself.

The Other

The concept of the Other is important not only to Cixous's writing but also to a strain of continental philosophy which informs post-structuralist thought. The concept of the Other was central to Simone de Beauvoir's work in *The Second Sex* [1953], where she argues that women are positioned as the Other in relation to a concept of Self which has been colonized by patriarchy. The Other, then, has an existential and phenomenological background and Cixous is informed by this philosophical heritage when she writes about the concept.

Importantly for women, who have been positioned within phal-locentric language as a subject in relation to men, writing the Other also involves reinventing or creating themselves as autonomous subjects. In this sense *écriture féminine* provides a space in which women can begin the process of creating an ontological autonomy, and begin to write a subjectivity which exceeds the phallocentric limits imposed on women. This is what Cixous means when she says that for women writing is about giving birth to the (m)other woman, the self as (m)other, which has been colonized by phallo-centrism.

A related concept is *alterity*. Alterity means in effect the other of the other, that is, a form of Otherness which is not reducible to the binary self/other. It is a concept of the other which is autonomous, that is, which exceeds the colonizing logic of the self/other binary. It is Otherness which is ontologically independent of the phallocentric binary that structures Western metaphysics. In this sense we might say that the other as alterity is difference also. Alterity signals a type of Otherness which exceeds the logic of, or exists independently of, the *A* (self)/not-*A* (other) binary; this is also the space of difference, a space which is different from the *A*/not-*A*. Cixous codes this space as maternal, for she argues that it exists prior to the formation of the subject within the Symbolic, or the space of phallocentric thought. As mater, the (m)other is also materiality, substance, the sensible, the living flesh of the world.

Moreover, when Cixous writes about the maternal body she is not writing about a literal body but a metaphoric one. Thus the (m)other is a metaphor for those subversive exiled energies which threaten the coherence of phallocentric thought. (M)other as subversion is also an intervention into common psychoanalytic and philosophical and cultural myths about the mother as a passive and conservative body, that which is acted upon, which nurtures and reproduces the subject but which is incapable of reproducing the subject otherwise.

On yet another level, the Other signifies the extreme limits of the knowable. In 'The Author in Truth', Cixous finds Lispector's texts profound because they so often contemplate the relationship between the human and the non-human Other, which is an alterity not easily contained within a sexual economy (1991f: 169). In a text by Lispector, *The Passion According to G.H.* (2000), the protagonist G.H. absurdly, but metaphorically, eats a cockroach (the *barata*). This revolting consumption is an attempt to connect with the extreme limits of the other. G.H., naturally enough, vomits. For Cixous, 'The text teaches us that the most difficult thing to do is to arrive at the most extreme proximity while guarding against the trap of projection, of identification. The other must remain absolutely strange within the greatest possible proximity' (1991f: 171). It is not possible to know the strangeness of the other by a process of incorporation. Difference cannot be fully incorporated. In *The Passion*, Lispector describes a confrontation with a cockroach (*barata*) which represents in the narrative the profane, the unclean, the extreme limits of the other. The narrator G.H.

comes to the point where she thinks that to come to terms with the barata's existence she has to overcome repulsion, since this prevents her from communicating with other people: she must exchange in the deepest way, translated into concrete fact by her 'courageous' decision to eat the barata. . . . She discovers that eating the other, cannibalism, is not the wisest way to fight back repulsion after all. So she thinks onwards. . . . Through death, towards the recognition of love. (Cixous 1993b: 40, 41)

To think through death is, in this context, to think through the desire to annihilate and incorporate the threat the others alterity poses to the self and move towards a more expansive, loving, or careful attention to the other which allows space and distance.

Love

Love is one of the central themes of most of Cixous's writing and before we dismiss this interest as prosaic or romantic or, dare we say it, feminine, it is important to recognize that the subject of love has a long philosophical and literary history. Early Greek philosophers such as Plato discussed the subject, canonical writers such as Stendhal devoted an entire book to trying to unravel its mysteries. Love and its scandals have the power to undo monarchies and political parties. Love is an important philosophical, literary and political subject and it would be a mistake to dismiss an enquiry into love as feminine and unimportant. Love is central to Cixous's exploration of ethical relationships between the sexes and also informs her understanding of writing and sexual difference. In 'Coming to Writing' Cixous asserts that 'writing is a gesture of love. *The Gesture*' (1991a: 42). What does she mean by this? In effect, 'love' here signifies an openness to the other which is demonstrated through writing. Writing is thus a loving meditation on the other within ourselves and the others we confront in the world. Love is bound up with thought, with the process of thinking.

For Cixous love is about receiving the strangeness of the other without being threatened by the difference; it is about a fidelity to the other, the passion of wonder, an openness to the unknown, the unthought. In an interview with Mireille Calle-Gruber Cixous writes:

It is to find one has arrived at the point where the immense foreign territory of the other will begin. We sense the immensity, the reach, the richness of it, this attracts us. This does not mean that we ever discover it. I can imagine that this infinite foreignness could be menacing, disturbing. It can also be quite the opposite: exalting, wonderful, and in the end, of the same species as God: we do not know what it is. It is the biggest; it is far off. At the end of the path of attention, of reception, which is not interrupted but which continues into what little by little becomes the opposite of comprehension. Loving not knowing. Loving: not knowing.   (Cixous and Calle-Gruber 1997: 17)

She also describes the paradoxical desires which govern love. The intensity of desire becomes a desire to know the other, to inhabit the other, to move within the other's skin. And yet this is acutely impossible.

So acute that a sort of paradoxical miracle is produced: right where we are unable to share, we share this non-sharing, this desire, this impossibility. Never before has what separates us united us with such tender ties. . . . Sexual difference is truly the goddess of desire. If she does not give 'herself', she gives us the most of us possible. She gives us to me by you, from you. She gives us the *jouissance* of our own body, of our own sex and our own *jouissance plus* the other one. *Plus* the mixture.   (Cixous and Calle-Gruber 1997: 54)

Once again Cixous emphasizes the exchange between one and the other as a third entity, something which exists in-between.

It is important to recognize that when Cixous writes about the other she is often stressing a loving, open relationship. It could be argued that the other often functions within post-structuralism as an idealized horizon towards which the subject must travel in order to evolve an ethics of sexual difference. In this sense the other risks becoming an empty category, evacuated of all historical or social content; the other could be anyone or anything. Surely the particularities of the other determine the relationship to a greater or lesser degree. To take an extreme and provocative example, what if the other was an abuser? Would be want to reach beyond the self to contact this other? It appears that Cixous is too free with love of the other. Eric Prenowitz puts it well in 'Aftermaths' when he writes the following.

> The presence of a 'further-than-myself in myself' naturally leads to a reconsideration of the mathematics of intersubjectivity. Because for all its extreme freedom Cixous's writing might be said to obey a uniquely supple rigour, it vows accountability with an arithmetic that promises a reckoning of the incalculable.   (1997: 249)

Love, perhaps, is the recognition of the incalculable other, writing an attempt to make accountable our attempts to account for the unknowable.

In Part II we shall apply Cixous's philosophy of writing and sexual difference to James Joyce, Virginia Woolf, Clarice Lispector and lastly, Angela Carter, in order to further explore her ideas. The chapters in this section are exercises in Cixousian readings, in the type of acrobatic thinking which her writing allows. We will be touching upon queer theory, ecofeminism, cyber-sex, post-human subjectivities, the materiality of the non-human, *jouissance*, the theorization of freedom and justice, and many other subjects which are opened up by reading with and through Cixous.

Part II
Undoing the Law: Reading with Cixous

3 Feminine Writing and Sexual Difference: James Joyce

> Sound is a difference, is it not? It is the rubbing of notes between two drops of water, the breath between the note and the silence, the sound of thought. I think that one perceives sexual difference, one receives it and one enjoys it in the same manner: like relationships between notes coming from instruments that are different but that are in harmony, of course. Music is also a sexual difference.
>
> Hélène Cixous, *Inter views* (in Cixous and Calle-Gruber 1997)

In this chapter we shall explore Cixous's critical and philosophical analyses of the work of James Joyce, which will necessarily involve an appreciation of the complexities of the Joycean text and a background analysis of the relationship between high modernism and sexual difference. In order to situate the last two subjects within the scope of this chapter we shall focus our thought on *Ulysses* [1922] (1993), and in particular the very last chapter, the 'Penelope' section or the (in)famous Molly monologue. Here questions about the relationship between the representation of sexual difference and high modernism will be thought through with reference to Cixous's philosophical analysis of feminine writing. In an important sense, the following chapters on specific authors are about testing the limits of Cixous's thought by establishing an on-going critical dialogue between her work and various texts. Some of the questions we shall be addressing are as follows. How does a modernist exploration of libidinality inform Cixous's theorization of feminine writing? What is the relationship between modernism and sexual difference? Can a thinker such as Joyce practise a feminine writing and if so what are the limits of this practice? How do we take up Cixous's thought when we read

Joyce? How do we think with and through Cixous when we read Joyce's Molly monologue?

Joyce seems the most appropriate to begin with as Cixous's doctoral dissertation was devoted to this writer. Published in 1976 as *The Exile of James Joyce*, the dissertation sets the ground for many of the philosophical concerns about writing and sexual difference which Cixous takes up later. Joyce, then, is central to Cixous's development as a literary critic and a thinker. His work stimulated her into thinking through a radical challenge to the proprieties of phallocentric thought and paved the way for a more complex analysis of the subversive potential of feminine writing. For Cixous, Joyce represented a major influence not just in terms of his preoccupations with the nature of the creative process but also as a poet-philosopher who sought to rethink the relationship between world and text. Discussing Joyce's subversive use of language in *Ulysses*, Cixous writes:

> Joyce does not imagine himself to be or to contain the world; what he is doing is refusing to pass to reality by way of an outworn culture. Reality tells itself to whoever will sincerely call upon it. This is why 'style' ceases to have any meaning for Joyce; he writes the world, but refuses to 'explain' it. The reader must read it. Reading and Writing are the two inseparable phases of creation.   (Cixous 1976: 687)

In other words, Joyce attempts a mode of representation which is free of the illusion of *autho*rity; the multiplicity of voices within *Ulysses* are not contained by a single perspective or interpretation but rather offer the reader a range of subject positions. The explosion of subjectivity which occurs in the text also draws attention to the way subjectivity is itself textual or a product of a polyphony of 'voices' or textual positions. Within *Ulysses* a subversion of subjectivity as the locus of a singular, authorial perception is achieved through the representation of interiority as an almost schizophrenic composition of contesting voices. With Joyce the focus shifts from a didactic singularity to the points of connection and disconnection between competing subject positions. Meaning is found in between systems of representation instead of being understood as the product of a dominant representation. In this context, and as Cixous suggests in the quote above, reading, or interpretation, becomes a creative activity, or a process of writing. To read a text like *Ulysses*, then, is to enter into a process of writing if writing is understood to be a form of thinking. The phenomenal amount of writing, some critical, some fictional, which has been spawned by *Ulysses* indicates the generative potential of such a text.

Likewise, Cixous's *écriture féminine* writing style can be understood as a Joycean subversion of subjectivity. Cixous argues that feminine subjectivity has been exiled by the singular authority of phallocentric representations and must be reclaimed and recovered by subverting the power such representations have through the opening up of female subjectivity to a Joycean multiplicity, a complex textuality which is generative rather than didactic. The authority of phallocentric representations of (female) subjectivity is subverted through the explosion of representation itself. The scene of writing, then, becomes that stage on which the boundaries of the subject are contested, opened up to the play of other voices, other readings, other bodies. Both Joyce and Cixous are, in this respect, dissidents, radicals, outlaws who resist the authority of the subject as the source of a singular truth through a writing which expands the limits of representation.

Joyce's outlaw status was confirmed when *Ulysses* erupted into print. First published in full in 1922, it was banned and burnt by those who were outraged by its manic irreverence for all forms of literary convention and its uncompromising exploration of social, sexual and religious taboos. Written in exile in France, *Ulysses* spans just one Dublin day (16 June 1904) of the transmogrifications of the wondering Harold Bloom, confused Jew and tortured husband of the adulterous Molly. A veritable encyclopaedia of facts and fantasies, 'a kind of critical anatomy of genres, myths, and modes', *Ulysses* represents the potentially infinite plasticity of the novel and indeed of human subjectivity (Cixous 1976: 675). Here, as W. B. Yeats once wrote, 'the centre cannot hold', everything is unstable, in flux, perpetually shifting under the reader's eyes. The effect is dizzy, confusing, notwithstanding Joyce's expressed intention to create a type of cabalistic symbolism to explain the noise of his writing/world. And here we have one of the paradoxes of the modernist text, the desire to order disorder, to find a centre, a structure in a world which is increasingly structureless.[1]

In a letter to the literary critic Carlo Linati, Joyce offers him a key to his monstrous 732-page novel, a 'summary-key-skeleton-scheme' to the book he describes as 'a sort of encyclopaedia'

(Cixous 1976: 673–4). 'Each adventure (that is, every hour, every organ, every art being interconnected and interrelated in the structural scheme of the whole) should not only condition but even create its own technique' (Cixous 1976: 674). Joyce wanted to write the novel to end all novels, a text which would incorporate and connect all texts. The book itself would function as an *imago mundi*, a womb space in which new techniques or forms of representation would be born. This ambition can be compared to the French Symbolist poet Rimbaud's experiments in poetry. In 'Second Delirium: The Alchemy of the Word' [1873] he describes inventing colours for the vowels, and writing as a type of sensual alchemy (Rimbaud 1976: 204–5). Or we could cite the British poet, visionary and painter William Blake who also invented complex mythological structures, and indeed Blake's influence on Joyce has been noted by many.[2] The point is that Joyce used language in *Ulysses* as a way of remapping the world, of creating new relations between words and things in an attempt to forge radically new representations. There is something of the shaman about Joyce – he uses language to experiment with new ways of being and thinking. Cixous's interest in reinventing subjectivity through an experimental writing owes a great deal to Joyce's careful violation of traditional literary conventions. She, too, takes up the position of a shaman who explores the alchemy of the word in order to liberate new meanings.

Commenting on Joyce's project in *Ulysses* Cixous writes:

> Joyce's programme, in its methodological formulation and with its encyclopaedic intention, is in its universality nothing less than a project to write the book of books, to find a form or 'structural scheme' in which everything must be said in relation to everything, in which each component part (art, organ, hour, etc.) should create its own language. This monstrous epiphany is to be the total manifestation of reality through language.   (1976: 674)

Of course the complete representation of reality through language is impossible, and perhaps this is one of the important messages of *Ulysses* too – reality continually escapes representation. Or rather, representation (writing) always fails to capture the totality of the real. Nevertheless Joyce tried. But his failure, ironically enough, successfully calls attention to the limits of representation and therefore the impossibility of a fixed truth. Any definition of the subject, in other words, is never total.

What are known as the 'Gilbert and Linati schemata' attempt to trace a series of correspondences between each chapter and moments in Bloom's day, various disciplines such as science or religion, colours, organs of the body, and symbols. These two critics, Gilbert and Linati, attempted to formalize Joyce's ideas in the book. For example, the section of *Ulysses* we will examine is tied to the following subjects in the Gilbert schemata: Penelope, bed, flesh, earth, monologue (female), Penelope: earth; Web: movement (Gilbert 1952: 735). For Linati the schemata for the same chapter looks like this: Penelope, starry, milky, the new dawn, Laertes, Ulysses, Penelope, monologue, resigned style, the past sleeps, fat (Gilbert 1952: 739). *Ulysses*, then, is both a novel and a symbolic system. Significantly for our purposes here, it is the body which functions as the locus of this symbolic system, generating a new type of writing which is subversive, playful, excessive. For Jeri Johnson, *Ulysses* is 'one gigantic textual body, a textual body which embraces and exults in the libidinal' (Jeri Johnson 1993: xxxvii). Nowhere is this more obvious than in the Penelope section where female desire is explored. However, Bloom's fantasies are also important to the movement of the novel. Joyce's frustration with the suffocating pieties of Irish Catholicism find expression in his humorous descriptions of Bloom's chaotic drives. From masturbatory fantasies to details of his shitting, Joyce spares the reader nothing in his quest to fully represent Bloom's interiority.

For Kristeva, following Mikhail Bahktin, *Ulysses* is a carnivalesque text which has its roots in the irreverent, scatological, taboo-breaking tradition of the picaresque novel which stretches back to the anonymous *Lazarillo de Tormes* (1533) and to *The Swindler* (1626), by the Spanish writer Francisco de Quevedo (Kristeva 1986a). The protagonist in this genre is known as the 'picaro', an exile, or misfit, who drifts through society. As Michael Alpert comments: 'On his wanderings, which can lead through several towns or even countries, the picaro meets and pits his wits against a variety of people, and in this way the writer builds up a portrait of contemporary society' (1969: 7). Like the picaro, Joyce's Bloom also drifts through different communities within Dublin and in doing so establishes a comprehensive representation of that culture. The picaresque began as a rejection of the constraints imposed by

Christianity, and Joyce too partakes of this sacrilegious rebellion in
Ulysses, openly criticizing the Catholic Church throughout his
lengthy novel. The picaresque or the carnivalesque narrative laid
the foundation for the novel. As Kristeva writes in her well-known
essay 'Word, Dialogue and Novel': 'This carnivalesque genre – as
pliant and variable as Proteus, capable of insinuating itself into
other genres – has an enormous influence on the development of
European literature and especially the formation of the novel'
(Kristeva 1986a: 52). If the novel was from its beginnings a subversive text, *Ulysses* reminds us that it is also capable of cannibalizing
genres and styles, that it is essentially an experimental form.

In her 1974 text 'Prénoms de personne' ('First Names of No-
One'), Cixous explores the way Joyce interrogates the process of
readability and naming and argues that his writing performs a
permanent revolution and is a text of the edge, of the outside
(Cixous, in Sellers 1997: 32). The Joycean text, argues Cixous, lays
open the workings of phallocentrism only to deconstruct or
destroy them. While he establishes a 'rapport with castration' he
also draws attention to the ways in which the phallocentric threat
of annihilation escapes the text: the very materiality of his writing
resists being consumed by the Law. In this respect Joyce can be
understood to escape the logic of capture. 'What I ask of writing',
states Cixous, 'is what I ask of desire: that it should have no link
with that logic which places desire on the side of possession, of
acquisition, or even of that consumption/consummation which,
so gloriously pushed to the limit, strikes up a (imaginary) relationship with death' (Cixous 1991a: 38). A writing which is vitalized by
the feminine libidinal economy will liberate desire from being
colonized by death, negativity, castration, the economy of phallocentric appropriation.

Modernism and libidinal writing

In order to increase our understanding of *Ulysses* and Cixous we
must consider some of the arguments made about the subversive
effects of the libidinal text. As Joseph Allen Boone argues in
Libidinal Currents: Sexuality and the Shaping of Modernism,
'mapping the instability and variability of psychosexual impulses
and . . . tracking the dispersive, wayward trajectories that the libido

etches in the subconscious, such modern fictions of sexuality have produced . . . a poetics and a politics of the perverse' (Boone 1998: 7). Many experimental avant-garde modernist texts match a celebration of the irrational forces of the unconscious with the fetishization of sexual perversion as a privileged form of creative resistance. In this context, a text acquires a radical status through a transgressive representation of the body, which emerges as the source of a new radical aesthetics.

During the 1960s in France the Tel Quel group focused on the works of Georges Bataille, Antonin Artaud and de Sade, establishing the political importance of (male) avant-garde writing. Bataille's work, for example, was heralded as a radical cultural transgression which exploded the limits of a repressive rationality by foregrounding the excesses of sexuality and madness. The avant-garde text became the locus of a radical subversion, a laboratory space in which transgressive investigations into sexuality are practised. An entire aesthetics of transgression is built upon the assumption that sex and text are symbiotically connected, so that an experimental textuality is always already the performance of an experimental sexuality. Erotic texts such as Bataille's *Histoire de l'oeil* [1928] (Bataille 1979) are heralded as symptomatic of a radical shift in representation; the subject is put into process by a transgressive libidinality, made productively incoherent by the excesses of a libidinal writing. The experimental text transgresses discursive norms, calls into question the limits of the Law, of meaning, of the sayable. In other words, this aesthetics of transgression depends upon a concept of the radically libidinal body, a body which disrupts conservative representational economies: the raw creativity of the libidinal body bursts through the limits of representation in moments of orgasmic *jouissance*, or sublime excess.

In his discussion of de Sade and Bataille, Philippe Sollers argues that modern literature is preoccupied with 'bodily writing' (*écriture corporelle*) such that the body has become the 'fundamental referent of [modern literature's] violation of discourse' (Sollers 1968: 1220). The libidinal body emerges as the privileged object of transgressive writing. Moreover, a critical attention to the textual organization of the libidinal body often assumes a correlation between sexual transgression, the disruption of linguistic norms, and radical political interventions. As Barthes put it: 'The transgression of values, that is the avowed principle of eroticism, is matched by – if not based on – a technical transgression of the forms of language' (Barthes 1976: 125–6). And such a technical transgression was coded as feminine. Within the pages of *Ulysses* we find a host of such transgressions. Words are scattered across the pages, disordered, exploded, the narrative flows in and out of different subjectivities, styles, genres, voices. Bodies have sex in many different positions, transgressive sexual fantasies are explored; bodies defecate, urinate, fart, menstruate, express breast milk; desire distorts, transforms, subverts, confuses identities.

But what relationship does this have to writing and sexual difference? Should we argue that experimental writing, because it calls into question the Law (order, syntax, religious and social proprieties), is therefore caught up in the subversive play of sexual difference? Should we say that subversion is inherently a feminine practice or energy? What about reactionary subversions? Is the question of feminine writing caught up in a normative evaluation of the avant-garde which is, ironically, conservative, fixed; in an insistence on what counts as radical literature? Again we have many of the issues which confronted us in the first chapter about the political worth of genre, and the problems of identifying a genre, or a type of writing, with a politics – of bestowing political worth to a particular form of writing or an aesthetics. As Felski observes, many writers 'transvalued sexual deviance by depicting it as a privileged epistemological standpoint from which to question social values and fixed truths' (Felski 1995: 177). Is this avant-garde transgression also a question of privilege? Is that why so many have not yet read *Ulysses* or why, indeed, this monstrous experimental work has gained the aura of being the very height of a literary complexity that only the very sophisticated can master?

It is not surprising that many of the claims made about the liberatory potential of the avant-garde text have fallen on deaf ears, or at least ears which are more attuned to the voices of everyday oppression than the cultured musing of the Parisian salons. Some have argued not only that the theoretical celebration of the subversive feminine text is the formulation of an elitist aesthetics, a sort of critical excuse for opaque avant-garde writing, but that it also betrays a masculine desire to colonize the feminine.[3] Just as women and feminism surge into discourse, the boys of the avant-garde, writers and theorists both, claim the feminine as their own, fashion a theory which finds this explosive energy in their own texts and set themselves up as masters of this new 'feminine' discourse. For Alice Jardine, while Cixous claims that feminine writing does not require the signature of a woman, 'women nonetheless, today (after psychoanalysis and Derrida), do have a privileged access to it' (Jardine 1985: 262). While we would not want to claim that Freud and Derrida are the midwives of a new feminine writing, birthing the female body into text as it were, it is important to recognize that challenges to representation made by male theorists should not necessarily be dismissed because they are signed by men. Such a dismissal too easily feeds a paranoia about the contaminatory effects of male texts and that paranoia has its roots in a sense of female lack which is fostered by a fear of being colonized by male writing. Cixous writes against that fear, refusing the lack and rewriting phallocentric colonizations of the feminine. Her writing can be more productively read as providing an antidote to female paranoia and not as a further cause of it.

Before we get too immersed in debates about the gender politics of writing, it is important to bring back the question of a feminine writing to thought, to recognize that the feminine is for Cixous an opening into thought itself. If this passage to thought is through the female body it is also, for many modernist writers and theorists of the avant-garde, through a poetics of eroticism. A libidinal poetics opens up a passage to thought precisely because it calls into focus the fluid, polymorphous potential of sexual identity. A thinking through sexual difference is not simply about debating the relative merits of the feminine and the masculine, rather it is about recognizing that difference is always already caught up in the resignification of sexuality. It is also about recognizing that we think with a sexually fluid body. Thinking through sexual difference is thus thinking through a libidinal poetics of the body. Writing provides a theatre in which such a thinking plays itself out.

In *Ulysses* writing provides such a theatre for the thinking through of sexual difference. Sexual identities are often subverted, turned about, shifted into strange new configurations. Molly imagines that she is a man: 'look how lily white they are the smoothest place is right there between this bit here how soft like a peach easy God I wouldn't mind being a man and get up on a lovely woman . . .' (Joyce 1993: 720). Bloom fantasizes, in the Circe episode, about becoming a prostitute who is ravaged my many men, 'You were a nice looking Miriam when you clipped off your backgate hairs and lay swooning in the thing across the bed as Mrs Dandrade, about to be violated By Lieutenant Smythe-Smythe, Mr Philip Augustus Blockwell, M.P., Signore Laci Daremono, the robust tenor, blueeyed Bert, the liftboy, Henry Fluery of Gordon Bennet fame', says Bello the sadistic brothel owner (502). 'Dr Bloom', asserts the voice of Dr Mulligan in the Circe episode, 'is bisexually abnormal' (465). The intimate currents which pass between consciousness and bodies which are continually negotiating sexual difference is what interests writers such as Cixous, Joyce and others. For Joseph Allen Boone, what is significant about *Ulysses* is 'Joyce's prying open of novelistic form to make narrative space for the representation of what he called those "ascending fumes of sex" – those incalculable psychosexual forces that shape even as they subvert human identity' (1998: 152). This subversion of identity is evident in Bloom's many transformations. Clearly sexual identification is made unstable in the text and it was precisely these taboo shifts which led to the novel being censored. But is a fluid, transgressive libido really a radical opening into thought itself?

There might appear something faintly absurd in the claim that a radical representation of libidinality is a passage to thought, for such a claim violates the classic Western metaphysical belief that thought is necessarily disembodied, evacuated of base passions, cut loose from the distracting ties of the flesh. To suggest that thought comes about through the play of sexual difference is to transgress the Cartesian mind/body split. However, it would be a mistake to read such a transgression in terms of a replacing of Descartes's famous, rather airy maxim 'I think therefore I am' with an earthy, hedonistic 'I desire therefore I am'. That would be to vulgarize a quite sophisticated post-structuralist critique of Western metaphysics. Consciousness, as Joyce shows us so relentlessly in *Ulysses*, is infinitely more complex. As Cixous states, *Ulysses* is 'a book of consciousness' (Cixous 1976: 699). *Ulysses* explores the limits of representing consciousness and it does so by thinking through the libidinal body.

A mollycixous drag act

It is the representation of consciousness streaming through the body of Molly which interests us here. The Molly/Penelope episode of *Ulysses* is known as the most powerful example of the literary technique of 'stream of consciousness'. Coined by William James in his *Principles of Psychology* (1890), 'stream of consciousness' is characterized by an uninterrupted, ironically self-aware interior monologue. Here Joyce stretched his experimental technique to the limit producing a writing which cast aside conventional punctuation and grammar. It is worth quoting the often quoted description of this episode which Joyce gave:

> *Penelope* is the clou of the book. The first sentence contains 2500 words. There are eight sentences in the episode. It begins and ends with the female word *yes*. It turns like the huge earth ball slowly surely and evenly round and round spinning, its four cardinal points being the female breasts, arse, womb and cunt expressed by the words *because, bottom* (in all senses bottom, button, bottom of the class, bottom of the sea, bottom of his heart), *woman, yes*. Though probably more obscene than any preceding episode it seems to me to be perfectly sane fully amoral fertilizable untrustworthy engaging shrewd limited prudent indifferent *Weib. Ich bin der. Fleisch der stets bejaht* [Woman. I am the flesh that always affirms]. (cited in Johnson 1993: xxxvi)

The body of Woman becomes a theatre for this play of consciousness in Joyce's turning, twisting, bottomless text, and it is to Molly's body and the consciousness which flows from her which we now turn.

What are we to do with the (in)famous menstruating, masturbatory Molly monologue *and* Cixous, shaman of the passage, voyager into the depths, trickster of the Law, and laughing Medusa? To read Molly through Cixous is to produce a new text: how do we think the play of sexual difference through the body of the Cixous-Molly text?

And Joyce? As Dorrit Cohn comments, the Molly section is '*the only moment of the novel where a figural voice totally obliterates the authorial voice throughout an entire chapter*' (Cohn 1978: 128). After Joyce had finished writing Molly he had a dream in which she appeared to him in a black opera cloak and flung a small coffin at him proclaiming loudly 'And I have done with you, too, Mr Joyce!' (Boone 1998: 171). Let's assume the 'death of the author' (Barthes 1976), and plunge into the text instead with Cixous to guide us.

When reading a text with or through Cixous we are faced with the challenge that her literary criticism does not conform to the norms of academic writing. When she writes about a text, she weaves through fiction, autobiographical reflections, philosophical musings, her own poetry, myth. Her readings are themselves creative practices, the graceful opening up of the text to more writing, of thoughts in the process of unfolding. Her method is as fluid and changeable as the thought she tracks down in the texts she reads. It is almost, but not quite, an anti-method: it is certainly posed against a critical mathematics. There is no formula, no stable critical economy at work. As such, there is no critical grid or method we can easily apply to a text in order to produce a Cixousian reading. What we are faced with is a challenge to create, to move beyond the distanced position of critic and enter the text fully with a sense of the immediacy of writing as the performance of sexual difference. This does not mean that we simply use free association in an attempt to reproduce an *écriture féminine*. Cixous demands that we think slowly, with a great reverence for detail.

With this in mind it is also important to add that I face a rather absurd situation as I think about how to enter this passage of writing. Do I attempt to impersonate Cixous while reading a text written by a man who is impersonating Molly who is herself a performer, an impersonator of songs written by others? There are several masks here, several layers of performance. It feels like bad faith to impersonate Cixous for a start. I risk vulgarizing her thinking, doing a drag act where delicate concepts are exaggerated, slightly misplaced, like lipstick too heavily applied which ends up drawing attention to the bad application rather than the beauty of the mouth. But isn't everything we do a bit like drag, a performance, the knowing acting out of roles, gestures, attitudes already circulating? Isn't every discourse, I hear Judith Butler and queer theorists ask, really like a second-hand dress, worn before by others?[4] Well, yes, but I don't want someone telling me my slip is showing. But then maybe a visible slip to one person is to another just part of the act.

Critical slips

Before I gather the courage to plunge myself and you into the promised molly-cixous passage/performance it is certainly worth considering some of the critical approaches taken towards Molly in order, perhaps, to provide the right sort of distance. Several feminist critics have argued that Joyce's representation of female desire in the Penelope episode is far from radical; but while the representation of female desire is stylistically radical the content is not. Bloom wanders through Dublin, interacting with many people, while Molly is alone in the house, confined to her bed. She fantasizes but does nothing. Elaine Unkeless argues that Molly represents 'conventional notions of the way a woman acts and thinks' (Unkeless and Hanke, *Women in Joyce*, 1982). She lacks a real career, she worries about becoming old and unattractive to men, preoccupies herself with petty vanities and anxieties, is bored with married life, complains about her husband Bloom – all in all a rather stereotypical picture of the frustrated lower middle-class house-bound woman. While she might offer the odd criticism about women's lot – 'whoever suggested that business for women what between clothes and cooking and children' (719) – and criticize male power – 'it'd be much better for the world to be governed by women' (727) – the narrative voice of Molly does not offer many insights into sexual politics in the way that, say, D. H. Lawrence's female protagonists do in *Women in Love* (1921) or *The Rainbow* (1915).[5]

On the other hand, one cannot ignore the force of Molly's desire in the text. She indulges in passionate fantasies, recalls her predatory sexual conquests with men, some of whom she forgets the names of, and all the while brings herself to orgasm. We could argue that Joyce's representation of female desire is subversive because it shatters long-held assumptions that women are sexually passive. As Boone points out, Molly's act of autoeroticism effectively excludes the reader even while his or her gaze is invited into a voyeuristic relationship with her (1998: 170). Molly's 'yes' is also an affirmation of sexual autonomy.

It could also be argued that the representation of Molly's female gaze challenges theoretical assumptions about the objectifying effects of the male gaze. Teresa de Lauretis in *Alice Doesn't* (1984), for example, and cultural critics such as Naomi Wolf and Susan Brownmiller, assert that women are the passive objects of the male gaze.[6] In stark contrast, Molly takes pleasure in looking back and teasing, manipulating and mocking the male gaze: 'those fine young men I could see down in Margate . . . standing up in the sun naked. . . . I could look at him all day' (725). 'I took off my glove slowly watching him' (698). 'I suppose there'll be the usual idiots of men gaping at us with their eyes as stupid as ever' (700). If Molly enjoys the pleasure of her own gaze, such a pleasure has evoked the disgust of many prudent readers. Molly's slightly disdainful and predatory relationship to the other sex has irritated many critics, who, as Bonnie Kime Scott notes, have dismissed her as a whore (Scott 1984: 157). In *The Conscience of James Joyce*, Darcy O'Brien claimed that 'For all Molly's vitality, for all her fleshy charms and engaging bravado she is at heart a thirty-shilling whore' (O'Brien 1968: 211). Here we see an example of the sort of moral censorship which confronts expressions of autonomous and vital female sexuality. As Scott notes, most critics have approached Molly as either a whore or a mythic earth mother. Caught between being read as a damned whore or as one of God's police, women are typically positioned as either slut or pure mother, violator of phallocentric propriety or the chaste upholder of those laws.

If many critics have dismissed Molly as whore or earth mother, others have celebrated her affirmation of female desire as a powerful contribution to feminism. However, the idea that Joyce offers a unique insight into female sexuality in Molly is rejected by Gayatri Spivak, who in her essay 'French Feminism in an International Frame', finds 'something even faintly amusing about Joyce rising above sexual identities and bequeathing the proper mindset to the women's movement' (Spivak 1987: 159–64). While Spivak's comment is rather harsh, it does call attention to a continuing issue with the fact that a man created Molly, and more broadly, issues to do with a mostly French feminist celebration of the femininity of avant-garde male writing. And yet this is not strictly true, for the French feminist Julia Kristeva reads Joyce's representation of Molly in the Penelope episode as a capitulation to a phallocentric metaphysics of feminine non-being. In *Desire in Language*, Kristeva argues that the Molly monologue is the glorification of female non-being: 'haloed, in all their nonsense, with a paternal aura, ironically but obstinately raising her towards that third-person-God – and filling her with a strange joy in the face of nothingness' (Kristeva 1980: 148–9). The 'yes' which punctuates the text with moments of shuddering *jouissance* lifts Molly towards a mystical but obliterating union with the Father. Significantly

Cixous herself even offers a similar reading in *The Exile of James Joyce*, in one of her few discussions of Molly in the thesis. 'The book ends', writes Cixous, 'on a naive glorification of the alliance between God and woman, expressed by Molly in metaphysical murmurings which lead her into a comfortable acquiescence' (1976: 82). Whore, earth mother or a modern St Teresa who swoons into nothingness before the Father, it seems Molly's monologue does little to breach the confines of phallocentrism. Molly's 'yes' is effectively read as a 'no'; a negation of female autonomy.

The singer and the song

> When I refer to music, it's because music lets us hear directly that language is produced in an interplay with the body. One writes with one's ears. It is absolutely essential. The ear does not hear a single detached note: it hears musical compositions, rhythms, scansions. Writing is a music that goes by, that trails off in part because what remains is not notes of music, it is words. But what remains of music in writing, and which exists also in music properly speaking, is indeed that scansion which *also* does its work on the body of the reader. The texts that touch me most strongly, to the point of making me shiver or laugh, are those that have not repressed their musical structure; I am not talking here simply of phonic signification, nor of alliterations, but indeed of the architecture, of the contraction and the relaxation, the variations of breath. . . . Who writes like that – like emotion itself, like the thought (of the) body, the thinking body? I have a passion for stops. But for there to be a stop, there must be a current, a coursing of the text. Always the mystery of difference, of *différance*. Never the one without the other.
>
> Hélène Cixous, *Inter views* (in Cixous and Calle-Gruber
> 1997: 64)

> . . . yes Ill sing . . .
>
> James Joyce, *Ulysses* (1993: 713)

It seems even harder to perform a Cixousian reading of the Molly text now that Cixous herself has all but dismissed it as 'a naive glorification' of woman's acquiescence to phallocentric transcendentalism. However, as Cixous so often asserts, it is important to bring forth a hidden feminine libidinal economy in the text, to explore the voice of the other which resonates within the text's underground chambers. Cixous's path towards thought involves opening up writing to this other voice. One way of opening up another reading of the Molly text is to explore the poetics and the performance of music in the monologue for Molly is, after all, a singer. Boone, following Kimberley Devlin, who writes that the monologue 'foregrounds [femininity as] theatricality' (1994), argues that the text confuses and resists any sense of the interior essence of femininity by producing a series of 'performative *surfaces*' (1998: 166, 168). Molly, suggests Boone, is a Diva, a prima donna, an actress, a performer who calls attention to the textual substance of the subject, the theatre of consciousness. This sense of the Molly text as dynamic theatre or performance also leads us into a consideration of the materiality of writing, of the ways in which writing is caught up in the materiality of a performing body. For Cixous the material texture of writing is produced through and with the body. This does not mean that there is a simple referential relationship between body and text, but rather that writing demonstrates the impossibility of sustaining the mind/body dichotomy, which is a symptom of a phallocentric will to mastery.

As Deborah Jensen writes, Cixous proposes a type of reading which is intimately connected to the senses, 'a sensualist capacity for reading. A sensuation of reading via the senses' (Jenson 1991: 190). Such a reading calls forth an embodied response, writing is felt and experienced as a living process rather than the distant object of a disembodied calculation. To read with the body and through the body is to ground writing as a process of embodiment. It is an approach to reading which is pitted against a dissociated perception, one that reads of suffering and joy and remains physically numb, untouched, unmoved. To read through the senses is not then to advocate a weeping feminine sentimentality, but rather to establish a responsive connection, one that opens up the possibility of a closer engagement with writing. We have all been moved by writing, have perhaps laughed or cried, been angered or inspired by what we have read. Cixous is on one level simply recognizing that embodied response to writing. We say that the most powerful writing 'moves' us; we are affected, we are changed by what we read. This physical openness to writing is for Cixous an important aspect of becoming for it is when we are 'touched' by

writing that we form particular understandings, perhaps epiphanies, new insights, new perceptions; these points of communication between body and text are also points of transformation. In a
sense the word does indeed become flesh, but Cixous would not
argue that we are merely imprinted by writing, a tabula rasa to be
inscribed on; rather, when we read we negotiate meanings. This
embodied negotiation of meaning is for Cixous a form of writing in
the sense that it produces new meanings. The Molly monologue, I
will argue, demonstrates the complexities of this embodied read-
ing/writing process.

One of the more overlooked aspects of the Molly text is the
sensualism of her singing voice and indeed of the flow of breath
and song in the monologue. In 'Coming to Writing' Cixous links
breath with the inspiration to write, establishing an embodied
poetics of breathing/writing to communicate the life-affirming
force of writing against negativity, lack. 'Who makes me write,
moan, sing, dance? Who gives me the body that is never afraid of
fear? Who writes me? Who makes my life into the carnal field of an
uprising of texts? Life in person' (Cixous 1991a: 44). In order to
explore a Cixousian poetics of breath and song in Molly I want to
take as a point of departure an essay by Mireille Calle-Gruber,
'Hélène Cixous: Music Forever or Short Treatise on a Poetics for a
Story to be Sung' (1999). Here she offers a lyrical reading of
Cixous's '*Beethoven à jamais, ou, L'Existence de Dieu*' (1993a). 'The
Cixousian sentence is, [here] pierced right through, perforated;
moving the breath in rests and quarter-rests, it creates suspirations
of air and aria; it embodies the rhythm of meaning, systole/diatole,
the cadence of nerves; it derives its inspiration from the volume of
the lungs' (Calle-Gruber 1999: 83). Calle-Gruber stresses the Cixous
text as a form of song: 'it is the voice – the guiding voice of lyrical
singing' (82).

Reading Molly, we too get a sense of a breathless singing, a background song which surges to the surface of the text as an *expiration*
and falls down into the depths again as *inspiration*, teasing us with
a sense of a song half-heard, half-remembered, an uncanny Siren
call which beckons us towards a sighing, singing body only
partially glimpsed; inspiring us with desire. The text sings a strange
seduction, pulling the reader onward through waves of thought in
process, never complete. The sense of breathless singing in the text
is performed through the lack of punctuation: the first speed into

Molly's consciousness ('yes because') in the opening sentence of 2500 words hardly pauses for breath so that we, the reader, must catch our breath *against* the tide of the text, catch our thinking *against* the tide of thought, as the text relentlessly draws us into a polyphony of images, people, sexual acts, fantasies, times, places, countries, bodies. The paragraphs grant us breath, only quickly, and then we are rapidly thrown back into the surging waves of the relentless monologue. It is overwhelming, we feel as though we are consumed by it, until we no longer know if we are inside it or outside it, if we are hearing Molly's interiority or her exteriority. It dissolves difference just as the endless sentence blurs disparate elements: 'I can see his face clean shaven Frseeeeeeeeefrong that train again weeping tone once in the dear deaead days beyondre call close my eyes breath my lips forward kiss sad look eyes open . . .' (Joyce 1993, 713). We swim through an image inside her head of a man's face, towards the sound outside of a train, to the sound of weeping, to a glimpse of her closing her eyes, the intimate sound of her breath, lips pouting forward, sad eyes, which open again, never knowing if this glimpsed body is inside her consciousness or on the surface of her face. The strange sound of the text pulls us into a becoming which liquefies the boundaries between elements, making those elements and bodies rhythmic. The sound of 'his face clean shaven' becomes a weeping train becomes the rhythm of breath becomes eyes closing, lips parting, eyes opening in sadness. The rhythm of the train becomes the rhythm of a nostalgic physical intimacy. The sound of the train sings the face as a weeping song and something more is created– a music so subtle we can hardly hear it as it rushes past our ears. Like the faint song barely heard when a wave crashes against you – catching your breath, your ears are full of the force and rhythm of the waves which seem to sing to you of depths never heard before.

The stream of consciousness in the monologue is a liquid sound machine which makes thought mobile, labile. It is a baroque opera of modernity, composed of a chaos of bodies, now stretched on a bed, now straining with urgent desire, now walking in another land, standing against a wall, on a stage singing; a cacophony of voices which speak over each other, a chorus which strains toward a harmony never quite reached.

The text transforms the singer Molly into song: she *is* singing:

he commenced kissing me on the choir stairs after I sang Gounods *Ave Maria* what are we waiting for O my heart kiss me straight on the brow and part which is my brown part he was pretty hot for all his tinny voice too my low notes he was always raving about if you can believe him I liked the way he used his mouth singing.   (697)

The song moves through the intimate sound of kissing through to the public singing of *Ave Maria* to a man's voice to the demand for kissing to a brow to a tinny man's voice, back to the low womanly notes of *Ave Maria*, to a man's voice raving in admiration of that song which now becomes a mouth moving sensually in a song which sounds tinny. We can barely hear the rush of notes, the rhythms, the resonating harmonies, the shifts in cadence. It's as though we have to attune our ears to hidden depths. As Calle-Gruber writes of Cixous: 'Writing through the music of speech means giving up and giving in. *In advance.* "La musique, c'est toujours d'advance"' [Music is ever in advance, advancing] (1999: 59). 'Giving up and giving in becomes a representation of a strange availability featuring extreme attention and tension' (1999: 87). Molly as song is also ever in advance, advancing, as song the text moves ahead of us so that in order to listen we have to give in to this movement. To halt the text, to cut it off from the source, is to break the song. The singing comes from the intensities produced when the elements of the text flow into each other so that, for example, the weeping sound of a train becomes the unique song of eyes opening in sadness. If we are to separate the sound of a train from the human sound of weeping and the image of eyes opening in sadness we miss the poetics of music in the text. We remain deaf to the Molly song.

In her landmark book *This Sex which is Not One*, Irigaray gestures towards a way of listening to the feminine text: 'One would have to listen with another ear, as if hearing an *"other meaning" always in the process of weaving itself, of embracing itself with words, but also of getting rid of words in order not to become fixed, congealed in them*' (Irigaray 1985a: 29). This other ear is cocked to the intimate sounds of poetry, listens carefully to the notes sung between words, to meanings otherwise muffled by the chant of a phallocentric loss. It is about listening to the current of life surging through the text.

In a quite powerful sense, the Molly song is sung in-between the elements of the text: the music comes from the liminal space between the sound of a train and eyes opening. It is from this space, which we previously referred to as the space of the other, which resonates in the underground chambers of the text, that the music pours forth. In this respect we can argue that the Molly song is caught up in the play of (sexual) difference and that what is produced is a type of feminine libidinal economy that moves beyond an economics of exchange which is mathematically precise in its dealings with negativity. Within the feminine libidinal economy of the Molly song, the gift is the music, which sings beyond the grasp of phallocentric logic.

Yes

> and O that awful deepdown torrent O and the sea the sea crimson sometimes like fire and the glorious sunsets and the figtrees in the Alameda gardens yes and all the queer little streets and pink and blue and yellow houses and all the rosegardens and the jessamine and geraniums and cactuses and Gibraltar as a girl where I was a Flower of the mountain yes when I put the rose in my hair like the Andulusian girls used or shall I wear a red yes and how he kissed me under the Moorish wall and I thought well as well him as another and then I asked him with my eyes to ask again and then he asked me would I yes to say yes my mountain flower and first I put my arms around him yes and drew him down on me so he could feel my breasts all perfume yes and his heart going like mad and yes I said yes I will Yes.
>
> James Joyce, *Ulysses* (1993)

There are several layers of 'yes' in the Molly song, the yes of private pleasure, a coming to thought, the yes which acknowledges the veracity of a thing remembered correctly, and finally the 'Yes' which ends *Ulysses*. For Joyce, the final 'Yes' which concludes the text signifies 'the end of all resistance' (Scott 1984: 182). This has been read as Molly's (and woman's) abandonment to the power of the Law, an annihilation of woman's sexual difference by a colonizing phallocentric desire which positions woman as no-thing, other to the male subject, the less than. Kristeva reads this final movement towards 'Yes' as an acceptance of the negativity of an annihilating phallocentric Law – Molly vanishes into nothing as she swoons over her orgasm, merging with the nothingness promised by a phallic God. And perhaps there might appear to be something rather irritating about this climax which fuses the acceptance of marriage, a mystical drift towards God and orgasm. The powerful repetition of 'yes' in the narrative, while an affirmation of feminine desire, appears limited – it is uttered inside a bedroom, does not travel outside and affirm social change. She says yes to her own passivity. However, such a reading forgets the materiality of the text and demands of it instead that it conform to a realist–political agenda. The poetics of yes are more complex than a simple affirmation of female abandon before the Law. We are within the domain of writing after all.

Moreover, even if we are to read Molly's 'Yes' as an abandonment of the self to the masculine, we are still confronted with the fact that even as she conjures up this final 'Yes' she is thinking otherwise: 'he asked me to say yes and I wouldn't answer first only looked out over the sea and the sky and *I was thinking of so many things he didn't know . . .*' (731, my emphasis). Molly says 'yes' to Bloom's proposal, accepting what might appear to be the constraints of phallocentrism, an acceptance of the marriage contract and her position as a subject of exchange within a masculine libidinal economy, but her consciousness wanders beyond this formal acceptance, subverting it and drawing attention to the different layers of performance which compose consciousness. Calling attention to the performative aspects of such a contract, the text demonstrates that consciousness is not contained or tamed by what appears on the surface as a giving over to the masculine.

The final word of *Ulysses* can also be read as the affirmation of an opening up to difference: a 'giving up and giving in', as Calle-Gruber might say, to the music of writing itself. Consciousness is represented as the remainder, the excess, the outside of the masculine libidinal economy. In a sense the whole of the Molly monologue is about singing excess. The refrain of 'yes' which begins the song, flows through it and concludes it, affirms the infinite registers of the other, those intimate liminal connections in the text where the music sings. The differences between the elements of the text (train, face) are no longer a source of loss but rather a gift through which to think the complex flows of writing sexual difference.

In conclusion, a Cixousian reading of the final and perhaps most

controversial episode of *Ulysses* would draw attention to the materiality of the writing, the sensual poetics of the text, and search out
a subterranean feminine libidinal economy which resists phallic
appropriation. What we have brought to bear in our reading of
Joyce with Cixous is an understanding of the importance of the
intimate connections between desire and writing. An appreciation
of the writing as caught up in the play of sexual difference also calls
our attention to the subtle sounds of meaning which are often
overlooked when one listens with an ear for sameness. Yes, in
many ways Molly can be read as a stereotype of frustrated femininity but 'she' is not a person, rather 'she' is the materiality of the
writing, and in this instance 'she' has become song. Molly finally
and forever sings herself into song.

In the next chapter we turn to a reading of Virginia Woolf's *The
Waves* [1931] in order to continue our exploration of the type of
reading Cixous opens up. As we have seen from this chapter, that
might entail actually reading against the grain of her writing. When
we examine *The Waves* we will be foregrounding Cixous's theorization of materiality and memory as part of the play of sexual difference in writing. Another key modernist text, *The Waves* is acutely
interested in the role of perception in the construction of identity
while also calling attention to the embodied nature of consciousness. Cixous's focus on the embodiment of perception seems very
applicable here. Both Woolf and Cixous, I will argue, construct a
phenomenological relationship between body, perception and
identity which opens up creative ways of thinking through writing
and sexual difference.

4 The Moment of the Third Body: Virginia Woolf and *The Waves*

> There is a time for listening to the vibrations that things produce
> in detaching themselves from the nothing-being to which our
> blindness relegates them, there is a time for letting things strug-
> gling with indifference give themselves to be heard.
>
> Hélène Cixous, 'To Live the Orange' (in Sellers 1997)

In this chapter we turn to one of Virginia Woolf's more experimental works, her 1931 novel *The Waves*, in order to explore, with
Cixous, how the relationship between representation and the
world is an effect of perception. Woolf's text is also a high
modernist meditation on the permeable nature of identity, which
describes the inner life of six characters as they interact through
childhood to old age: the perceptions of the characters intermin-
gle, creating 'waves' of consciousness. For Woolf, such 'waves' of
consciousness continually break against and overcome the limits
of representation. Within *The Waves* the relationship between self
and other, word and thing, time and memory is opened up to 'the
eternal renewal, the incessant rise and fall and fall and rise again'
of life (1989: 200). Woolf's understanding of this dynamic renewal
of representation bears some affinities with Cixous's approach.
Indeed the philosophy of post-structuralism has an affinity with
high-modernist writers such as Joyce and Woolf in so far as there is
often a common interest in interrogating spaces of excess within
language as passages into new dimensions of thought.[1]

In order to anchor our Cixousian reading of Woolf it is appropriate that we begin by thinking through some of our guiding
concerns with the relationship between writing and sexual difference. How might a Cixousian reading of Woolf's focus on perception allow us to clarify this relationship? If our perception of sexual

difference can be said to produce a knowledge or writing of sexual difference, the creative and positive expansion of perception becomes a vital goal in the production of new ways of writing sexual difference. As such, Cixous's work is preoccupied with the process of perception or *reading* as a creative, positive and dynamic activity. To expand the limits of perception, to create a dynamic, active and creative perception, is to also subvert dominant forms of subjectivity, perception and knowledge: to read differently is also then to take up new subject positions and produce new representations. As Cixous argues, this opening up of perception depends upon a recognition of the object as a form of positivity which is in the process of becoming. What I perceive is not lacking because it is not-I, but rather it is a positive becoming which my point of view cannot fully know. The strangeness of the object, it's difference, is perceived as a positive form of becoming rather than an inert lack.

Perception and time

In Cixous's 'To Live the Orange' (in Sellers 1997), the limited point of view is tied to temporality; we can only ever glimpse moments of becoming: our perception is temporary, only ever a moment in time. Woolf has a similar understanding of perception, which intensifies into a form of revelation or a 'moment of being'. Indeed, Morag Schiach reads a similarity between Woolf's 'moments of being', Joyce's 'epiphanies' and what Cixous terms 'quasacles' or 'quasi-miracle-instants', or attempts to express the intensity of a moment in which consciousness becomes aware of difference (1991: 34). If perception is a moment in time, such a moment is not simply a pure present, a moment of pure awakening free of past perceptions, but it is also made up of the memory of perceptions. The relationship between time, memory and perception is a major theme is much of Woolf's writing, but it is perhaps in *The Waves* that her exploration of this relationship is at its most sophisticated. The symbolism of the waves in the text conjures up a fluid relationship between perception, time and memory and can be read as a continuation of the 'stream of consciousness' conceit found in much high modernist writing.

It is important to recall that many high modernists, such as

Woolf, were greatly influenced by the work of Henri Bergson who wrote extensively on time as a process of *duration*, of fluidity, in classic works like *Matter and Memory* (1911). Bergson has experienced something of a revival through Deleuze's interest in his work. Commenting on Bergson, Deleuze writes: 'Duration essentially defines a virtual multiplicity (*what differs in nature*). Memory then appears as the coexistence of all *the degrees of difference* in this multiplicity, in this virtuality' (1988: 112). By 'virtual', Deleuze means the image or representation. Duration as memory is composed of images or representations. With Bergson, linear, mathematically precise concepts of time were complicated by ideas about time as a process of almost organic unfolding, by the idea that time is subjective and thus caught up in recollection, punctuated by moments of intensity. Time stopped it's mechanical ticking and melted, like one of Salvador Dali's clocks, under the heat of subjective experience.

However, Bergson's challenge does not simply result in a morally bankrupt subjectivism nor can we rightly argue that for Cixous or Woolf perception is merely subjective, or a form of relativism (pure subjectivism, pure difference, would only be intelligible to itself: subjectivity signifies because it is understood by others). Rather, what these intimate connections between perception, time and memory foreground is the virtual nature of reality, or the way reality is composed of images. This does not mean that the body does not exist but rather that our perception of the body is also a representation of the body. Perhaps one way of understanding this is through the concept of morphology. As Gatens has argued, the concept of morphology highlights the way various discourses produce representations or images of the body. For example, the discourse of medicine produces particular representations of the female body across time. The female body is not some brute essence which exists outside representation, but a system of representations, and is, as such, virtual. I perceive my hand and I am able to say that my hand contains bones, blood, nerves and muscle because I recall that this is the way hands have been represented or named. The perception of the bones in my hand depends upon the memory of a virtual hand, on a particular biological representation of the human body. Perception is therefore dynamically connected to memory or the virtual.

For Cixous, and Woolf as we shall see, recognition of the object as a form of positivity which is in the process of becoming opens up a creative mode of perception. The multiplicity of representations which layer the perception of a hand are experienced as a positivity in the process of becoming and not as a final perception. The object of perception, in other words, is never reducible to the perception. Another way of understanding this is to say that materiality exceeds perception. As Woolf asks in *The Waves*: ' "Like" and "like" and "like" – but what is the thing that lies beneath the semblance of the thing?' (1989: 110). In other words: What lies beneath representation?

One central connection between Woolf and Cixous is a shared interest in a contemplative perception of materiality which foregrounds a receptive, dynamic intimacy. Cixous's writing describes a proximity with the non-human as a productive, creative engagement with materiality which demands slow and careful concentration. Meditating on the materiality of the orange, Cixous writes:

> The orange is a moment. Not forgetting the orange is one thing. Recalling the orange is another thing. Rejoining it is another. At least three times are needed in order to begin to understand the infinite immensity of the moment. . . . I am beginning to measure its importance. . . . The orange is a beginning. Starting out from the voyage all voyages are possible. All voices that go her way are good.   (in Sellers 1997: 88)

Here the orange as an object of perception is a moment which is layered with different temporal modes, described as 'not forgetting', 'recalling' and 'rejoining'. Such a moment is infinite and a beginning, a becoming or a voyage. Cixous is trying to move beyond a commonsense understanding of what an orange is, in order to meditate on our perception of materiality or the thing. To live the orange is to respond to the call of materiality without violence.

As Susan Sellers comments, we can compare Cixous's approach to a Heideggerian insistence that we 'step back from the thinking that merely represents – that is, explains – to the thinking that responds and recalls' (1997: 83). A receptive perception of the thing would open up the possibility that it is in the process of becoming and is therefore something deserving of responsive thought. Receptive perception is therefore a type of responsive thought.

Such a perception, as Woolf suggests, challenges the foundations of identity. In *The Waves*, the character Neville sits on a river bank in the sun. ' "In a world which contains the present moment," said Neville, "why discriminate? Nothing should be named lest by so doing we change it. Let it exist, this bank, this beauty, and I, for one instant, steeped in pleasure" ' (55). Words inevitably rise up within him. ' "I see it all. I feel it all. I am inspired. My eyes fill with tears. Yet even as I feel this, I lash my frenzy higher and higher. It foams. It becomes artificial, insincere. Words and words and words, how they gallop . . . I do not know myself sometimes, or how to measure and name and count out the grains that make me what I am" ' (56). An awareness that representations cannot capture the world leads to an awareness that self-representation is based on the same uncertain relationship between word and thing. A friend approaches and Neville's identity undergoes a further change. 'Yet how painful to be recalled, to be mitigated, to have one's self adulterated, mixed up, become part of another. As he approaches I become not myself but Neville mixed with somebody – with whom? – with Bernard?' (56). A receptive perception opens up into an awareness of the contingent relationship between world, representation and identity.

Such a mode of perception can be contrasted with what we have earlier described as an alienated relationship to matter in our discussion of Cixous's rewriting of what we might call the morbid poetics of existential alienation. In Sartre's *Nausea*, for example, the protagonist Roquentin experiences alienation and dread when contemplating the thingness of a pebble in his hand. Instead of experiencing wonder before the immense strangeness of the thing, fear narrows perception so that the force of the pebble is experienced as negative. When Woolf urges us to 'Think of things in themselves' in *A Room of Ones Own* (1987: 105) she does so in order to push thinking beyond the limits of representation, but such a thinking beyond is understood to be a positive, creative practice and not one which leads to dread or alienation. Woolf's writing, like Cixous's, moves beyond an alienating fear of the strangeness of the thing into a receptive contemplation. A morbid existential alienation involves a pulling towards the objectification of the self as death-bound matter. In this context, the body becomes a thing when the contingent connection between representation and object is perceived: contingency or the perception of uncertainty leads to alienation. Cixous, on the other hand, views the contemplation of materiality as an opening up into a life-affirming thinking otherwise: the negativity of a death-bound alienation is passed through. The arbitrary relationship between representation and materiality is perceived as a form of positivity. For Cixous, a feminine thinking describes a passing through such alienation into a creative affirmation of materiality as the source of a poetics of becoming. Another way of putting this, is to say that Cixous affirms life and the pleasures and challenges of becoming rather than the morbid contemplation of limits, boundaries, laws. Both Woolf and Cixous affirm writing as a positive mode of perception.

Thinking responsively

The receptive mode of perception which both Woolf and Cixous favour is also a type of responsive thinking. Cixous often highlights the word 'approach' when describing a non-violent feminine response to the human or non-human Other. In many ways we can understand her life work as the exploration of an ethics of non-violence towards difference, which she argues is vital if we are to transform dominant modes of destructive thinking. Such a concern informs many post-structuralist meditations on the relationship between the body and representation: how do we form non-alienating and liberatory representations? Instead of resorting to censorship, perhaps we need to explore how thinking is itself an embodied process. One of Woolf's achievements in *The Waves* is the location of an embodied thought within the passage of time so that a thinking through the body becomes a thinking through the process of time and memory. Before we explore Woolf's *The Waves* with Cixous in more depth it is necessary to sketch out some further connections between the two writers and to locate Woolf as a thinker of embodiment.

Woolf's famous *A Room of One's Own* (1928) is generally recognized as the founding text of a tradition of feminist literary criticism which centres on the woman writer. Here Woolf explores the possibilities open to the woman writer and urges women to rewrite numerous discourses. Elaine Showalter, in her landmark essay 'Towards a Feminist Poetics' (1979), uses the term 'gynocritics' to describe a type of feminist literary criticism which focuses on the woman as writer, 'woman as the producer of textual meaning, with the history, themes, genres, and structures of literature by women' (1992: 128). For Showalter, however, Woolf is finally little more than an aesthete whose poetics are inward looking and rather too precious: Woolf's writing retreats into a 'celebration of consciousness' which conveys a sense of 'uterine withdrawal and containment'. In other words, for Showalter, Woolf's poetics of consciousness is a return to the comfort zone of the womb, a return to the mystical maternal. Indeed she writes that 'In this sense, the Room of One's Own becomes a kind of Amazon utopia, population 1' (1992: 139). This rather harsh dismissal avoids a deeper engagement with Woolf's description of writing and consciousness in *A Room of One's Own*, and indeed the rest of her work. Apart from the fact that Woolf argues that economic independence is necessary if women are to write, and has a quite pragmatic approach to the difficulties confronting women writers, her more subtle descriptions of consciousness as a thinking through sexual difference also make it difficult to agree with Showalter's negative appraisal. Woolf simply does not espouse a withdrawal into aesthetics any more than Cixous does, and indeed the similarity between Woolf and Cixous and the criticism launched against them is significant for it indicates, yet again, the power a prescriptive politics of reading has on attempts to think otherwise. It is not insignificant that both Woolf and Cixous have been read as aesthetes, priestesses of exquisite sensibility who remain aloof from the hard realities of the everyday. For many of Woolf's critics, her writing is too deli-cate, too mannered, lacking the muscular strength of a more politically engaged writing.

There are many conceptual overlaps between Woolf's manifesto and Cixous's much later manifesto 'The Laugh of the Medusa'. Both discuss the exclusion of the female voice and body within patriarchal writing and insist that women must reclaim their own speaking position. Both dream of a newly born woman poet who will revitalize thought. Woolf imagines that Shakespeare had a sister called Judith, just as brilliant, but who died unknown, never having been able to put pen to paper because she was a woman. 'She lives in me,' writes Woolf, 'and in many other women who are not here to-night, for they are washing-up the dishes and putting the children to bed' (1987: 107–8). If we create another way of thinking, argues Woolf, 'the dead poet who was Shakespeare's sister will put on the body which she has so often laid down. Drawing her life from the lives of the unknown who were her fore-runners ... she will be born' (108). In contrast to Showalter's dismissal of Woolf's work as a uterine withdrawal into a precious poetics of consciousness we can argue more convincingly that Woolf imagines the birth of a new consciousness through the woman writer.

Both Cixous and Woolf argue that the female imagination has not yet been fully explored and yet both also refuse a crude egalitarian collapse between the sexes and offer a concept of thinking as something which transcends the confines of masculine and feminine and which is itself a type of femininity or openness: for Cixous this type of thinking is linked to the 'other bisexuality', among other things, and for Woolf it is the 'androgynous mind'. Following on from the Romantic poet Coleridge who claimed that a great mind is androgynous, Woolf argues that such a mind is 'resonant and porous', 'transmits emotion without impediment', is 'naturally creative, incandescent and undivided' and would, significantly, 'not think specially or separately of sex' (1987: 94).[2] 'Sex-consciousness', argues Woolf in *A Room of One's Own*, leads to sterile writing: 'It is fatal to be a man or a woman pure and simple; one must be woman-manly or man-womanly' (99). She provides an example of the type of thinking which separates sex in her brief description of a contemporary novel by 'Mr A': 'After reading a chapter or two a shadow seemed to lie across the page. It was a straight dark bar, a shadow shaped something like the letter "I". One began dodging this way and that to catch a glimpse of the landscape behind it' (95). This 'I' is the signifier of a colonizing phallocentric imaginary. This phallic identity 'blocked the fountain of creative energy and shored it within narrow limits' (96). Men, she summarizes, are today mostly writing 'only with the male side of their brains'. Such writing is sterile and remains trapped in a reactive denial of the feminine, while androgynous writing 'explodes and gives birth to all kinds of other ideas, and that is the only sort of writing of which one can say that it has the secret of perpetual life' (97). Again, it is not so much a uterine withdrawal from the world, which Woolf envisages, but rather a consciousness that gives birth to new thought, producing effects in the world rather than retreating from it.

In *Reading Woman: Essays in Feminist Criticism*, Mary Jacobus explores Woolf's concept of mind in *A Room of One's Own*, which is, she argues, an 'essentially Utopian vision of undivided consciousness' (1986: 39). Yet she also argues that within Woolf's description of androgynous writing there is a sense of the 'play of diference perpetually enacted within writing. . . . And in holding open other possibilities – otherness itself – such writing posits "the difference of view" as a matter of rewriting' (1986: 39). However, these two readings seem to contradict one another. One describes the final synthesis of masculine and feminine into a totality called 'androgyny', while the other describes the androgynous mind as fluid, 'porous' or penetrable, and productive. One suggests stasis, the other a dynamic growth. The former 'undivided consciousness' could be read as corresponding to Showalter's 'uterine withdrawal' in so far as there is a retreat from productivity, while the latter is outward-directed, a creative engagement with difference and not a final synthesis of difference.

It is this last description of Woolf's concept of the androgynous mind which I want to take up here for it offers a productive way of opening up Woolf's writing to Cixous's concept of thinking. The conceptual subtlety of Woolf's writing on consciousness is too easily missed, I would argue, simply because she was using a language which had only just began to struggle with ways of think-ing through the writing of sexual difference, and it would be a mistake to dismiss her thought on the grounds that she used terms like 'androgyny' to describe this process. This is to approach her writing with a sense of respect for the struggle towards thinking which it performs. And it is also to open up the writing to thinking, to let it 'explode and give birth to all kinds of other ideas'. This, to me, is also a Cixousian approach, a reading/writing which refuses the negativity of lack, and instead explores the life current within the text.

Woolf's representation of the creative mind is not determined by a biological understanding of male and female brains or sexed identities. Such a mind is capable of a receptive perspective and a responsive thinking precisely because it is not limited to the point of view of a male or female mind. Woolf's exploration of perception in her writing seeks to achieve a thinking which is continually fluid, undergoing a process of becoming.

Waves of becoming

By emphasizing Woolf's description of consciousness as a birth
into the spaciousness of new possibilities for thinking rather than
a withdrawal into the comfort zone of the maternal I hope to foreground the approach I have taken to *The Waves*, a text which could
too easily be read as drowned by a mannered emphasis on maternal metaphors. The sea, after all, and the element of water, has long
been associated with the maternal and the feminine. We could
argue that every metaphor of fluidity in the text is simply a continuation of a Romantic mystification of the maternal as the oceanic
sublime.[3] However, the text also describes a phenomenology of
perception that connects memory with consciousness in ways
which open up into Cixous's thinking. For Cixous, as we recall, the
maternal signifies far more than a nostalgia for an undivided
consciousness or a pre-lapsarian unity, and nor does the maternal
simply signify an idealized political position from which to speak of
an authentic female consciousness. As a poet-philosopher Cixous
explores the way the maternal functions as the source of a thinking
through the *matter* of sexual difference.[4] In this sense the maternal
is not just simply tied to a host of myths and legends about the
maternal body, but rather the maternal is approached as the very
substance, the matter, of that which calls on us to think.[5] To call
this substance 'maternal' is simply to recognize the *gift* of a living
thought which is *generated* through contemplation. Like Woolf's
concept of an androgynous thought which 'explodes and gives
birth to all kinds of other ideas', Cixous understands feminine writing as something which nourishes thought.

   If consciousness is fluid, so too is the perception of time. Many
modernist writers explored the dynamic relationship between
interior and exterior senses of temporality in their work. The
impact of Freudian psychoanalysis and the resulting emphasis on
the importance of childhood memories also led to literary explorations of the time of the child. Marcel Proust begins his first of
seven novels known collectively as *Remembrance of Things Past*
[1913] with the famous line 'For a long time I used to go to bed
early'. *The Waves* also opens with the perceptions of a child. More
than simply part of an historical interest in childhood though, writers such as Proust and Woolf (and indeed Cixous with her frequent
focus on her childhood) explore how an examination of the early

awakening of consciousness leads us into a contemplation of the process of cognition. The phenomenologist Maurice Merleau-Ponty puts it like this: 'With the first vision, the first contact, the first pleasure, there is initiation, that is, not the positing of content, but the opening of a dimension that can never again be closed, the establishment of a level in terms of which every other experience will henceforth be situated' (1992: 151). It is the maternal body which initiates us into this opening up of the dimension of a thinking, which, as Merleau-Ponty stresses, is sensual, tactile, born of desire and never simply a disembodied cogito. The opening of our perception, then, is mediated through the maternal.

Throughout Woolf's novel the relationship between time and subjectivity is communicated through metaphors of water. Memory especially is linked to fluidity, to waves of becoming, ripples of moments across time. Woolf is not alone in connecting memory and time to water, for in *The Poetics of Reverie: Childhood, Language, and the Cosmos* (1971), Gaston Bachelard argues that the poetics of memory are tied to a sense of depth, of water. Bachelard attempts to create a philosophy of the anima or the feminine through his exploration of the poetics of reverie. Water becomes a metaphor for the process of a feminine contemplation of the depths of memory and it is also an element which can function as a metaphor for the flow between exterior and interior temporality, for the very permeability of being.

Like many modernist writers Woolf was acutely aware of the importance of symbolism and the very title of *The Waves* signifies her approach to consciousness here. Like her better known novel *To the Lighthouse* (1992), the text is divided into sections, each of which symbolizes a particular stage in the narrative. In *The Waves* each of the seven stages in the narrative (which represent stages of the characters' lives as they progress towards death) begins with a lyrical description of the relationship between the sea and the sun. The passage of a day is linked to the passage of the characters' lives. For example, the text opens with the following, '*The sun had not yet risen. The sea was indistinguishable from the sky, except that the sea was slightly creased as if a cloth had wrinkles in it*' (1989: 5), and goes on to explore the detailed perceptions of the characters as children in a garden by the sea. The sense of a separate consciousness slowly emerges in the characters just as the subtle distinction between sea and sky is formed as the sun rises. Finally the sun sets:

'*Now the sun had sunk. Sky and sea were indistinguishable*' (159).
The distinction between sun and sky is once more blurred, just as
separate consciousness vanishes into death. This final section ends
with a description of the eternal return of the seasons, of the
endless rhythm of life, of the waves of becoming which flow
through consciousness. There is also, finally, a courageous movement against death. 'And in me too the wave rises. . . . It is death. .
. . Against you I will fling myself, unvanquished and unyielding, O
Death!' (200). As the sun sinks, symbolizing the close of a day and
a life cycle, consciousness moves against death. The final sentence
of the novel, '*The waves broke on the shore*' (200), produces a
connection between consciousness and the movement of the
waves against the shore.

This slippery symbolism saturates the text with a sense of the
permeability of the boundaries between self and other, a continual
exploration of the flows between interiority and exteriority. 'There
is no division between me and them. As I talked I felt "I am you"'
(195). Bodies are traced by the memory of other bodies – 'Here on
the nape of my neck is the kiss Jinny gave Louis. My eyes fill with
Susan's tears' (195). Even the experience of flesh is something
which is produced through contact with another: a childhood
memory of being bathed by a nurse becomes a baptism into the
experience of flesh – 'ever since old Mrs Constable lifted her
sponge and pouring warm water over me covered me with flesh'
(195). Identity becomes multiple, unstable: 'nor do I always know
if I am man or woman, Bernard or Neville, Louis, Susan, Jinny or
Rhoda – so strange is the contact of one with another' (190).
Elsewhere Woolf writes 'so fluid has my body become, forming
even at the touch of a finger into one full drop, which fills itself,
which quivers, which flashes, which falls in ecstasy' (149). The
boundaries of the body are read as permeable, liminal zones which
incorporate and transform other bodies.

In *A Thousand Plateaus*, Deleuze and Guattari offer an interesting reading of *The Waves*:

> Waves are vibrations, shifting borderlines inscribed on the plane of
> consistency as so many abstractions. The abstract machine of the
> waves. In *The Waves*, Virginia Woolf – who made all of her life and
> work a passage, a becoming, all kinds of becomings between ages,
> sexes, elements, and kingdoms – intermingles seven characters. But

each of these characters with his or her name, its individuality, designates a multiplicity (for example, Bernard and the school of fish). Each is simultaneously in this multiplicity and at its edge, and crosses over into the others. Percival is like the ultimate multiplicity enveloping the greatest number of dimensions. But he is not yet the plane of consistency. Although Rhoda thinks she sees him rising out of the sea, no, it is not he. . . . Each advances like a wave, but on the plane of consistency they are a single abstract Wave whose vibration progates following a line of flight or deterritorialization traversing the entire plane (each chapter of Woolf's novel is preceded by a meditation on an aspect of the waves, on one of their hours, on one of their becomings).   (1991: 252)

Their reading calls attention to the affinity between this novel and post-structural projects such as theirs which seek to elaborate a resistant, creative or 'nomadic' thinking. By 'plane of consistency' they mean immanence, the substance of materiality. The waves which Deleuze and Guattari read in the text are like movements of energy flowing through this immanence, just as energy passes through bodies. Memory composes here a *virtual body*: although Percival dies early in the novel he lives on through the other characters and becomes part of their substance of being. As memory, Percival is a virtual subject but one which has a material effect on the waves of becoming (or duration) of the other characters.

Deleuze and Guattari emphasize the way Woolf describes the interconnections between the characters. Each character is like a wave which moves into the others; together they function as a fluid substance, a wave of becoming composed of the multiplicity of other waves of becoming.[6] For Woolf, such a wave of becoming is caught up in the passage of time. There is a sense of repetition here too, for a wave is never a singular event in time, it breaks, pulls back and breaks again, and this sense of movement is tied in the text to the shifts between the past and the present. The moment of the wave of becoming describes a movement between the past and the present: memory pulls consciousness back only to release it again into a becoming, such that the very pulling back, the recollection or reverie, becomes the source of a movement forward. The moment of becoming is also a type of perpetual returning, or recollection.

The third body

One way of approaching the complex fluidity of *The Waves* is through Cixous's writing on the 'third body'. We recall from the chapter on her concepts, that the 'third body' represents a type of liminality which is produced through the exchange or connection between the self and other. Instead of seeing the connection between the self and other as one which results in a form of alienating negation (the other is negated by the identity of the self, or the self is negated by the fear of the other), Cixous understands this exchange as creative. Openness does not signify a passivity that is vulnerable to incorporation and annihilation but rather a generous productivity. What is produced in the exchange is something Cixous calls 'the third body'.

Cixous's writing is preoccupied with the poetics of the *passage* between bodies as the process of becoming. She offers a careful and slow interrogation of the passage, of the third term. This third term is always already virtual in the sense that it is a form of representation. All forms of representation create virtual bodies, or as Gatens points out, knowledge produces a morphology of the body, a conceptual map of the body. The exchange between two bodies, suggests Cixous, produces a third representation of self and other which exceeds both: this third body is the space of multiplicity. Within *The Waves*, images and recollections of the longed for and dead Percival permeate the other characters: as he is continually recomposed through their desire for him he becomes multiple, capable of endless movement. As Deleuze and Guattari put it: 'Percival is like the ultimate multiplicity enveloping the greatest number of dimensions.' Or we might argue that Percival signifies the virtual body produced through memory, as a third body he is as multiple as the memories which compose him. His identity is quite radically an effect of representation.

Cixous's concept of the third body can be compared to what Merleau-Ponty calls the *chiasm*, the intertwining between the visible and the invisible, flesh and idea.[7] Discussing the relationship between the flesh of the body and the flesh of the world, he writes that 'there is a reciprocal insertion and intertwining of one with the other' (1992: 138). Or to put it another way, our understanding of the world is not limited to the self-present moment of a sensory experience, rather we inhabit bodies which are capable of folding back, or recollecting past sensations and re-anchoring them in our flesh. To use a simple example, we have an ability to recall the touch of a lover with such force that it makes our body shudder with desire. Or to conjure up the memory of pain so that our heart races with fear. Deep within the present we can trigger an experience from the past. This embodiment of memory suggests that memory is much more than an abstract representation, it is a form of embodiment. The temporality of the body is thus complex, never linear, always in the process of negotiating several temporal horizons at once. In this sense the third body is a type of echo chamber for past sensations and thoughts. However, Cixous suggests that the third body is not simply a retrospective form of embodied representation; it is also a space through which new representations are embodied.

We have a *mind's eye* which can 'see' images, representations from the past, just as we can 'hear' our internal dialogue, or composers can 'hear' new musical compositions. The ability to recollect or relive sensory experiences also provides us with the ability to imagine new ones, to fantasize and create, to 'hear' conversations which have not yet been uttered, music that has not yet been played, to 'see' images that have not yet been seen, pictures not yet painted, to 'taste' sensations which have not yet been tasted. These spectral but creative senses are what Cixous means by the third body. The third body might be understood quite simply as the body of the imagination. Dreams would be third-body experiences. The third body is also capable of tasting sound, hearing color, feeling words, of a receptive and dynamic perception of the world which produces creative connections, reinventing the relationship between the body and materiality. In other words, we can argue that the third body also describes the passage from which are born new experiments in thinking. Indeed, the third body is the space of thinking itself.

For Cixous the third body exists in a moment which exceeds the law: 'there came to us a third body, at a place where there is no law'. The third body not only exceeds the constraints of physical limitations (and biologically sexed identities) but moves, with an almost imperceptible speed, through the constraints of representation into the spaciousness of difference. The moment of the third body is thus a type of non-linear flight through time. Writing can barely capture this intensity, it forever escapes representation.

Commenting on Woolf's philosophy of the moment of writing, Deleuze and Guattari write:

> She says that it is necessary to 'saturate every atom,' and to do that it is necessary to eliminate, to eliminate all that is resemblance and analogy, but also 'to put everything into it': eliminate everything that exceeds the moment, but put in everything that it includes – and the moment is not the instantaneous, it is a haecceity into which one slips and that slips into other haecceities by transparency. To be present at the dawn of the world.   (1987: 280)

In other words, the moment is not a singular or self-present event in time but rather is saturated with haecceity. The moment of the third body is the movement of thinking through time. Or as Deleuze argues, 'the present *is not*; rather, it is pure becoming, always outside itself' (1988: 55).

The Waves can be read in this way as a stream of consciousness play-poem about what Cixous calls the third body. Composed of multiply identities which speak across and through each other, each 'I' attests to the virtuality and multiplicity of the third body. In *The Marine Lover*, Irigaray offers a way of thinking of the many surfaces of the sea, not as some depth which can finally be penetrated and arrived at, but rather as 'supple living envelopes for specular alchemy' (1991: 46), and indeed there is a sense in Woolf's text in which each character becomes a reflective surface in which such a specular alchemy occurs. 'I am made and remade continually,' says one of the characters (1989: 90). ' "Yes," said Jinny, "our senses have widened. Membranes, webs of nerve that lay white and limp, have filled and spread themselves and float round us like filaments, making the air tangible and catching in them far-away sounds unheard before" ' (91). The nerves of the third body extend beyond the flesh, suggesting a sensory thinking which is capable of multiple connections, multiple transformations. Jinny says 'I cannot tell you if life is this or that. I am going to push out into the heterogeneous crowd,' and enters into a surreal process of becoming in which her subjectivity unfolds into many different bodes (119). Louis meditates on his name and his identity, which appears to be 'clear-cut and unequivocal', and then goes on to say that 'a vast inheritance of experience is packed in me. I have lived thousands of years' (112). Louis becomes a duke, now Plato, companion of Socrates; the tramp of dark men and yellow men migrating east, west, north and south; the eternal procession, women going with attaché cases down the Strand as they went once with pitchers to the Nile; all the furled and close-packed leaves of my many-folded life are now summed in my name; incised cleanly and barely on the sheet.   (112–13)

The proper name or the subject is revealed to be a moment of intensity which harbours a multiplicity of identities and movements. Within the proper name lies the potential of an endless unfolding which is not just tied to personal experiences but reaches beyond, imaginatively, into anything the subject has encountered. The vast moment of the third body is not limited to individual memory but also encapsulates numerous histories. 'We are forever mixing ourselves with unknown quantities' (79), writes Woolf. The third body extends itself beyond the limits of the actual body, it is capable of collective movement, infinite plasticity. It is even capable of becoming post-human: 'I am not a woman, but the light that falls on this gate, on this ground. I am the seasons, I think sometimes January, May, November; the mud, the mist, the dawn' (66).

Escaping the confines of sexual identity, this third body often takes on the third person singular 'it,' which is evident in the following sections from Woolf and Cixous. As Woolf writes:

> Our bodies communicate. . . . I feel a thousand capacities spring up in me. I am arch, gay, languid, melancholy by turns. I am rooted, but I flow. . . . I flutter, I ripple. I stream like a plant in the river, flowing this way, flowing that way, but rooted, so that he may come to me. . . . I am broken off: I fall with him: I am carried off. We yield to this slow flood. We go in and out of this hesitating music. Rocks break the current of the dance; it jars, it shivers. In and out, we are swept now into this *large figure*; it holds us together; we cannot step outside its sinuous, its hesitating, its abrupt, its perfectly encircling walls. Our bodies, his hard, mine flowing, are pressed together within *its body*; it holds us together; and then lengthening out, in smooth, in sinuous folds, rolls us between it, on and on.   (68–9, emphasis mine)

Here the third body is compared to 'the current of the dance', a flowing movement which enfolds and unfolds two bodies, pulling them into a multiplicity which exceeds their boundaries.

Throughout the novel it is most often desire which is described as
the force which creates this third body, this fluid substance born of
the communication between self, other and world.

The language of the third body resists being captured by representation even as it is born of representation, of the endless mirroring of the other. To remain trapped in the representation of the
other, in the mirror of the other's eyes, as Cixous suggests, is to
destroy the creative force of the third body. Rather, the third body
is that which exchanges representation by translating resemblance
until it becomes something other. The language of the third body
is potentially limitless, capable of perpetuating 'us' without end,
for sexual difference is kept in play by the continual deferment of a
final synthesis. The language of desire never arrives at a final point
of meaning but is continually being born through the third body. In
this sense then, the moment of the third body is capable of bearing
a language of sexual difference which is continually in the process
of becoming.

The poetics of matter

> Senses flow, circulate, messages as divinely complicated as the
> strange microphonetic signals, conveyed to the ears from the
> blood, tumults, calls, inaudible answers vibrate, mysterious
> connections are established. It is not impossible in the unre-
> strained conversing that among disjunct, remote, disproportion-
> ate ensembles, at moments, harmonies of incalculable resonance
> occur.
>
> Hélène Cixous, 'To Love the Orange' (in Sellers 1997: 92)

In 'To Live the Orange' Cixous explores the moment of contemplation, the intensity of thought, which is produced through a meditation on an orange. Her essay is not so much a description of what
an orange is, as a description of the process of feminine thinking
and writing which unfolds through a meditation on materiality or
the thing. The poetry of the orange wells up through this careful
contemplation and nourishes the writer with thought. In a sense
she moves towards the orange by peeling back the layers of
language which have encased it. Cixous also describes this meditation on materiality as a turning towards the '*source*' of going
'*further into the birth-voice*' (87). Again we have a metaphoric link

between matter and the maternal – both are figured as the source of a feminine writing practice which is capable of rethinking subjectivity. And again this process of thinking back to the source of thought through a deep meditation on materiality is described as an intimately sensory experience, one which engages the senses on an acute third-body level. Cixous writes of her 'ears of meditation. . . . That listen to the growing of poetry when it is still subterranean, but struggling slowly in the breast to bring itself forth to the incantation of the outside, rejuicing and suffering from being only the breathing of matter' (87–8). Here we could argue that the polymorphous senses of the third body are evoked, and that it is this liminal body which listens to the subtle voice of the poetics of matter which, barely audible, are called forth through this sensory meditation until what is finally 'heard' (and written) is the becoming ('the breathing') of matter. On a less subtle level, Cixous is drawing attention to the importance of a slow and respectful thinking through the body, a thinking which engages the body through a contemplation with the materiality of the other, which in this case happens to be an orange.

Cixous also draws attention to the multiplicity of this moment of thinking: 'I have been living around an orange for three days. . . . The instant breathes, deepens, comes and goes, approaches, waits, continually' (88). Woolf's moments of being describe a similar process, a flickering intensity in which the moment of matter, the time of the thing, offers a subtle opening into the immensity of consciousness. The moment is a passage into the uncanny strangeness of the latent consciousness of matter. For Cixous this deep contemplation is about 'learning the thing' (89), it describes a mode of seeing beyond ways of seeing which are determined by representation – to see the orange beyond the word 'orange' involves listening to the poetry of matter.[8]

Towards the end of *The Waves*, Bernard observes that in order to see things in themselves it is necessary to forget the self, words, the linguistic apparatus which structures our perception (178, 194). This is only achieved very fleetingly, for quickly 'blindness returns' and the gaze pulls with it a 'train of phantom phrases' (194). Language hides the shining truth of matter, blinding us with phrases. One could argue that Woolf and Cixous maintain that an authentic truth lies behind the artificial layers of language and that all one has to do is peel back language to reveal the thing in itself, which will communicate, on an almost sublime level, the purity of an intense self-presence. And yet, as Cixous reminds us in 'To Live the Orange', the labour of thinking, even when it is caught up in the moment of an orange, is a labour towards freedom, towards a greater awareness of the process of respectful attention to the other. As she contemplates the orange, indulging in what some might term a form of navel gazing, a woman telephones her to remind her of the plight of women in Iran. This call to action is for Cixous also part of 'the work of un-forgetting, of un-silencing, of un-earthing, of un-blinding oneself, and of un-deafening oneself' which the contemplation of the materiality of the orange demands (in Sellers 1997: 78). In order to understand the materiality of the other (the women in Iran) one has to think responsively. As Cixous puts it, '*the love of the orange is political too*' (90).

In conclusion, our Cixousian reading of Woolf highlights the importance of understanding perception as a dynamic and creativity activity. Our discussion of the 'third body' drew comparisons between Woolf and Cixous, suggesting that both understand thinking as an embodied, creative process which occurs within a complex temporality. Our reading can be summarized as follows.

1. Perception or point of view is an active process which negotiates and produces knowledge or representations. For Cixous, reading is a form of writing.
2. Receptive perception recognizes the object as a form of positivity undergoing a process of becoming. In this context, sexual difference is perceived as a positivity that is in the process of becoming.
3. Receptive perception is a form of responsive thinking. A non-violent responsive thinking opens up into a recognition that the object of perception is never reducible to the perception. Point of view is always a partial perspective.
4. Understanding that the object of perception is not reducible to the perception is to be distinguished from perspectivism and anti-representationalism. A recognition that representations and perception are limited opens thinking up to a more productive and creative process and not a reactive denial of the force of representation and perspective.
5. A recognition of the contingent relationship between word and thing opens up writing to the play of difference. Both Woolf and

Cixous approach this contingency as the source of new ways of thinking.

6. Woolf's concept of mind is not tied to biological sexed identities. For Woolf, the point of view or perspective of male or female sexed identities cuts off responsive thinking. Receptive perception is therefore caught up in a fluid writing of sexual difference and moves beyond sexed identity.

7. The opening up of perception is mediated through the maternal, which stands in for a materiality which exceeds perception. Responsive thinking is nurtured by an intimacy with a world which can never be fully represented.

8. Cixous's concept of the third body can be understood through Woolf's representation of fluid morphology in *The Waves*. The third body is the virtual body of thinking; it is an embodied consciousness which is mobile, creative, and productive. Such a virtual body exceeds fixed images of self-present, stable sexual identity: it is porous, fluid, transformative, nomadic.

9. Cixous's writing on the third body offers a way of understanding thinking as an embodied process which, like Woolf's idea of the mind, is not fixed by the perspective of male or female biological sexed identities. The third body is the space of a receptive perception and a responsive thinking because it expands the limits of representation.

A question remains, however. What drives this opening up of perception? What force activates third-body transformations of systems of representation? Cixous's text *The Third Body* is also an elaborate and disjointed meditation on desire as an active force which is continually generating representations, connections between disparate elements, fractured memories, sensations. In a sense the third body is the zone of an experimental desire. Moreover, Cixous suggests that the third body *is* desire itself, but it is a desire without a single author; rather it is a field of desire which is crossed by different intensities, temporalities, the subtle language born of numerous connections. Perhaps we can understand the third body as a force. In the next chapter we turn to Clarice Lispector, a writer who had a profoundly enriching effect on Cixous's work and her understanding of the force of desire. Desire can blind but it can also open up perception and it is this difference Cixous investigates through her writing on Lispector. By focusing on the many essays Cixous has written about Clarice we shall achieve a greater intimacy with Cixous's thought. It was Clarice who inspired Cixous's meditation on the poetics of matter and memory and it is to Clarice that we now turn, in order to explore the ways in which Cixous understands her work as a form of libidinal education.

5 Libidinal Education:
Lispector and Cixous

At the school of Clarice Lispector, we learn the approach. We take
lessons of things. The lessons of calling, letting ourselves be
called. The lessons of letting come, receiving. The two great
lessons of living: *slowness and ugliness.*

Hélène Cixous, 'Clarice Lispector: The Approach' (1991b)

My vast night takes place in a primary state of latency. My hand
rests upon the earth and listens hotly to the beating of a heart. I
see the large white slug with a woman's breasts: is it a human
entity? I burn it in an inquisitional fire. I possess the mysticism of
the shadows of a remote past. And I leave these tortures of a
victim with the indescribable mark that symbolises life.
Elementary creatures surround me, dwarfs, goblins, gnomes, and
genies. I sacrifice animals to take from them the blood I need for
my own occult ceremonies. In my fury I offer up the soul in its
own blackness. The Mass terrifies me – I who perform it. And the
turbid mind dominates all matter. The beast bares its teeth, and
horses of allegorical chariots gallop through the distant air.

In my night I idolize the secret meaning of the world. Mouth
and tongue. And a loose horse, running free. I keep his hoof as a
fetish. In the depths of my night there blows a crazed wind that
brings me threads of cries.

Clarice Lispector, The Stream of Life (1989)

Here, according to the poet, was the cave which afforded access
to the infernal regions, and here Aeneas offered sacrifice to the
infernal deities, Proserpine, Hecate, and the Furies. Then a roar-
ing was heard in the earth, the woods on the hill-tops were
shaken, and the howling of dogs announced the approach of the
deities. 'Now,' said the Sibyl, 'summon up your courage, for you
will need it.' She descended into the cave, and Aeneas followed.

Thomas Bullfinch, The Golden Age of Myth and Legend (1985)

In this chapter we shall explore Cixous's substantial writings on the Brazilian author Clarice Lispector, in order to explore her concept of a libidinal education. Compared with Joyce and Woolf, Clarice Lispector is a relatively unknown writer, but for Cixous Lispector's writing is the most profound example of a feminine textual economy she has encountered. Lispector died in 1977 having published nine novels, four children's books and seven collections of short stories. Her first and critically acclaimed novel, *Close to the Savage Heart* (1944), was followed by, among others, *The Passion According to G.H.* (1964), *The Apple in the Dark* (1967), *An Apprenticeship, or The Book of Delights* (1969), and her last novel, *The Hour of the Star* (1977). In 1976 she presented Brazil at the World Witchcraft Congress in Bogota, Columbia. Most of her work is written in the first person singular and concerned with interior consciousness and its relationship to the non-human. Influenced by existentialism and the phenomenological exploration of the materiality of the thing, her work is also modernist in the sense that she uses the stream of consciousness to express epiphanic moments and deploys experimental prose fragments to disrupt the conventional novelistic form. Lispector, then, is another poet-philosopher, a thinker who uses prose to explore questions which are central to the Cixousian universe. Among Cixous's works on Lispector there are *Reading with Clarice Lispector* (1990), *Three Steps on the Ladder of Writing* (1993), and the essays 'Clarice Lispector: The Approach', 'By the Light of an Apple', 'The Author in Truth', 'Extreme Fidelity' and 'To Live the Orange'.

Lispector is a poet-philosopher who offers a particular 'approach' or 'passage' into a form of transgressive writing which is productive rather than reactionary, subversive without being violent, and in this sense Cixous understands her writing to be profoundly feminine. Lispector's libidinal education involves the refinement of libidinal energies and the creation of non-dominative desire through a receptive contemplation of the materiality of the ugly and profane. As Cixous comments, much of Lispector's work is on the abominable, the abject, or what Lispector herself calls the *imund*. However, as we shall explore later, Lispector's approach exceeds an extolling of the transgressive powers of the abject in the way perhaps that Kristeva's by now classic work on the subject, *Powers of Horror* (1982), achieves.[1] For Cixous, Lispector's libidinal education takes us beyond a romantic reification of the abject or the *imund* as the source of subversion and oppositionality. The 'apprenticeship' which Lispector's writing offers is essentially about forming a non-dominative, non-appropriative relationship to what has been coded as impure. It is not an easy apprenticeship. However, as Verena Andermatt Conley comments, '[a]pprentice-ship is not the same as submission, for within it, a path towards transformation and change is open' (1984: 77).

It is vital that we think through the phallocentric logic which governs the desire to purify and appropriate if we are to challenge the libidinality of domination and this is why, argues Cixous, Lispector's libidinal education has so much to offer us, for within her writing we learn a non-violent approach to the impure. And the impure or the profane, as both Lispector and Cixous point out, is not simply pollution, but it is also the subject out of place, the outsider, those bodies who transgress cultural definitions of the clean and proper.[2] For example, the coding of homosexuality as impure depends on a homophobic revulsion against what are read as unclean sexual acts. Such a concept of the unclean motivates homophobic attacks and a general reduction of democratic rights for subjects who identify as homosexuals. Racist discourses also often depend on concepts of the unclean body. The term 'ethnic cleansing' aptly describes the violent effects such concepts have. Women's bodies have also been subjected to discrimination because they have been coded as unclean; for example, menstru-ating women are read as a source of pollution and social disorder. In other words, representations of the unclean body are caught up in a complex politics of exclusion while the pure and clean body often signifies the ideal subject of power, which in the West would be the white, heterosexual middle-class male. Deviations from this clean norm will be subjected to the discourse of pollution as culture attempts to limit and contain threats to the body politic of the ruling subject.

To forge a non-violent relationship with the impure is also in this context to create a more respectful and creative relationship with materiality in general. Both Lispector and Cixous suggest that a reverence for materiality is inseparable from a reverence for difference. If the central binary which has dominated Western metaphysics is the Cartesian division of mind and body, one way of overcoming the violence such a dichotomoy produces is to create a more responsive approach to the body. We might argue that for Cixous and Lipsector such an approach involves thinking through the various fictions which imagine the body (and materiality in general) as a source of contamination and impurity. To think through abjection, and our fear of the impure, is to think against a disembodied phallocentric metaphysics which supports undemocratic exclusions.

'Nature'

Before we explore Cixous's particular reading of materiality it is worth considering some of the conceptual problems which some critics have identified in her uptake of Lispector. As Conley puts it, with the discovery of Lispector: 'A new pluralism, of different sexes, species, and cultures is discovered. Apprenticeship of the world leads to that of alterity, of cultures and languages' (1984: 82). Conley's way of describing the shift in Cixous's thought suggests a certain naivety in the poet-philosopher, as though Cixous has suddenly noticed a world outside, full of other cultures, languages, species. Indeed it is worth signalling some of the reservations Conley expresses about Cixous's work on Lispector now, so that we can spend some time exploring the possible limitations of Cixous's Lispectorian philosophy.

Conley is certainly dubious about the conceptual worth of Cixous's uptake of Lispector and expresses several reservations most of which stem from her critique of what she perceives to be Cixous's romantic mysticism. She accuses Cixous of orientalizing Lispector's Brazilian voice, of downplaying the historical and social context of her writing by laying too much emphasis on its exotic qualities (Conley 1984: 83). Conley also argues that Cixous canonizes Lispector, framing her as a saint or a mystic, and that Cixous is excessively and narcissistically identified with Lispector's writing (84, 85). She argues that Cixous indulges in a nostalgic anthropomorphism, longing for a world in which nature communicated directly, in the moment, its pure essence (86, 89). In summary, Conley finds Cixous's writing on Lispector a form of arrogant Romanticism riddled with conceptual problems which arise from Cixous's belief in the privileged knowledge of poets and their relationship to nature.

> Cixous writes about other cultures by allusion to proper names, mainly 'poets' in the widest sense, who write or live through historical circumstances with an inner vision. . . . Ordinary mortals do not belong because theirs is neither an extraordinary politics nor a politics of the impossible. Seeking the same visionary stage, Cixous chooses to close her eyes in order to dream of an imaginary politics.
> (Conley 1984: 92)

Yet again the argument about the poetic and the political surfaces in a critique of Cixous – she is simply too poetic.

If Cixous's praise of Lispector and other 'poets' can be dismissed for being elitist, or rather, for overestimating the philosophical and political value of a select few, it is also worth recognizing, in her defence, that she doesn't write in a typically academic way about literature. It is important to recognize that Cixous's work on various writers does not conform to what we would usually expect of academic literary criticism. Like Heidegger's meditations on the poet Holderlin, Lispector provides Cixous with a way of enriching her own philosophical meditations.[3] I would also argue that the self-consciously personal relationship she establishes towards the writer means that if would be an error to confuse her praise of Lispector with the type of veneration for an author we find in literary critics such as F. R. Leavis or Harold Bloom, who attempt to disguise a personal preference with statements about the cultural importance of various writers.[4] If Cixous can at times be accused of genuflection in her writing on Lispector (and Conley is also certainly right to notice a certain 'etherealization' of the author), then perhaps we should also accuse Heidegger of genuflection in his writing on Holderlin, or Sartre of lionizing Jean Genet, or Foucault of making far too much of the significance of Baudelaire for modernity. Perhaps Cixous's passion for the philosophical richness of Lispector's writing transgresses a sense of propriety, but then maybe it is important that a female poet-philosopher should find such inspiration from another woman writer.

Conley's other reservation about Cixous's romantic anthropomorphism also needs addressing. There are several reasons why we might argue that such a romantic mystification of the natural world is conceptually flawed. Broadly speaking, Romanticism developed as a critique of the dehumanizing effects of the

Industrial Revolution and was generally opposed to the scientism of the Enlightenment, or the faith placed in reason and technological progress. In this context, texts such as Rousseau's *Emile* (1762) stressed the importance of a return to the natural world, to the instinctual body, and longed for the uncorrupted simplicity of an Edenic, pre-industrial past. The organic, intuitive and instinctual were valued over the mechanistic, rational and artificial. Poetry was often heralded (by Novalis in particular) as an antidote to the pathology of scientific reason.[5] As Foucault points out in 'What is Enlightenment?' one of the central problems attendant with what is essentially a rejection of the Enlightenment, is the danger of a reactionary dismissal of the emancipatory impulses which have shaped modernity. Extreme forms of Romanticism result in the entire representational system of modernity being rejected in favour of the impossible task of remaking the world. The desire to remake the world, as history has shown, leads to extreme politics and the formation of an intellectual or political elite which is unable to enter into a democratic dialogue with the masses. However, it would be a mistake to assume that Cixous is not aware of the historical load of various concepts for she is, after all, a writer who is acutely aware of the process of writing, the subtle dynamics of textuality.

In the context of our discussion of Cixous's Romanticism and what Conley argues is her essentialist approach to nature, it is worth examining a section from *Three Steps on the Ladder of Writing* where she draws attention to the word 'nature'. Here Cixous writes:

> The natural word, the word *nature*, has a sad fate: it was taken up in the great disputes, aimed in particular at people like myself who work on the sexual scene and who have been accused by a certain group of unenlightened people of using this word to mean a feminine or masculine nature – something I have never been able to conceive of – as if 'nature' existed in opposition to 'culture' or there were such a thing as pure nature. . . . For a while, to flee the field of these sterile disputes, I no longer used the word *nature*, even though I adore it. Then I adopted it again. As soon as I use it in the domain of writing it begins to move, to twist a little, because in *writing* this is what it's all about. As soon as there is writing, it becomes a matter of *passage*, of all kinds of passages, of delimitations, of overflowing. (1993: 128–9)

nto what exists between the number one and the
ow I saw the mysterious, fiery line, how it is a surrep-
tween two musical notes there exists another note,
acts there exists another fact, between two grains of
r how close together they are, there exists an interval
exists a sensing between sensing – in the interstices
matter there is the mysterious, fiery line that is the
ng, and the world's continual breathing is what we
lence.   (2000: 90)

ilence is also what she calls variously neutrality,
byss, Hell, the demonic, the non-human and
writing strives toward a point where identity
s why she names this point neutrality, nothing-
human, for it represents the extreme limits of
lls this Hell and the demonic because it is pre-
han and not because it signifies an encounter
ell is essentially the abyss or the nether realms,
encounters the profane or the impure and in
the non-human. For Lispector, the encounter
n leads to the 'destruction of layers and layers
ogy' (62), while she also writes that 'to be
constraint' (166). Human sentiments are utili-
r is not alone in her perception of the finite
. In *The Order of Things: An Archaeology of the
91a), Foucault writes of the disappearance of
wn in sand at the edge of the sea' (386); new
elling the future Ocean; man will disappear'
e writes, man is something to be overcome.[7]
is overcoming of the human is achieved
to the liminal materiality of the non-human.
ty of the non-human can only be encountered
h which enters into the deconstruction of
nd an exploration of a post-human imagi-
ing, suggests Cixous, is a libidinal education
s on the ethics of approaching the liminal.
human archaeology is the materiality of the

lity of things. Humanity is steeped in humaniza-
t were necessary; and that false humanization

Cixous is drawing attention to the ways in which writing always
already transforms or re-signifies the word 'nature'. In a sense the
purity of the concept or word 'nature' is put into play through writing. Within writing 'nature' has no pure or static meaning. She is
also careful to defend herself against the accusation of essentialism
which was mounted against her work in the 1980s when the big
debates about essentialism took centre stage within feminist
theory. Clearly, she is still touched by these accusations and admits
to even dropping the word 'nature' from her writing to avoid being
misread. But the overall point here is that 'nature' exists within
writing and as such is open to 'passages', transmutations, transformations, to the play of difference.

She goes on to argue that within Lispector's work 'nature'
signifies the extraordinary multiplicity of the ordinary:

> By the word *nature* I don't necessarily mean the concept. I don't
> want to return here to philosophic thinking and the subject theme of
> crossing in its intersection and articulation with culture, I prefer to
> remain in the poetic space, which is also philosophical, naturally.
> When I say 'I adopt again' I am rehabilitating, I am enjoying afresh
> the word *nature*, without being unaware that all kinds of adven*tures*
> happen to it in the text, including rhyme, and without being
> unaware of language clichés or on the contrary of great linguistic
> advances and impressions. . . . Again, in Clarice's work we have a
> magnificent leitmotif that highlights nature. Here there is nature of
> all kinds. She designates nature as 'supernature,' a 'supernatural.'
> She stresses that there is nothing more supernatural than nature. We
> could change that and say: there is nothing more marvellous than
> the ordinary, but this is already more difficult to think. In Clarice
> Lispector's writing it is a question of rehabilitating what *is*.   (1993:
> 129–30)

Here Cixous is careful to point out that her use of the word 'nature'
is writerly or poetic and is not limited to the philosophical debates
about the relationship between nature and culture although she is,
of course, aware of the conceptual load of such debates. Rather,
Cixous's knowing use of the word 'nature' attempts to open it up to
new configurations and meanings. Lispector's use of the word,
argues Cixous, highlights the fecund immediacy of a nature which
is excessive, 'supernatural', 'marvellous', and, importantly, this is
read as the 'nature' of the ordinary – 'the quotidian is supernatural'

(1990: 99); or as Lispector writes in *The Passion*: 'That supernatural thing that is living' (2000: 10). Nature or matter is understood as something which is radiant with an agency that challenges the limits of representation.

There are several points worth exploring here. First, when Cixous writes 'Here there is nature of all kinds', and that within Lispector's writing 'it is a question of rehabilitating what *is*', she is not suggesting that nature (or materiality) itself contains an immediate self-presence. Rather she is referring to the *event of writing* 'nature'. This subtle distinction calls attention to the difference between the 'presence' of 'nature' within the writing and Romantic assumptions that the true meaning of nature exists outside writing, signification, representation, language, the Symbolic and so on. If Cixous discusses 'nature' she does so within the context of a poetic exploration of the process of writing. If, within the domain of writing, 'nature' becomes, it does so because it occupies a place within writing and instead of understanding this position as a retreat into semantics, we should rather understand it as a call for ethical responsibility in the domain of representation. In this context it is the Romantic definition of nature as pre-discursive which avoids a responsible and ethical engagement with the place of 'nature' within writing. And this, as I hope I have shown, is very far from what Cixous is doing with the concept of nature.

In 'Ecofeminist Literary Criticism: Reading the Orange' (1998), Josephine Donovan finds Cixous's theorization of Lispector an important contribution to an eco-feminist metaphysics. Donovan's main argument consists in recuperating the concept of the 'absent referent' in order to argue for an eco-feminism which foregrounds an 'epistemological awakening' such that a dominative relationship to the other as 'it' is replaced with 'thou'.[6] Donovan argues that 'Cixous sees Lispector as a writer who attempted to remain faithful to the literal by capturing immediate, unmediated, and sacramental encounters with the world' (1998: 82). Eco-feminism, argues Donovan, attempts to achieve such a non-dominant epistemology. Donovan argues that Lispector 'seems to express a desire for the restoration of the absent referent in the text, its restoration as a living being, a thou' (84). Donovan also suggests that such an approach offers the possibility of developing a '*meditative attentiveness* ... in the hope that such a reawakening to the reality of the literal [the material], constructed

as a spiritual presen
world, including anin
mental respect' (89).
many affinities with
more useful, I think,
philosophical descri
is non-dominative a
finally, at the truth c
this reading is certa
are within the dom
unmediated encou

The materiality of

Another way of
through Lispecto
human; as Conley
the human altoge
self and other (19
focused primarily
we arrive at a p
explodes into a r
leave behind se>
contemplation
emphasis shifts
materiality of se
the materiality c
tion of a mor
comments in 'T
Lispector, the m
ated between t
(1991f: 169). In
with a cockroa
and subjectivit
It is through
the human an
Lispector's libi
apprenticeshij
Lispector writ

How I went i
number two, h
titious line. Be
between two f
sand, no matte
of space, there
of primordial
world's breath
hear and call si

For Lispector this s
nothingness, the a
grace. Lispector's
dissolves and this i
ness and the non-
identity. She also ca
human or non-hun
with the satanic. He
a place where one
doing so confronts
with the non-huma
of human archaeo
human has been a
tarian (61). Lispecto
nature of the humar
Human Sciences (19
man, 'like a face dra
gods 'are already sw
(385). Or as Nietzsch
For Lispector, th
through an attention
The liminal materiali
through an approac
human subjectivity
nary. Lispector's wri
or a series of lesson
Beneath the layers o
non-human:

I want the materi
tion, as though i

impedes man and impedes his humanity. There exists a thing that is broader, deafer, and deeper, less good, less bad, less pretty.   (1988: 150)

Lispector's writing strains against the limits of what it means to be human because she is attempting to explore an ethics that moves beyond the constraints of human morality, of concepts of good and bad which have led to the exclusion of bodies that are coded as profane or non-human. To think of ourselves as merely human, to remain limited by human subjectivity is, for Lispector, to perpetuate a reactionary morality. Such a morality is reactionary because it is formed against what is figured as non-human. Lispector argues that a fear of the non-human thing, of the profane, the impure, the liminal, closes off a reverential contact with the materiality of our own bodies and the bodies of others, because she understands materiality in general as something which exceeds the concept of the human. In other words, human subjectivity and human morality are limited by a definition of the non-human as a form of impure materiality: the freeing up of human moralism depends upon a more ethical opening towards the non-human through a non-reactionary relationship to liminality.

But what are the ethics of such an approach? As a brief answer we might say that such an ethics is about writing difference, the undecidable, the exploration of a non-violent, non-appropriative approach. In order to challenge the violence of dichotomous thought we need to create a writing (or a metaphysics or practice) which explores the ethical potentials of the in-between or liminal. Lispector's writing becomes a conduit for Cixous's philosophical explorations of alterity and the working through of an ethics of (sexual) difference. Both ground their exploration of the liminal through a careful attention to the materiality of the non-human in order to write a poetics of matter. Indeed, matter is frequently associated with the liminal, as the very substance of fluidity, or that which is always already in-between.

In her reading of Cixous's theorization of Lispector's *The Passion*, Rosi Braidotti argues the following: 'the term "approach" defines for Cixous the basis of her ethical system: it designates the way in which self and other can be connected in a new world-view where all living matter is a sensitive web of mutually receptive entities. The key terms are affinity and receptivity' (2002: 164–5).

Matter then is not simply coded as either human or inhuman but as mutually receptive, capable of productive exchanges and becomings. Lispector's and Cixous's understanding of materiality might also be compared to Spinoza's concept of Substance.[8] In *Collective Imaginings: Spinoza, Past and Present*, Moira Gatens and Genevieve Lloyd comment: '[e]ach singular finite thing is in this philosophy a particular determination of the power of God as Substance; each mediates the power of Substance and is itself acted upon and changed by the power mediated through other finite things' (1999: 13). Such an understanding of Substance or matter as mutually receptive – not simply acted upon or acting against – as mediating or acting with the other, is certainly akin to a Cixousian concept of matter. Braidotti goes on to write that 'adoration' is 'the best mode of approach and perception of the other' (2000: 166). By adoration we mean here a form of open respect, a loving attention to the other, and not a romantic and ultimately a pious self-serving sentimentalization of difference. Such an approach also involves the releasing of an anthropomorphic perception which sees in matter the reflection of human desire. To adore, to take up an approach to matter which is mutually receptive, entails a forgetting of human perspective.

With Lispector, Cixous discovers the possibility of a feminine writing which is courageously open to materiality. In *Illa*, Cixous writes: 'Seeing all that enters through the Clarice window, the marvellous quantity of things of all kinds, of all human, vegetal, animal species of all sexes, of all cultures, one feels with what loving force she holds herself open, with what frightened joy, to let herself be approached by the sudden' (1980b: 135). Cixous describes this perception as *claricéant* or 'clariseeing'. Clariseeing is an epistemological mode which strains towards a non-dominant relationship to the other. Clariseeing describes a sacramental encounter with the non-human, which is achieved through a slow and careful exploration of the many seductions to dominate and appropriate that the subject invariably comes across when facing the other. Or to put it more simply, in order to 'see' the other, one has to resist the many seductions to appropriate. For Cixous this approach is based on what Lispector calls 'clandestine felicity' – 'one can really have only if one knows how to have in a way that does not destroy, does not possess' (1991f: 160). Cixous goes on to write:

> One of the first lessons about living is the one that consists of know-
> ing how not to know, which does not mean not knowing, but *know-
> ing how not to know*, knowing how to avoid getting closed in by
> knowledge, knowing more and less than what one knows, knowing
> how not to understand, while never being on the side of ignorance.
> It is not a question of not having understood anything, but of not
> letting oneself get locked into comprehension. Each time that we
> come to know something, in reality it is a step. Then we have to
> strike out for the un-known, to make our way along in the dark, with
> an 'apple in our hand' like a candle. To see the world with the
> fingers: isn't this actually writing *par excellence*?   (161)

Another way of putting it is that we must continually ask questions
about the limits of knowledge, to keep alive our desire to discover
the unknown. To imagine that we can ever fully arrive at a point of
total comprehension is to close off thought, to remain deaf to the
question of the other.

What Cixous and Lispector are arguing for is a feminine epistemology that remains responsive to the question of the other, which
is also the question of thinking. Such a feminine epistemology or
knowledge is based on the materiality of difference and springs
from a careful and open contemplation of a materiality which is
always already impure, profane, and exceeds concepts of the
human and of what counts as human identity. Cixous also argues
that part of Lispector's libidinal education is a profound recognition of the difference between having and knowing. To *have* an
experience of the other does not mean that you *know* the other, for
the experience is too often a product of the desire to dominate.
Lispector's libidinal education is about the impossibility of fully
knowing and having the other or rather, about the spectral 'nature'
of the knowledge and possession of the other which is produced
through a blindness towards the contingent exclusions that form
identity: to know, to claim knowledge of an identity, is to forget
these exclusions.[9] As Elizabeth Grosz writes, 'ethics is a response to
the recognition of the primacy of alterity over identity' (1989a:
xvii). In the end, all we can hope to achieve is the right sort of
distance from our predatory desires to dominate. That distance
can only come about through a recognition of the phallocentric
libidinality of domination which governs the articulation of the
subject. Lispector's libidinal education is about achieving a type of
courageous disrespect for the Law in order to create a greater

respect for that which is outlawed *without* being caught in a reactionary binary. For Cixous, what is most profound about Lispector is that she does not construct an anti-Law. Reacting against the Law only makes the Law erect more powerful barriers. The challenge has to come from somewhere more subtle and feminine.

Ugliness

> At Clarice's school we have the most beautiful of lessons: the lesson of ugliness. Have I in effect abandoned a whole system of good taste? But is that my own gain? How imprisoned I must have been that I feel myself freer just because I no longer fear a lack of aesthetics. . . . For now, the first timid pleasure that I feel is being able to say that I have lost my fear of the ugly. And that loss is a very great good. It is a delight.
>
>   Hélène Cixous, 'Clarice Lispector: the Approach' (1991b: 75)

> Beauty would be at the mercy of a definition as classical as that of the common measure. But each individual form escapes this common measure and is, to a certain degree, a monster.
>
>   Georges Bataille, 'The Deviations of Nature' (1991a: 55)

Cixous offers a provocative interpretation of Lispector's understanding of the ugly in the final section of *Three Steps*, called 'The School of Roots'. This school represents an initiation into the depths of writing. She draws heavily on Lispector in order to explore a feminine libidinal economy which is open to the transgressive powers of the profane. She begins by exploring a chapter in Leviticus where distinctions are made between clean and unclean meat in order to open up a philosophical discussion of Lispector's confrontation with the unclean in *The Passion*.[10] Here the protagonist G.H. confronts a cockroach which 'becomes the focus for a type of fantastic, total, emotional, spiritual, and intellectual revolution' in which she 'must deal with the phobia, with the horror we have of so-called abominable beings' (1993b: 112). Cixous argues that what Lispector explores here is the phallocentric prohibition against contact with the unclean, and more profoundly, how a phallocentric Law, expressed in such texts as the Bible, defines what is unclean and abominable. In this sense the

Law describes a boundary between the unclean and the clean, and for Cixous this boundary has political and poetic significance for what is outlawed is not just a cockroach but rather those subjects who possess the uncanny power of the profane. 'I associate women and writing with this abomination. . . . It is my way of indicating the reserved, secluded, or excluded path or place where you meet those beings I think are worth knowing while we are alive' (1993b: 113). These beings are exiled by the Law, existing outside or else-where: 'Outside we shall find all those precious people who have not worried about respecting the law that separates what is and is not abominable according to Those Bible' (1993b: 113). In other words, the 'ugly' is the subject in exile, the outsider, dissident, the subversive feminine writer, the profane other.

Ugliness is also attached to sexual, racial, cultural and class difference, to people who are coded as social 'dirt', hybrid beings who do not fit into the clean and proper social body. In other words, ugliness is not simply a deviation from a standard of beauty, but it is also what is coded as social and political deviation. For example, representations of the ugly Jew were stock images in Nazi propaganda, which also represented the Jewish body as a source of physical and social filth. Similar connections between physical ugliness and social ugliness are also often made in representations of homosexuals, feminists, Muslims, and the working classes. In this way, ugliness can be understood as pivotal in the generation of prejudice. We might even argue that ugliness is the materiality of difference. Ugliness is that which doesn't fit, which exceeds the clean and proper, it is defilement, taboo, pollution, excess, an improper identity. Lispector's lesson about appreciating the ugly is essentially about remaining open to the gift these exiled subjects can give to thought, to a writing which is able to pass down into what Cixous calls the 'nether realms'. Lispector, Jean Genet, Anna Akhmatova, Marina Tsvetaeva, Ingeborg Bachmann and Ossip Mandelstam are all writers Cixous claims dwell in 'this risky coun-try', the 'nether realms', hell, or the place of a radical exile (1993b: 114).

For Cixous, Lispector's use of the word '*imund*' in *The Passion* brings into focus the powers of the unclean. *Imund* is Brazilian for unclean, and within the narrative the cockroach represents the imund. Attempting a connection with the profane, the protagonist G.H. corners the cockroach in the kitchen and squeezes it until a thick white substance seeps from it. As Lispector writes: 'I opened my mouth in fright to ask for help. Why? Because I did not want to become imund like the cockroach. What ideal held me from the sensing of an idea? Why should I not make myself imund? Exactly as I was revealing my whole self, what was I afraid of? Being imund? With what? Being imund with joy' (2000: 116). As Cixous goes on to comment, the etymological connection between *imund* and *immonde* – 'out of the *mundus* (the *world*) – suggests that the profane or the unclean possesses a joy which is out of this world. The world, the mundas, is the domain of the Law, the clean and proper, the good, the ordered, while that which is beyond the world (the *imundi*) is the domain of the excluded feminine, of improper and unclean bodies which are prohibited by the Law. To enter into this 'nether realm', this hell world outside the Law, is to become profane. However, we have forgotten the secret joy of the prohibited. 'Joy is out-of-the-world – this is what Clarice wants us to understand. It is true that what is really forbidden is enjoyment; jubilation' (1993b: 117). I want to stress that it is important that we recognize that Cixous is not urging us to discover the outlawed pleasures of squeezing a cockroach – this is not an initiation into the world of the imund she suggests we perform. Rather, Cixous is examining, through Lispector's writing, the compelling power of the profane or the ugly as a source of joy and not a signifier of death, corruption. And it is worth pointing out that neither is Lispector advocating indulging in perverse practices simply because they are outlawed. Lispector's protagonist comes up against the boundary which prohibits contact with the ugly or unclean and questions what that boundary in general (and not simply in relation to the cockroach) prohibits. The cockroach is a metaphor for the imund.

Another way of thinking through this profane joy or this joy of the profane is to link the idea to carnivalesque laughter, which Bakhtin argues arises when the ugly or the prohibited brings into relief the fragile, self-important solemnity of the Law.[11] Carnivalesque laughter challenges the boundary the Law erects to keep out the powers of the unclean. It is the laughter of Cixous's Medusa, an irreverent enjoyment, a Dadaist mocking of the proper: a black humour which ultimately liberates and expands and has the potential to transform repressive boundaries. It is the laughter of an excluded joy and the joy of an excluded laughter. We can also understand this joy as *jouissance*, a moment in which phallocentric representations are exploded by the eruption of a prohibited libidinality.

Cixous is also describing the importance of entering into this profane, exiled space through writing. Such a writing, which ventures into these 'nether realms', is feminine for it breaks the Law, transgresses the phallocentric boundary between the proper and the improper. This writing process demands courage. We must master our fear of exclusion and contamination if we are to enter into the realm of the excluded. This demands a certain disrespect for the group and a pleasure in being wild, outlawed. 'The trouble', writes Cixous, 'is that we are not taught that it pays, that it is beneficial. We are not taught the pain nor that in pain is hidden joy' (1993b: 119). In another sense it requires mastering the fear of non-being, or being out of this world, of castration and becoming feminine.

The descent into the exiled realms through writing involves a libidinal choice. It is important to recognize that this libidinal choice is non-violent, and while it might be transgressive, it is not reactionary. Discussing the libidinal economies of Genet and Lispector, Cixous writes:

> Their economies are both similar and different, and I feel they are exemplary, Genet and Clarice are inhabitants of those countries that Genet deliberately and magnificently calls the 'nether realms' and that Clarice calls not the 'nether realms' but 'hell'. . . . There is not a single text by Clarice in which hell does not arise and arise jubilantly. Hell is a place of *jouissance*, a place of happiness; we might imagine that hell, despite its name, is situated celestially, though it is situated in the lower realms.   (1993b: 121)

The difference between the two libidinal economies is located in an approach to materiality which can be summarized in the following way. Genet exalts the profane, venerates the inferior, the polluted, the abject, corporeal deformities and taboo practices. He is a provocative picaresque writer whose outlawed status as a criminal and a homosexual fuels a transgressive poetics of the body. For Cixous, however, his writing is caught within a series of reversals in which the pure is replaced by the impure, the high with the low, so that ultimately his transgression is limited to the creation of 'another hierarchy which is libidinal and imaginary' (1993b: 150). His defiance against the Law leads to the creation of an anti-law.

Lispector, on the other hand, moves beyond a provocative defiance or exaltation of the ignoble and profane. In *The Passion*, Lispector concludes that 'kissing a leper isn't even goodness' (2000: 162) because such an extreme approach to the profane materiality of the other is still caught up in the desire to appropriate. As Cixous comments in 'The Author in Truth': 'Communing with the material of the *barata* [cockroach] is a kind of grandiloquence. Too much desire and too much knowledge taint the act and cause G.H. t*o fall* into heroism' (1991f: 170). Genet (whom Sartre called Saint Genet) plucks the lice from his lover's diseased body but does so in order to exalt himself, to position himself as a sovereign subject within the anti-law of the profane. For Lispector, this approach simplifies materiality and is still caught within the utilitarian sentiments of human subjectivity: the materiality of the non-human is appropriated as a resource for the exaltation of an outlawed subjectivity, which on closer inspection remains within a conservative, even reactionary libidinal economy. Lispector, suggests Cixous, resists this underworld self-serving piety by a careful attention to the complexities of matter. 'Matter for her is not abstract but intelligent, alive and powerful' (1993b: 150). This recognition entails a respect for materiality which prevents an easy appropriation. 'For Genet, everything is defiance. There is no defiance in Clarice except of herself, she only attacks one enemy: the distortion and remoteness that are in her as they are in every human being' (1993b: 150). Quite simply, Cixous understands Genet's libidinal economy to be masculine while Lispector's is feminine. Genet's approach could be argued to be typical of the subversive male avant-garde writer who in his defiance of the Law of the Father retains a phallocentric approach to materiality. Matter remains something to be appropriated, colonized and consumed, and not something which is intelligent, autonomous, alive and powerful. The lesson of ugliness which is central to Lispector's libidinal education or apprenticeship is about passing through the desire to appropriate the materiality of the other in order to reach a 'scene of meeting without consuming' (1991f: 166).

The unbearable slowness of becoming

By now we should be clearer about the particular approach towards thinking which Cixous argues is central to Lispector's libidinal education. For Cixous the reading/writing process, which is inseparable from an approach to living, requires a tender and slow attention to the ugly, to the abject, the taboo, the *imundi*, the unspeakable, that which exists on the margins of the Phallocentric Clean Machine. If we have already described how, in 'To Live the Orange', Cixous writes about approaching the orange as a thing in itself prior to language, we can now refine that approach as a process in which the libidinal impulses which drive the subject's desire to appropriate the other are re-educated. Such an approach is acutely aware of the minute temptations to appropriate the other and attempts a knowing detachment from the desire to consume. In Lispector's writing this detachment comes about through moments in the text that both interrupt and interrogate the workings of desire, which is why Lispector (and Cixous) emphasize 'slowness' as a quality of thinking which is necessary in the libidinal education of the subject. If a feminine approach is an ethical contemplation of alterity, such a contemplation can only come about through a careful process of self-reflection. Commenting on her approach, Lispector writes: 'My fear was that, out of impatience with the slowness that I have in understanding myself, I would be hurrying to bring about a meaning before its time' (cited in Cixous 1990: 104). In other words, it is easy to reach meaning, far harder to practise the patience required for deep thought. Quite simply, rigorous, careful and ethical thinking takes time.

This 'lesson' can be understood as a corrective to the speed thinking which tends to dominate our culture. In order to think for ourselves perhaps we need to resist the seductive security of the already thought, which presents us with meaning too quickly, before we have even had a chance to examine how that meaning is produced or whose interests such meaning serves. We have been taught to take, to consume, and that the speed of consumption is a type of beauty, a victory over the ugliness of social exclusion. Thinking is too often lost in the rapid white noise of post-modern communication. As Morag Schiach comments, Cixous's concept of slowness 'is the antithesis of dominant political and cultural discourses, which offer volume and speed of communication at the expense of knowledge and understanding' (1991: 62). Soundbites replace thought, feelings become commodified, identity is mass-marketed, information replaces wisdom, consumption replaces creativity. As Cixous writes:

> We are living in the time of the flat thought-screen, of newspaper-thinking, which does not leave time to think the littlest thing according to its living mode. We must save the approach that opens and leaves space for *the other*. But we live mass-mediatised, pressed, hard-pressed, blackmailed. Acceleration is one of the tricks of intimidation. (1991b: 62)

Here Cixous is suggesting that speed is the antithesis of a non-dominative thinking – a thinking which is able to resist the numerous seductions to colonize and appropriate the object must practise patience.

On another level we can understand the Lispectorian emphasis on slowness in relation to post-structuralist understandings of becoming. Generally speaking, post-structuralism has popularized phenomenological and psychoanalytical understandings that truth, meaning and the subject are involved in a continual process of becoming. *Jouissance*, or moments of (libidinal) excess, drive the process of becoming by exploding the stasis of the subject of the Symbolic or the Law. Avant-garde writing, for example, calls into question the limits of representation (meaning, truth and the subject) by introducing libidinal excess, or *jouissance*, into discourse. *Jouissance* is privileged within post-structuralism as a transgressive libidinal force which is capable of undoing the violence of representation: *jouissance* revitalizes meaning and in doing so subverts fundamentalist closure. *Jouissance*, then, opens up representation to becoming by exploding limits. For Lacan 'thought is *jouissance*' (1982: 142). We could also argue that if becoming is associated with *jouissance* and the subversion of fixed meanings, such a *jouissance* is often figured as a type of speed, with the ecstatic flash of new meaning, with the jolt of new thinking, the electrifying of representation with the current of an excess libidinality, the intense delirium of the new. *Jouissance* punctuates representation with moments of subversion which are then gradually contained until another moment of *jouissance* shatters that containment or meaning. In other words, becoming depends upon moments of *jouissance*: without *jouissance* (or thinking), becoming would reach a final point of closure or meaning. But is there a normative value attached to the force of *jouissance*? Has a post-structural celebration of the force of *jouissance*, or the transgressive power of libidinal excess, assumed a correlation between subversion and the liberation of the subject which remains blind to a respectful attention to the materiality of the other that is the source of this profane explosion of the Law? And if so, how might this appropriation remain within a masculine libidinal economy, a sort of Jean Genet defiance, a rapid rebellious reversal of the good, clean and proper? Perhaps it is a matter of steering an ethical course between delirium and tyranny, between catharsis and exclusion.

For Cixous, the value of Lispector's libidinal education is a recognition that the moment of libidinal excess needs to be examined carefully and that in order for that moment to be carefully considered one has to slow down and resist the temptation to suddenly enter transgression, to be suddenly overcome by an intoxicating contact with the materiality of the other. It is far harder to slow down and examine carefully the approach or the path one takes towards transgression in order to make sure that one is not, through the many seductions to colonize which face the subject, merely appropriating the intoxicating difference of the other in order to achieve a position of rebellious piety or subversive delirium. Championing the excluded, suggests Lispector, can also lead to the exploitation of the excluded and a blindness to the other's materiality. Slowness is then, in this context, intimately tied to a careful and respectful attention to the other: slowness is the essence of an approach which recognizes that desire always carries a debt to the materiality of the other.

A floribunda writing

Lispector's approach to the materiality of the other is not simply concerned with the darker dynamics which motivate appropriation, or with the ugly. Much of her writing is also about the importance of practising a gentle humility towards the mystery of matter, and she writes about flowers. Not all of the rooms in Lispector's writing contain cockroaches. In her essay 'Clarice Lispector: the Approach', Cixous explores Lispector's 'The Imitation of the Rose':

Clarice maintains that in the room, the rose spreads itself out in presence. It roses. It enters into the trance of its own presence and with all of its strength it is there, and with all of its contained roses, it makes the rose, for us, it delivers itself up to its I-am-a-rose in the flux of its own vitality. If we observe it in slow motion, we see that at each second the seemingly immobile rose is in full flight at the height of its presence towards our love, and enters in full radiance. (1991b: 73)

Here the materiality of the rose is understood as dynamic, active, possessing an agency which calls towards the subject that perceives it. As Cixous also writes: 'We have forgotten that it is plants that call us, when we think about calling them, that come to meet our bodies in blossom' (1991b: 65). Again, materiality has a presence which is framed as independent of the subject's relationship to it. As Calle-Gruber notes in her 'Afterword', much of Cixous's writing 'abounds in flowers' and 'the flowers of these books are not embellishments but essences. They bear fruit: beauty and *intelligence* (of the text)' (1997: 211–12). Flowers are also for Cixous part of the 'school of roots', or a passage into the depths of a writing–becoming which finally confronts death and the loss of self not as an end but as a flowering into the other. She wonders in *Three Steps* whether, at moments of physical extremity 'we admit to having a relationship to the vegetal' and the writing hand which has left the self behind 'leads to the flowers' (1993b: 156).

There are several ways of reading Cixous's thoughts on flowers here. For example, we might find the quote from the essay on Lispector about letting the flower meet our bodies in blossom slightly absurd, a little too precious, feminine and flimsy. And even, perhaps, read into Cixous the faded scent of a Wordsworthian Romanticism offering us a fleeting nostalgia for an age in which nodding daffodils were more populous than endlessly multiplying motorways. It would be very charming if we could allow the flower to meet our bodies in blossom but really the time of flowers is past. In a competitive age dominated by the speed philosophy of advertising slogans like 'Just do It!', pausing to open up to the intimate blossom of a flower is absurdly anachronistic; charming but silly; we must pass over the time of the flower and 'move on'. Who could possibly take flowers seriously today? They are simply too romantic, too feminine. Or we could approach Cixous's writing about flowers within the context of her work and recognize it as a metaphor for a connection to materiality which nourishes creative and productive thinking.

'But the problem of flowers', writes Cixous, 'is the problem of maternal and indispensable women: they are there. They are so much there' (1991b: 73). Here she seems to suggest that we take for granted certain materialities, certain bodies, simply because they are always there, radiating with a giving presence. Flowers are also metaphors for the materiality of the gift, for a feminine libidinal economy in which the gift circulates without debt. As Cixous goes on to write:

> the soft giving of a rose today helps us to take the giving of all presence. By its way of containing while overflowing, of making us feel the rose of the rose, of making us think in its blossoming of the mystery of the birth of the living in each instant we do not forget to share. To receive sharing. Our loving souls are descendants of roses. (1991b: 74)

Through the contemplation of the rose in Lispector's writing, Cixous opens her own writing into a meditation on the libidinal economy of a maternal, in the sense of an open, materiality. To be open to the gift of the rose is to be open to the giving of all presence, to an understanding of materiality as something which presents us with the mystery of giving. It is to avoid understanding materiality (or things in the world) as merely objects to be used, appropriated, colonized and exchanged, but to see it rather as suffused with a luminous generosity. Materiality gives to us. But can we receive the gift of materiality? And how do we receive this gift without consuming it? How do we receive the other without appropriating its difference? In a sense, Cixous is calling attention to the importance of reaching a relationship of appreciation and gratitude towards the materiality of the other and the non-human.

It is not so much the object which is important though, as the approach to it, which is why although both Lispector and Cixous write about such disparate things as cockroaches and roses, the ugly and the beautiful, the careful formulation of an approach is what is most important. It is not so much a question of aesthetics which concerns their writing but the relationship to the object, to the thing, to materiality. For both, such a relationship has the potential to be filled with a certain joy or ecstatic wonder which is the product of a non-appropriative desire. Such a state is akin to Heidegger's understanding of rapture. In an essay on the subject he writes the following:

> Rapture as a state of feeling explodes the very subjectivity of the subject. . . . Beauty breaks through the confinement of the 'object' placed at a distance, standing on its own, and brings it into essential and original correlation to the 'subject'. Beauty is no longer objective, no longer an object. The aesthetic state is neither subjective nor objective.   (1991: 123)

Cixous, with Lispector, would add that such a rapture is possible towards materiality in general and is not just confined to what is thought to be beautiful. Lispector's approach receives matter without objectifying by engaging in the rapture of a receiving which goes beyond a desire to appropriate.

What then does Cixous mean by Lispector's *apprenticeship*? At the very end of 'The School of Roots' she writes: 'We must work. The earth of writing. To the point of becoming the earth. Humble work. Without reward. Except joy. School is interminable' (1993: 156). For Cixous the essential lesson of Lispector's libidinal education is an attitude of true humility and respect towards the other, a respect and humility which is able to resist the numerous seductions of appropriation. This also means recognizing the latent egoism of a pious giving towards the other: 'We think we are holding out a hand? We hit. The work of Clarice Lispector is an immense book of *respect. Book of the right distance*' (1991f: 156). Too close and we appropriate, too far and the other is lost. For Cixous it is the desire of the appropriating ego which stands as an obstacle to the awakening of a feminine libidinal economy in which excess circulates without debt. As Cixous writes in 'The Author in Truth', we are all atoms, minute matter among a multiplicity of other matters, other beings.

Paradoxically, when the self is humbled by a recognition of the plurality of being, the self is capable of infinite expansion and metamorphosis, for the subject is recognized as a 'thing', as matter among matter. To recognize the materiality of one's own subjectivity, one's own body is not to enter into an objectifying and alienating relationship with the self, to fall into Sartre's nothingness. As we have already seen, Cixous deftly ironizes the traditional concept of alienation in which a recognition of the self as thing or matter is equated with a paralysis of the subject and a loss of self. Instead, a humble recognition of the self as matter among matter leads to an expansion of being, to a lightness of being which opens up the possibility of a poetic transformation. Lispector writes of a 'full void' which one reaches through meditation. Cixous writes against an empiricism that remains blind to the invisible forces which govern our lives: 'Yes, and not to forget that the structure of the atom is not visible. But we're informed. I'm aware of many things I haven't seen, and you too. One cannot give a proof of the existence of what is truer, the trick is to believe. To believe weeping' (1991f: 159). To believe in the materiality of tears and all they mean is not to indulge in a sentimental romanticism but rather to humble oneself before the other, to inhabit a body which remains open to the gift of the infinite mysteries of matter.

6 The Question of Transgression: Angela Carter

She applied herself to the task of writing an antiwar letter, like this: thinking very hard about every word, bearing down on each word with all her angers in order to transfuse them into it.

Thus she got to the point of thinking that she was going to give this love letter a graver emphasis than she had planned.

Since in these dire political circumstances, it was right not to be content just to love, but to arm love as well. Which stood to reason moreover. For a person well loved is a person well armed.

Because war will never stop them from living. But robs them of the rich hours of silence and immobility. With its boorish sounds blurs the refined ultrasounds of joy. Because one of the objectives of modern warfare is the development of unbelievably perfected, in other words perverse, psychological weapons: being a war of the nullification of women and similar beings, but not of liquidation; being a shameful but global, methodological war; being undeclared but public, state-sponsored, transcultural; being a hypocritical war, the first great war for the voluntary devaluation of civilisations; being a war aimed at weakening and reducing half of the world, and at enslaving nine tenths of the other half of the world.

And the modernity of this war being defined precisely – by the dissimulation of its murderous power beneath civil, non-bellicose outward appearances – above all, in a basely inventive way, by the utilisation of means of aggression which are strictly insidious, invisible, inaudible, and which have a radical force of destruction hitherto never attained; because acting down at the deepest levels, having as target beings with souls, being able to annihilate entire populations without ever seeming to touch them. By repressing the zones of sensitivity. By deafening, debasing, besotting . . . by the total foreclosure of all evidence of libidinal, sexual, cultural difference.

Hélène Cixous, *Lemonade, or Everything Was So Infinite*
(in Sellers 1997)

In this chapter we return to an exploration of feminist avant-garde practices through a Cixousian reading of Angela Carter's *The War of Dreams* (1972). In doing so we will also be challenging some of the assumptions which underpin contemporary post-modern celebrations of the subversive force of transgressive desire. Carter's text can be usefully read as a narrative about the post-modern crisis of reason.[1] Using a barrage of consciousness-warping representations derived from 'eroto-energy' or desire, Doctor Hoffman is 'waging a massive campaign against human reason itself' (11). Hoffman's war against Enlightenment rationalism can be understood as an allegory for the counter-discourse of post-modernism, but as Carter so deftly points out, this discourse depends upon a phallocentric concept of desire. In other words, Carter calls attention to the problems associated with a post-modern opposition to Enlightenment rationality when such an opposition is articulated through a phallocentric libidinal economy. A Cixousian reading of Carter, then, opens up questions about the limitations of post-modern oppositionality and moves towards what we might term a post-modern feminine libidinal economy. Rosi Braidotti suggests that Carter explores 'a new "post-human" techno-teratological phenomenon that privileges the deviant or the mutant over the more conventional versions of the human' (2002: 179). Indeed, throughout her writing Carter has explored the contorted cartography of the post-modern subject while retaining an earthy suspicion about the effectiveness of such transgressions and the debt to materiality of so many of these monsters of the liminal silence. Reading Carter with Cixous will allow us to work towards imagining how a post-modern feminine libidinal economy offers a paradigm shift within the post-modern counter-discourse of transgressive desire.

Carter's exploration of the limits of the ideology of liberatory desire in *The War of Dreams* brings into focus some of the conceptual problems associated with an anti-rationalist, post-modern celebration of the subversive force of the libidinally awakened imagination. According to Suleiman, Carter specifically explores the limits of a Surrealist faith in the emancipatory effects of the libidinal imagination (1994: 126–7) which have informed a postmodern celebration of sexual transgression. In brief, avant-garde movements such as Surrealism, which flourished in the early part of the last century, glorified transgressive desire as a force capable of liberating the subject from the repressive constraints of

Enlightenment Reason, freeing the imagination, energizing an oppositional creativity, and overcoming psycho-political oppression. This faith in the liberatory effects of transgressive desire influenced a range of intellectuals whose work informs the broad project of post-modern literary theory.[2] Julia Kristeva's *The Revolution in Poetic Language* (1984), Roland Barthes's *The Pleasure of the Text* (1974), Georges Bataille's work, and Deleuze and Guattari's monumental *Capitalism and Schizophrenia*, among others, became central references in the analysis of subversive desire and the repressive effects of Enlightenment rationality.

In their influential *Dialectic of Enlightenment* (1944) the cultural theorists Theodor Adorno and Max Horkheimer stated boldly that 'Enlightenment is totalitarian' (1979: 6). In *Anti-Oedipus*, Deleuze and Guattari state that 'desire is in its essence revolutionary' (1992: 34). Dystopian accounts of modernity as a sexually repressive condition also informed psychoanalytic critiques of culture proposed by theorists such as Norman O. Brown, Wilhelm Reich, Erich Fromm and Herbert Marcuse. Just as Enlightenment reason became pathologized as the aetiology of the ills of modernity, the libidinally awakened body became privileged as the source of healthy resistance, excess and creativity. Anti-rationalism, in other words, heralded transgressive desire as an antidote to the repressive effects of reason, a redemptive force capable of restoring a primary connection to the body which the alienating effects of modernity had severed. A conflict between reason and desire emerged as one of the central narratives in post-modern explanations of contemporary consciousness. In this context, the figure of the pervert became the new anti-hero, his paraphilic desires emblematic of a dissident challenge to the propriety of repressive reason. As Rita Felski writes, sexual transgression emerged 'as a privileged emblem of refusal' (1995: 177).

But where do we situate Cixous and Carter in all of this? Carter's *The War of Dreams* (1972) can easily be read as a post-modern parody of transgression and subversion, for much of the text lampoons the exaggerated postures of a libidinally generated war against repressive reason. Within it we find a range of intertextual references to Surrealism, psychoanalysis, theories of perversion, post-modernism, and darlings of the avant-garde such as de Sade, Baudelaire and Proust. The text is also itself post-modern. Suleiman offers a succinct description of post-modernist fiction:

> Postmodernist fiction can be defined formally as a hyper-selfcon-
> scious mode of writing that insistently points to literary and cultural
> antecedents or (as we say in the trade) intertexts, and thematically as
> a kind of fiction that reflects, implicitly or explicitly, on the historical
> and social present in its relation to the past and, if possible, the
> future.   (1994: 129)

However, the text is much more than a post-modern parody of
transgression, for Carter offers a salient and unflinching critique of
the totalitarian desires lurking within the heart of the oppositional
imagination. As Joan Cocks (1989) and others have pointed out, it
is naive to assume that the oppositional imagination is free of
fundamentalist ideologies, and within every counter-discourse
there often lurks the desire for power, the lust for a take-over.[3] With
Cixous, we can argue that Carter is calling into question the ethics
of a phallocentric libidinal economy in which a defiance against
the Law ends up in the creation of an equally oppressive anti-Law.
Post-modern anti-rationalism risks becoming reactionary when
the materiality of the other is appropriated as an oppositional
resource. In other words, the Hegelian master–slave dialectic
remains intact, desire still remains caught up in a phallocentric
'Logic of Destruction'. As we shall see, this is precisely how Carter
reads desire in *The War of Dreams*.

As Cixous so carefully reminds us, it is not enough to desire freedom, one must apply a delicate ethical attention to the language of
our desire and remain wary of confusing a desire for freedom with
a desire to dominate. As history so often shows us, the desire for
freedom too often falls into terrorism and war. Cixous's writing is
about deconstructing the violence of phallogocentrism, which cuts
consciousness into antagonistic, hierarchical dichotomies. For
Cixous, the deconstruction of phallogocentrism also depends
upon a careful, ethical attention to the workings of death or negation. Phallogocentrism is:

> a universal battlefield. Each time, a war is let loose. Death is always
> at work.
> Father/Son Relations of authority, privilege, force.
> The Word/Writing Relations: opposition, conflict, sublation, return.
> Master/Slave Violence. Repression.
> We see that 'victory' always comes down to the same thing: things
> get hierarchical.   (Cixous and Clement 1991: 64)

The desire for liberation expressed by the counter-discourse of the patriarchal avant-garde, as Suleiman argues, remains complicit with phallocentric power, locked into a battle between a tyrannical father and an outlawed son. Indeed, the theory and politics of avant-garde oppositionality is often saturated with the rhetoric of war. Arch avant-garde writer Robbe-Grillet, for example, described his work as a 'machine of war against order' (cited in Suleiman 1990: 43). Many avant-garde manifestos use the rhetoric of violence, perhaps none so much as Marinetti's Futurist Manifesto which glorified war as a method of cleansing society of the burdens of the past.[4] The Surrealist Manifesto declared a revolution against reason with 'material hammers' if necessary – the 'war for freedom must be waged with anger' (cited in Nadeau 1973: 113, 121–2).

While we might dismiss such language as ineffectual, it would be a mistake to assume that the paper weapons of the intellectual are innocent. Ideas have a habit of materializing. Carter draws attention to the inherent violence of a reactionary post-modern irrationalism through her representation of the Promethian anti-hero Doctor Hoffman: aristocrat, philosopher, scientist, poet and technological wizard, although he champions the liberation of desire and the unconscious, Hoffmann is a terrorist, his evangelical politics of the liberated libido thinly disguised totalitarianism. Indeed, it is precisely the point of overlap between transgression and terrorism, liberation and oppression, which concerns Carter. And Cixous, as we have seen, is a deconstructive philosopher and writer who is also acutely aware of the seductions of power which inform oppositional practices. Desire, even when it is expressed through the discourse of liberation, is not immune from totalitarian impulses. This chapter explores the often occluded logic which informs the crossing over of the desire for liberatory transgression into the violence of terrorist violations. How is it that the desire for liberation so often, and so easily, becomes a form of terrorism, a form of violence? Such a question has wider socio-political significance of course, but here we will be examining it through a Cixousian reading of Carter's critique of the logic of the post-modern phallocentric libidinal economy.

In 'First Names of No One' Cixous states: 'I ask of writing what I ask of desire: that it have no relation to the logic which puts desire on the side of possession, of acquisition, or even of that consumption-consummation which, when pushed to its limits with such exultation, links (false) consciousness with death' (in Sellers 1997: 27). Writers who put the logic of phallocentrism into question are, for Cixous, 'artists of deconstruction' who 'denounce the playacting which is constituted around the threat of castration, and whose real "author" is the little anti-life calculation' (1997: 29). In this context we can argue that Carter is such an 'artist of deconstruction', for *The War of Dreams* exposes the death-driven logic of phallocentric desire relentlessly, passionately, with wicked erudite humour and an iconoclastic irreverence. In summary, then, this chapter will explore the question of desire as it arises in Carter's text by applying Cixous's insights into the dynamics of domination which govern a phallocentric libidinal economy. We also return to the theme of a feminist avant-garde politics and poetics and explore the ways in which Cixous's work can be used to illuminate some of the strategies available to such a practice by focusing on Carter's writing. But first some words on the British writer Angela Carter and why reading her with Cixous can offer us some insights into the contemporary scene of desire.

Like Cixous in some ways, Carter has written within many genres: she has produced radio plays, film scripts, essays, literary and cultural criticism, short stories, novels, journalistic pieces, polemics about modern sexual politics, fairy tales, gothic tales, science fiction, and strange picaresque romances about mad bohemians.[5] Carter's first novel, *Shadow Dance* (1966), which was rapidly followed by *The Magic Toyshop* (1967), explores her interest in sexuality, the unconscious, myth, fairy tale and the gothic. The text in question here, *The War of Dreams* (1972), continues her exploration of these themes with a particular emphasis on the difference between aggression and eroticism. *Love* (1971), *The Passion of New Eve* (1977), *The Sadeian Woman* (1979), *The Bloody Chamber* (1979), *Nights at the Circus* (1984), *Nothing Sacred* (1982), *Heroes and Villains* (1969), and *Wise Children* (1991) are among her other texts. Braidotti offers a useful description of Carter's preoccupations: she is a 'shrewd tracker of the kind of genetico-ethical mutations that are currently taking place in post-industrial urban landscapes, and in the psychic horizons of those human and post-human subjects that inhabit them' (2002: 134). Both Cixous and Carter can be understood as avant-garde feminists, as eclectic thinkers who work on the boundaries of genres and traditions in order to destabilize and invigorate discourses. Both do so from a position within the avant-garde, that is they are not merely avant-garde writers, but they are also subverting a particular avant-garde tradition which has been dominated by the ideas of men. Both use laughter as a way of subverting phallocentric representations. Parody, irony, carnivalesque inversions, a playful use of myth, all characterize the texture of such laughter. In her essay on the surrealist imagination, 'The Alchemy of the Word' (1993), Carter writes that although she became disillusioned with the Surrealists' constant positioning of woman as other, beauty and mystery, it is the attention to the convulsive or embodied potential of language which she found so useful in their work. And as we have discussed in a previous chapter, Cixous's manifesto 'The Laugh of the Medusa' also appropriates and subverts Surrealism.

While I don't want to stretch the correspondences between these two writers too far, it should also be noted that like that of Cixous, Carter's position as a feminist writer is a contested one. Indeed, Carter's irreverent pen often lampoons forms of political correctness and refuses the comfort zone of any orthodoxy. This very refusal to occupy a clearly demarcated political position can be read not as an ethical lack but rather as a recognition that orthodoxy of any kind has a habit of stagnating thought, of fixing ideas into rigid structures. And when the imagination is imprisoned by orthodoxy it often follows that the freedom of thought necessary to work through forms of liberation is also blocked, limited, and denied. It is all, in a nutshell, about the effects of negation. This brings us to *The War of Dreams*, which, ironically enough, is among many things a satire on libertarian ideologies which equate sexual repression with political oppression, a liberated libido with a liberated body politic, and which, preferring the speed of conquest to careful thought, ends up performing yet another negation, another drama enacted around the spectral threat of castration.

Spectres of negation

> It is a very simple war. There is a battlefield. . . . You, wretched Death, whom I attack, I don't bear you any ill will, creature of our anguishes, vast illusion we have sculpted in nightmare lining, to then revere you with hatred, monster child of our entrails, in whom we swear we see our assassin, powerless thing transported

on the blazing throne, fruit of our pallors, poor divinity we make
in the image of our terror and our sickness, condemned innocent,
you whom we beg to help us live basely, to live slowly and
pinched in little shoes, and to whom we dedicate piles of smok-
ing lies, how will I forget you, obedient fierceness we make a show
of obeying.

No, Death you are not this, this dragon denture. You can go in
peace, you can disperse. Go, I don't need to run against you to
live and revive. (Cixous, in Sellers 1997: 186)

In many ways Carter's text can be read as an allegory of the challenges facing the (male) subject as he confronts the post-modern
crisis of reason. Carter's protagonist Desiderio (Italian for desire) is
caught between two masters, the Minister of Determination, who
represents Enlightenment rationality, singular truth, empiricism
and order, and Doctor Hoffman, who represents anti-rationalism,
transgressive desire, imagination and anarchy. Hoffman has
waged a war against reason and is terrorizing Desiderio's city with
a carnival of disordered representations which have been 'liberated' from the citizens' unconscious. Every mind projects a fantasy
until the fabric of the city begins to morph and distort into a
rippling surface of competing unrealities. 'This phantasmagoric
redefinition of the city was constantly fluctuating for it was now the
kingdom of the instantaneous' (1972: 20–1). The post-modern
collapsed future tense has taken over, the image has replaced the
real, and history has been dissolved. As one of Hoffman's minions
puts it:

Hoffman's philosophy is not so much transcendental as incidental.
It utilises all the incidents that ripple the depthless surface of, you
understand, the sensual world. When the sensual world uncondi-
tionally surrenders to the intermittency of mutability, men will be
freed in perpetuity from the tyranny of the single present. And we
will live on as many layers of consciousness as we can, all at the same
time. (Carter 1972: 127)

Here we have a rather apt description of the temporality of post-
modern consciousness along with a rather sarcastic comment on
the tendency towards the verbose within much post-modern
theory.

And yet, within all of this whirling post-modern excitement

Desiderio remains indifferent, bored, cynical. Desiderio is chosen by the Minister to hunt down Hoffman and assassinate him because he remains detached and largely immune to the chaos of representations that have infected the city: 'Boredom was my first reaction to incipient delirium' (19). Desiderio suffers from post-modern ennui. The systematic disordering of the senses, the proliferation of representations, the collapse between the real and the virtual, the circulation of transgressive desire, leave Desiderio indifferent. It is only the elusive spectre of Albertina, Hoffman's daughter, who is able to pierce the shell of his nihilism. If the Minister of Determination has employed him to hunt down Hoffman, Hoffman retaliates by attempts to seduce him through his daughter. Caught within the crises of reason the subject must choose desire for the feminine and private pleasure or reason and the public good. As he travels towards his goal, Desiderio as post-modern picaro encounters a motley group of exiled and perverse subjects all of whom are somehow symptomatic of Hoffman's corruption of Enlightenment rationality. In the chapter 'Acrobats of Desire', for example, he encounters a troop of morphing, poly-morphous desiring bodies who, four times a day 'transcend their own bodies and made of themselves plastic anagrams' (144). In 'The Erotic Traveller' he meets a Sadeian figure called 'the Count' who is desperately in search of the ultimate, transcendental orgasm.

Albertina haunts his travels, masquerading as a number of different, alluring identities until finally she escorts him to her father's gothic castle and his infernal desire machines. Refusing to consummate his desire for Albertina after confronting the full inhumanity which lies behind Hoffman's dream of liberation, he murders both daughter and father in a bid to escape. Within this post-modern Gothic the path of excess has led to a palace of exploitation where the only wisdom is the negation of tyranny through violence. He returns to the city a hero, having restored reason and order, but remains in a permanent state of nostalgia for the lost object of his desire. The crisis of reason is over but the (male) subject remains nostalgic, unsatisfied, haunted by the spectre of his murdered love, hallucinating her return.

The climax of the novel occurs when Desiderio faces Hoffman's infernal desire machines, which are the source of the irrationalism which has been unleashed on Desiderio's city. (The connection between sexual desire and the liberation of the unconscious is obviously Freudian.) For Hoffmann, eroto-energy is the key to liberating the unconscious and the imagination and overthrowing the tyranny of reason. As Hoffman states:

> I can make you perceive ideas with your senses because I do not acknowledge any essential difference in the phenomenological bases of the two modes of thought. All things co-exist in pairs but mine is not an either/or world.
> 'Mine is an and + and world.
> 'I alone have discovered the key to the inexhaustible plus.   (265)

Fulfilling the desires of so many theorists of libidinal oppositionality, Hoffman has apparently overcome dichotomous thought by harnessing desire as pure productivity, the inexhaustible plus, or excess, so that consciousness enters into a 'complex becoming' (269): identity is radically subverted by desire, bodies become monstrous hybrid beings, gender becomes fluid and endlessly transformative. However, this post-modern utopia of complex becomings is orchestrated by a totalitarian: 'He might know the nature of the inexhaustible plus but, all the same, he was a totalitarian' (267). Hoffman is a totalitarian who wants to enforce a regime of total excess for as Desiderio states, 'he was a man who wanted to establish a dictatorship of desire' (274). Here desire is idealized as an autonomous force, unfettered by physical constraints; it is strangely disembodied, disconnected from material needs. Within Desiderio's besieged city, people starve and commit suicide under the regime of 'complex becoming'. Desire might unleash a complex post-modern becoming but when the materiality of the flesh is ignored, such transformations are a form of negation.

The irony of Hoffman's project is also conjured up when Desiderio comments, 'he penned desire in a cage and said: "Look: I have liberated desire"' (268). The desire machines, which are strange cage-like pens located within a sterile labyrinthian laboratory/factory, farm the 'eroto-energy' of hundreds of endlessly copulating couples who are fed hormones intravenously and continually sexually stimulated. Here desire has become a product, which is harvested from chemically enhanced meat. The body has become a brute resource, desire a product which is farmed by a

totalitarian to be used as a weapon against Enlightenment rationality – the body as resource, desire as commodity, chemically
dependent sex: the dystopian underbelly of the psycho-sexual
liberation conjured by the political Freudians.

Carter is also expressing a pessimism about the commodification of desire through post-modern technologies of representation. She offers a neat parody of Hoffman's post-modern desire
technology in the following section:

> Inside the reality modifying machines, in the medium of essential
> undifferentiation, these germinal molecules are agitated until,
> according to certain innate determinative tendencies, they form
> themselves into divergent sequences which act as what I call 'trans-
> formation groups'. Eventually a multi-dimensional body is brought
> into being which operates only upon an uncertainty principle. These
> bodies appear on the screen ... over there ... expressed in a
> complex notation of blips and bleeps. It requires extreme persis-
> tence of vision to make sense of the code at this stage. Nevertheless,
> those formless blobs are, as it were, the embryos of palpable appear-
> ances. Once these undifferentiated yet apprehendable ideas of
> objectified desire reach a reciprocating object, the appearance is
> organically restructured by the desires subsisting in latency in the
> object itself. These desires must, of course, subsist, since to desire is
> to be.   (272)

Desire has become the virtual plaything of technology, manipulated on computer screens, reduced to abstract bytes of information, only to be remade when an object activates its becoming. The
desire of the object determines the body's virtual becoming. Carter
describes a radical receptivity in which the materiality of the
object's desire governs the representation of the body. However,
the source flesh, as it were, of this infinitely pliable and productive
desire is left behind, imprisoned in a desire machine, drugged and
seduced into an endless production. Desiderio exclaims, 'So that
was the Doctor's version of the cogito! I DESIRE THEREFORE I EXIST'
(272). Is this the post-modern cogito? Within Carter's post-modern
dystopia Descartes's infamous mind/body split has been replaced
by a desire/body split. The new dichotomy is between desire and
the body – the ghost in the machine is no longer reason but desire.
The materiality of the body is colonized by post-industrial technologies of representation, reduced to meat, farmed for desire.

Hoffman's technological wizardry might have made desire virtual and viral, capable of an endless nomadic becoming, but the body which gave birth to this desire remains trapped in the postures of exploitation. Cut off from the source, distilled by the post-modern representational technology of phallocentrism into an essential energy, desire forgets its origins, carries no trace of the body which gave birth to it. Its becomings bear no trace of the source flesh. An orphaned imaginary of desire, as Carter suggests, is vulnerable to exploitation. Balanced against post-modern celebrations of the revolutionary potential of new representational technologies, Carter's desire machines also offer a warning about the techno-elite subject who is able to use radical technology to manipulate and exploit others, for Hoffman is an aristocratic scientist, his machines, the product of wealth and elite information, and his resources are drugged bodies.

In some ways we can compare Hoffman's desire machines to contemporary representational technology, specifically the inter-net. In the virtual world of the net, desire is truly nomadic, open to a continual transformation, to endless acrobatics of becoming. However, Fredric Jameson's sober point that in a consumer society sexual transgressions are increasingly exploited and exhausted is worth considering in this context (1979: 169). As the range of pornography on the internet demonstrates, within the world of cyber-desire there is no repression. However, this lack of repres-sion has less to do with the liberation of the subject from the repressive constraints of Enlightenment rationality and more to do with a cynical commodification of sexual desire and the mass marketing of representations of what are too often, in reality, drugged, exploited and underage bodies. Sexual boundaries are commodified, exploited, exhausted and shifted into increasingly perverse markets. While the representational scene of the internet can be read as the 'liberation' of the libido, and the post-modern desiring subject, as a cool cyborg who downloads his transgres-sions with a few clicks, this 'liberation' often depends on the subjection of other bodies. The debt to materiality that these repre-sentations occlude is something which underpins this particular post-modern libidinal economy, just as the farmed bodies in Hoffman's desire factories enable the 'liberation' of the uncon-scious from the tyranny of repressive reason. In an article on cyber-sex Sadie Plant argues that the internet has deregulated the entire sexual economy: 'sex disperses into drugs, trance and dance possession; androgyny, hermaphroditism and transsexualism become increasingly perceptible; paraphilia, body engineering, queer sex, and what Foucault calls "the slow motions of pleasure and pain" or SM – already "high technology sex" (Califia 1993: 175) – proliferate' (2000: 460–1). There are no more boundaries; sexual repression is a pre-cyborg concept; in the world of post-human desire there are no limits. Want it: click it. But as Plant also writes, this is so much ' "macho bullshit", a discourse which admits nothing beyond subjection, a perspective which cannot accept any other relation' (2000: 466–7). Unable to cross over into a libidinality without subjection, the transgression folds back on itself, becoming, as Cixous puts it, yet another 'playacting which is constituted around the threat of castration, and whose real "author" is the little anti-life calculation' (in Sellers 1997: 29). Within this Utopia of the liberated libido, desire falls back into negation.

If Carter's text can be read as a critique of the phallocentric libidinal economy as it now enters into the realm of radical representational technology, it is also a deconstruction of the potency of phallocentric desire, for throughout the text the central male characters are oddly lacking in desire, essentially anaesthetized, gripped by an unshakeable ennui. Trapped within the phallocentric libidinal economy, transgressive desire remains in dialogue with death, a form of negation. Despite being the engineer of new technologies of desire, the new Master of the liberated libido, Hoffman is 'a man without desires', Desiderio is terminally bored, and the hyper-sexuality of his travelling companion, the Count, masks a deep emotional frigidity (1972: 272). The character of the Count allows Carter to critique the Sadeian libertine sensibility, which she later developed in *The Sadeian Woman* (1992). Here she writes that 'the conquest of morality and aesthetics, of shame, disgust and fear, the pursuit of greater and greater sexual sophistication in terms of private sensation lead [the libertine] directly to the satisfactions of a child; transgression becomes regression' (1992: 147). Sexual transgression becomes a form of solipsistic hedonism, a failed counter-discourse which eventually drifts into a complicity with the very power it sought to overthrow and becomes yet another marketable commodity

Carter's point is that the post-modern war against Enlightenment rationality, this fetishization of the transgressive force of desire, is, finally, a masculine fantasy, and as such still very much caught up in a reactionary relationship to paternal Law. The liberatory force of transgression results in inversion: power merely shifts to the other side and the exchange, as both Carter and Cixous argue, remains among men. Commenting on the libidinal economy at work in the avant-garde writer Genet, Cixous argues that he shatters the propriety of the Law through a process of reversal which is 'moving, magnificent, and magnifying. At the same time it is disquieting, since it undoes, undermines, and saps a social hierarchy, though this is in order to replace it with another hierarchy that is libidinal and imaginary' (1993b: 150). For Cixous, the phallocentric libidinal economy, even when it is expressed by exiled subjects such as Genet, remains hierarchical and thus a form of violence. This is the central problem of phallocentric oppositional movements and it is one which both Carter and Cixous are writing against.

The idealization of desire as an autonomous force which remains unhampered by any responsibility to the flesh, as both an emblem of the revolt against Enlightenment rationality and the means by which all repressions will be overcome in a moment of orgasmic triumph, appears to be, at least within the context of Carter's deconstruction of the post-modern fantasy, the dream of the power-hungry elite. It is precisely the severing of desire from the body which enables this idealization: the reification of desire as revolt leaves behind the materiality of the flesh. This materiality is woven by history, culture, politics, a whole social fabric which cannot easily be torn apart by the eruption of *jouissance* into discourse. This radical over-estimation of the virile power of desire, the fantasy of a desire which is capable of conquering the Enlightenment, seems to be yet another Phallic inflation. Within this high drama, the questions of love, compassion, care and the ethics of sexual difference, are overshadowed by the spectre of Phallic desire: confined to the shadows of femininity, the ethics of sexual difference are barely visible.

While Cixous is committed to undoing the effects of phallogocentrism and, throughout her writing, champions feminine desire as a potentially liberatory force, she does anchor what can be read as a Utopian celebration of *jouissance*, in an ethics of sexual difference which is in turn grounded in materiality.

Within a feminine libidinal economy desire is always already a process of transformative exchange between material bodies, a non-violent opening towards the other and alterity in general. In order for desire to circulate between bodies in a non-violent way, we have to think through or against a libidinal economy which frames desire as a commodity, which reads the other as a resource to be appropriated. Such a libidinal economy is caught up with Enlightenment concepts of justice, freedom and equality and so cannot be simply read as yet another post-modern break with Enlightenment rationalism. Indeed, the assumption that a total break with the Enlightenment is possible or that such a break constitutes progress is an oddly other-wordly position. As Foucault argues in 'What is Enlightenment?', we cannot simply escape the fact that we are, to a greater or lesser extent, historically determined by the Enlightenment. Instead of reverting to an adolescent refusal, we must, rather, explore the limits which are imposed on us and begin the patient work of freedom (1991: 50).[8] In a conversation with Geoffrey Bennington, Derrida also makes clear that deconstruction is not a form of anti-rationalism:

> We ... have to deconstruct, to take time to deconstruct Enlightenment. But when I say we have to deconstruct a thing, I do not say we are *against* it, or that in any situation I will fight it, be on the other side. I think we should be on the side of Enlightenment without being too naive, and on some occasions be able to question its philosophy.   (1985: 69)

We might say that Cixous is on the side of the Enlightenment but that she deconstructs the libidinal economy of phallocentric sameness which has emerged from it. In this context, her theorization of desire has more to do with Enlightenment concepts of liberation than it does with an anti-rationalist idealization of oppositional desire. In this sense Cixous's writing on desire can be understood as an ethics of difference, for it is through a proximity to alterity that writing plays out the decision to either destroy or nurture, to limit or remain open – that delicate and careful tolerance before the immense facticity of the other's materiality must continually strive towards a justice which remains free of the already written.

Love of/as difference

> I write also with an incessant drive for re-establishing the truth,
> justice. I want to use this word: justice. We do not think with
> justice. The world is not just. The world-wide non-justice that we
> all know politically has spread all the way to our imagination. It
> goes so far that we are not just with the earth, with the stars, with
> ground, with blood, with skin. In advance, and without our even
> being informed, everything is already ordered – classed according
> to a scale which gives primacy to one element over another. And
> power to one thing, or to one being over another. All the time.
> And in an unfounded manner.
>
> Hélène Cixous, *Inter views* (in Cixous and Calle-Gruber
> 1997: 11)

In Cixous's 'Lemonade, Everything was so Infinite', a woman writes
an anti-war letter which becomes a love letter directed against the
'Great Logic of Destruction'. 'And this letter would begin with
"listen . . .". It would be magical, it would play a little melody of
peace right in the midst of the cacophony, she encouraged herself.
"Even if there was a war going on, especially because of the war" '
(in Sellers 1997: 109). The war is the expression of the Logic of
Destruction, the severing of the flesh from feeling, a numbing of
thinking which occurs when the body has been processed by what
we might also call the phallocentric logic of disembodiment.
Resisting this deathly logic requires "the ultrasensitive intelligence
of proximities", a careful sensory embodied attention to the other
which is able to hear the unheard' (Sellers 1997: 110).

> But war stuns it, deafens it, war makes its stupidity reign over the
> world. Power is given to the forbidden over everything capable of
> feeling. And nevertheless we feel. With what tenderness, with what
> fierceness we have to work every day in order to reattach living
> importance to the very delicate things which we are constantly torn
> away from by the forces of war.   (in Sellers 1997: 110–11)

The war which Cixous is describing here is the war against life, it is
a global war driven by the desire for power and destruction

> – by its supranational, and supramilitary, supraracial extent, this war
> being superior to all other wars in that it has the unanimous support
> of all the peoples who appear to be the most violently opposed, in

that it secretly reconciles colors, religions, classes, continents, the truly toxic powers, the model monsters and the mimetic states, in the ardor of a single common hostility; which is why it must be kept relatively secret: because in this war all the men-men would risk finding themselves on the same side; would be in a disastrously fraternal alliance.   (1997: 112)

Alliances between different subjects are forged in the name of a common hostility but this alliance, suggests Cixous, is not based on a democratic respect for difference or a reverence for life but rather is driven by the lust for destruction. The Great Logic of Destruction reconciles difference in order to annihilate life just as, perhaps, political differences are subsumed by the military indus-trial complex, which, as post-industrial capitalism's most success-ful global business, indiscriminately sells weapons of mass destruction to whoever can afford to buy them.

In a sense Cixous is writing about the meta-logic of war, the logics of the death drive, or *Thanatos*. She goes on to invoke the discourse of Darwinism which naturalizes the Great Logic of Destruction and is part of the meta-logics of war – 'one species destroys a species which destroys another species which destroys another species' (Sellers 1997: 113). And yet, if this appeal to the imagined barbarism of the animal kingdom is used to naturalize the war against life, Cixous also writes about the dangerous sophis-tication of modern war, which masks 'its murderous power beneath civil, non-bellicose outward appearances'. The mannered civility of a smiling politician who makes a sentimental appeal to our shared humanity and the need to respect life unleashes carnage, ripping life from its roots. Modern war is 'able to annihi-late entire populations without ever seeming to touch them. By repressing the zones of sensitivity. By deafening, debasing, besot-ting . . . by the total foreclosure of all evidence of libidinal, sexual, cultural difference' (1997: 166). It is precisely this foreclosure of difference which enables war and such a foreclosure of difference also depends on the repression of a sensory, embodied connection to the other. Cixous is not advocating desire or sensualism as the antidote but rather a loving, rigorous, careful attention to the other which is able to respect the materiality of life through an 'ultrasen-sitive intelligence of proximity's' (Sellers 1997: 110). Love of the other, writes Cixous, is not enough to resist destruction, one must

strengthen that love through the careful ethical writing of difference. In this context, the writing of (sexual) difference is an anti-
war letter directed against the Great Logic of Destruction.

For Cixous love opens up a horizon towards an ethical relationship to the other, to difference, to alterity, and holds the possibility
of a profoundly intimate non-violent encounter with difference.
Such an encounter entails letting go of the desire to know, moving
beyond the already written knowledge of the other and opening up
into the creative possibilities of not-knowing, of incomprehension.[6] In *The Book of Promothea*, which is one of Cixous's more
sustained texts on the subject, she argues that a loving encounter
with the other entails 'learning dispossession' and as such, the
writing of love is also a 'book on relinquishment, dispossession'
(1991a: 85).

Elsewhere, in '(With) Or the Art of Innocence' (in Sellers 1997),
she again writes about not-knowing as the wisdom of innocence –
'the supreme knowledge: the knowing-not-to-know' is also understood as a strategic innocence of lack. In this context innocence is
a form of positivity which strategically refuses the power of a phallocentric knowledge of lack and in doing so moves beyond the Law.
Innocence as not-knowing is a form of positive disbelief: the feminine subject refuses to believe that she lacks and in doing so over-
throws the negative knowledge of the Law which would draw her
into narratives about her disempowerment. It is refusing to be
intimidated by a lack of knowledge and the knowledge of lack.
Charlotte Perkins Gilman's poem 'An Obstacle' conjures up this
relationship to lack. She writes

> I was climbing up a mountain-path
>   With many things to do,
> Important business of my own,
>   And other people's too,
> When I ran across a Prejudice
>   That quite cut off the view.
>
> My work was such as could not wait
>   My path quite clearly showed.
> My strength and time were limited,
>   I carried quite a load;
> And there that hulking Prejudice
>   Sat all across the road.

She reasons with him politely but he does not move; she becomes passionate, hysterical and angry and he still remains blocking her path, until 'a sudden inspiration came' and she 'walked directly through him,/As if he wasn't there!' (1992a). Walking through Prejudice, through the many cultural and social knowledges about the subject's lack, demands courage but it also requires a recognition that such knowledges are intimidating spectres thrown up by power. Refusing to be intimidated and simply moving through the space of lack (the Prejudice) also for Cixous entails a strategic and deconstructive innocence.

If the Law might prohibit subjects from entering various spaces because they have been coded as lacking, perhaps the first step in overcoming this often internalized sense of lack is to refuse to 'know' or accept the knowledge of one's lack. The first step which transgresses the boundary of the Law is taken with a gesture of positive innocence, with the wisdom of 'knowing-not-to-know'. Because such an approach moves beyond a provocative defiance of the Law it potentially avoids engaging in a reactive dispute about the proper place of the subject. As Gilman's poem points out, reasoning with the Law about the injustice of a prejudice or railing passionately against this injustice prevents movement, and sometimes the way forward is simply to take a leap of faith across the abyss confronting us, with the knowledge that such an abyss or lack is merely a spectre, something that can be passed through precisely because it is not the lack it appears to be. Such a leap requires faith in our own positivity, our own agency. Ultimately we are confronting fear, fear of our own lack, the spectre of our own negation, those phantoms of racial, class, and sexual inequalities that can make us avert our eyes and submit our bodies to the savage inscriptions of power. 'One might as well know', writes Cixous, 'that the principal enemy in life is fear' (Cixous and Calle-Gruber 1997: 26). And as Cixous writes in 'The Laugh of the Medusa', it is the belief in our lack which supports power: men want to make women believe they are castrated ('And we believed') but this belief can be withdrawn – with a laugh (1980a: 255). 'I think laughter is set off', writes Cixous, 'when we are not afraid. When we see that the immense is not overwhelming; and also, perhaps, when the maternal in us can manifest itself' (Cixous and Calle-Gruber 1997: 21). The laugh of the Medusa is also the laughter of a mother who knows she has never been, and never will be, castrated.

In an interview with Mireille Calle-Gruber, Cixous talks about the difference between a negative and positive incomprehension of alterity. Negative incomprehension is a state in which the alterity, the foreign difference of the other, results in fear: difference is perceived as a threat to the autonomy of the self, as loss or death. Ultimately difference is limited to a mirroring of the self's lack. Positive Incomprehension, on the other hand, describes an open wonder towards difference: 'it is to find one has arrived at the point where the immense foreign territory of the other will begin' (17), and to experience this incomprehension as exaltation (Cixous and Calle-Gruber 1997: 17); 'Loving not knowing. Loving: not knowing' (ibid.). The desire to know finally the ultimate truth of the other is for Cixous caught up in a desire to dominate and appropriate, to control the threat of lack. Positive incomprehension allows difference to circulate, instead of imposing the already known, the already written, such an approach leaves space for what has yet to be written. In other words, positive incomprehension as love is tied up with a feminine writing of (sexual) difference. Cultural, racial, social, or sexual difference is respected as something which is not yet known and which is open to an infinite writing. In her meditation on love as an encounter with alterity in 'What is it o'clock?' Cixous writes that when we are in love we are 'strangers to the world, we are held in the fragile arms of foreignness, each in the other's foreignness' (1998a: 77). Through love one encounters the alterity of the other as a positivity. 'I don't understand you with an incomprehension so vast it surpasses all my great understanding of you' (1998a: 81).

For Cixous, love holds the possibility of an intimate deconstruction; the many fictions of alterity, the writing or understanding of the other, is undone through a loving encounter with the strangeness of the other's materiality. Love is also an opening into the infinite, to the possibility of an endless feminine textual economy. The world expands under the lover's gaze, it is reborn, made new; difference is exalted; the boundary between the interior and the exterior becomes permeable; love becomes that which passes through, the liminal space of the limitless; anything is now possible, everything can be overcome, there are no barriers. We fall in love and fall into the infinity of the other's alterity, we are released from the burden of our singularity and open into the fecundity of difference.

For Cixous, love is also the possibility of an ethics of sexual difference – 'what the sexes have in common is the heart. . . . As if the heart were the sex common to the two sexes. The human sex' (Cixous and Calle-Gruber 1997: 31). Cixous is not writing of a sentimental love that is easily commodified, easily manipulated by power, the worn out discourses of bourgeois courtship rituals. Rather, the word 'heart' here must be read in the context of her writing about alterity. It is a 'heart' which is open to the play of difference, which is able to sense, feel and respect with careful attention to the other. We might say that for Cixous, writing against the Logic of Destruction, against the war which is consuming life, is also affirming a writing of the heart which honours our shared need for love, our shared vulnerability within the proximities of intimacy, and which fearlessly believes in the possibility of ethical connections across the boundaries of race, gender, class and nationality which are based on an opening up of the gifts of difference. Utopian? But then so too is the Enlightenment dream of freedom and equality and justice.

In praise of a writing of tolerance

> The thinking that addresses the undecidable is the thinking of tolerance, the thinking that does not sever, the thinking capable of concavity, of turning in on itself to make room for difference.
> Hélène Cixous, *Inter views* (in Cixous and Calle-Gruber 1997: 83)

Cixous suggests there is always a choice between destruction and protection and that this choice should be recognized as an ethical one because to choose destruction is to also be on the side of violence, to let words close off meaning, to retreat into the prison of inscriptions ordering hierarchies. For Cixous love is not just a personal, private encounter with the lover but the space of an intimacy in which a post-foundational ethics of difference can be played out. Far from being an irresponsible escape from the politics of the material world or a lapse into sentimental semantics, Cixous's ethics of difference requires a rigorous and a continually vigilant responsibility for the language we use because our language has an impact on the materiality of the bodies of others. We can no longer think of ourselves as the simple victims of power;

we must take responsibility for the violent way we use power against others and that means taking responsibility for the writing of difference. She puts it this way:

> It is we, with our language, who make the law. Who draw the borders and produce the exclusion. Who grant admittance. Who are the custom officers of communication: we admit or we reject. One of the roots of *Neutre* was a reflection on the destiny of the 'human' mystery – a mystery that is settled violently most of the time. Because ordinary human beings do not like mystery since you cannot put a bridle on it, and therefore, in general they exclude it, they repress it, they eliminate it – and it's *settled*. But, if on the contrary one remains open and susceptible to all the phenomena of overflowing, beginning with natural phenomena, one discovers the immense landscape of the *trans-*, of the passage. Which does not mean that everything will be adrift: our thinking, our choices, etc. But it means that the factor of instability, the factor of uncertainty, or what Derrida calls the *undecidable*, is indissociable from human life. This ought to oblige us to have an attitude that is at once rigorous and tolerant and double so on each side: all the more rigorous than open, all the more demanding since it must lead to openness, leave passage; all the more mobile and rapid as the ground will always give way, always. A thought which leads to what is the element of writing: the necessity of being only the citizen of an extremely inappropriable, unmasterable country or ground. (Cixous and Calle-Gruber 1997: 51–2)

Cixous's understanding of the shifting and unmasterable grounds of ethics has many affinities with a post-structuralist theorization of post-foundational politics. Judith Butler has offered ways of understanding what we are calling here a post-foundational ethics of difference. It is worth considering some of the main elements of this approach in order to situate Cixous within this re-framing of the ethics of difference. We will return to this issue in more depth in the final chapter, but for now it is worth mapping out some of the central points.

Butler's work has called attention to the ways in which a melancholia over the so-called death of the subject, and of the grand emancipatory narratives, has led to a reactive pessimism. Within feminism, for example, there has been an anxiety expressed over what is seen as a disembodied theorization of subjectivity.[7] A post-structuralist destabilization of the category of woman has led to the accusation that pluralism is a form of ethical relativism, that the explosion of identity has disabled a politics of position. We've lost our ground, we are cast adrift in a lactic sea of theory, retreating from any real intervention into the mounting violence on the shore, while we might offer the occasional sentimental piety about injustice we prefer the soporific circularity of our endless debates about the self and the other. And yet, as Butler goes on to argue, if we neglect to deconstruct the grounds of our ethics then feminism risks losing it's 'democratising potential through refusing to engage – take stock of, and become transformed by – the exclusion which put it into play' (1993: 29). If feminism is founded on a particular identity (for woman) then because that identity can only ever be normative and the product of a series of exclusions it follows for Butler that an ethics which is built on this foundation will also be normative and exclusionary (1995: 50). It is important to recognize that Butler's position is not reactionary, she is not advocating the total erasure of all foundations (hers is not a post-modern irrationalism) but rather she is calling attention to the democratic importance of remaining aware of the contested boundaries of any foundation and the strategic possibilities that are opened up once one takes into account these contestations. 'That such foundations exist only to be put into question is, as it were, the permanent risk of the process of democratisation. To refuse that contest is to sacrifice the radical democratic impetus of feminist politics' (1995: 51).

In relation to Cixous we can argue that like Butler she is advocating a writing which interrogates the '*settled*' grounds or foundation of knowledge and so therefore remains open to difference precisely because such an openness is part of a democratic ethics in which concepts of justice, equality and freedom are vital concerns, vital writing practices. In a sense both Butler and Cixous are arguing for a writing which is driven by an obligation to continually call attention to the exclusions that articulate foundations. Tolerance for difference means questioning the ethics of our foundations and refusing to be seduced by a self-righteous piety which endows the oppositional with an ethical purity. Indeed, as John D. Caputo points out in *Against Ethics* (1993), such a purity is impious for it depends upon the abjection, the exclusion, of the other. A post-foundational ethics of (sexual) difference entails careful attention to detail, a certain minimalist perception which is able to locate points of exclusion, moments when the Logic of Destruction attempts to suppress 'the zones of sensitivity', those zones of the heart which are capable of feeling across those spectral barriers of negation, those Prejudices that block the way – that is, able to recognize with a heartfelt laugh the impotence of an abyss which threatens to pull down all difference into the hell of non-being. Perhaps a post-modern feminine libidinal economy is nothing other than the working through of a post-foundational ethics of (sexual) difference.

As our Cixousian reading of Carter has suggested, oppositionality is not without violence, dreams of liberation are often driven by the lust for destruction. Carter's critique of the post-modern reification of desire in *The War of Dreams* is significant in the way it calls attention to the violence of post-modern representational technologies which sever desire from the body, (mis)appropriating desire as an autonomous force, harnessing its workings while the body is left behind, caged and exploited. If, for Carter, a phallocentric post-modern libidinal economy has orphaned desire precisely because it has confused the source body, as it were, with the repressive foundations of Enlightenment rationality, Cixous reminds us that the foundation has been misrecognized. We cannot leave the body behind and nor can we achieve an aristocratic break with the Enlightenment. What we have left are bodies who have been born of the Enlightenment dream of reason, a monstrous materiality perhaps, but one which we have ethical obligation towards. The freak is the norm writes Carter in *The War of Dreams*. We are all more or less freaks depending on how the Law frames us. If our sameness is contingent upon a shared foundation, a shared identity, then as Cixous argues, that very foundation is continually open to contestation: we are already within the passage of difference whether we realize it or not. We are already the citizens 'of an extremely inappropriable, unmasterable country or ground (Cixous and Calle-Gruber 1997: 51–2). Instead of lapsing into a melancholic nostalgia for a lost ground, or adopting a reactive adolescent refusal, it might be more strategic to begin the patient writing of an ethics of the passage of difference. A democratic obligation to others requires a certain decision to write with heart, with a careful self-reflexive sensitivity to the singularity of the other's materiality, which moves beyond the fictions of racial, national, religious, sexual and class prejudices and overcomes the self-defensive lust for destruction which blocks the path to freedom.

Part III
Writing, Theory and Beyond

7 Where Do We Go from Here? (Moving towards Freedom)

The gorgeous journey without horizon, beyond everything, the appalling yet intoxicating excursion towards the never-yet-said.
Hélène Cixous, 'Coming to Writing' (1991a)

Nothing seems to me to be less outdated that the classic emancipatory ideal.
Jacques Derrida, 'The Force of Law: The "Mystical Foundations of Authority"' (1992)

A fear takes hold of us. Calls us: 'There are nothing but ways.'
Hélène Cixous, 'Coming to Writing' (1991a)

When I close my eyes the passage opens, the dark gorge, I descend. Or rather there is descent. I entrust myself to the primitive space, I do not resist the forces that carry me off. There is no more *genre*.
Hélène Cixous, 'Writing Blind' (1998c)

For 'woman', well imprinted with the sociocultural heritage, has been inculcated with the spirit of 'restraint' She is in fact 'restraint' itself, socially. She restrains herself, and is restrained, by a thousand bonds, hitched, conjugated, strings, chains, nets, leashes, feeding dish, network of servile, reassuring dependencies. . . . They have taught you to be afraid of the abyss, of the infinite, which is nonetheless more familiar to you than it is to man. Don't go near the abyss! If she should discover its (her) force! If she should, suddenly, take pleasure in, profit from its immensity!

If she should take the leap! And fall not like a stone, but like a bird.
If she should discover herself to be a swimmer of the unlimited!'
Hélène Cixous, 'Coming to Writing' (1991a)

Cixous's writing is concerned with the movement of thinking, with
the ebb and flow of meaning, points of stagnation, stillness, with
the delicate, hesitant movements of an approach to alterity, with
flight, descent, border crossings, movements which circle the
abyss, which pass through and come towards. Her writing is also
concerned with the space of thinking, with interiorities, exteriori-
ties, the in-between, the nether realms, distances, proximities,
with the space of dreams, writing, bodies, Elsewhere, the realms of
the not yet written or thought. In a sense her (unfinished) *oeuvre* is
a contemplation of the passage of difference as the opening up of
thought. In the last chapter we ended by arguing that for Cixous
writing and sexual difference (and the writing of sexual difference)
are inseparable from questions to do with justice and freedom, and
that Cixous understands writing as a rigorous and ethical attempt
to move beyond the spectres of negation which block the path to
freedom. But what might Cixous mean by freedom?

The descent into freedom, or, against transcendence

You must climb down in order to go in the direction of that place.
Hélène Cixous, *Three Steps on the Ladder of Writing*
(1993b: 118)

Within feminist theory and criticism the concept of freedom usually
circulates as a synonym for liberation and emancipation and such
concepts are usually articulated within a socio-political framework.
Such a framework is a product of feminist appropriations of the
classic Enlightenment ideals of emancipation: First Wave feminist
texts such as Mary Wollstonecraft's *A Vindication of the Rights of
Woman* (1792) applied egalitarian principles to women, arguing for
greater political and economic freedom. Subsequent waves of feminist thought have refined (and at times, contested) her basic egalitarian premises, and although not all will acknowledge her as the
'mother' of feminism, we can generalize that most feminist thought
is informed by an Enlightenment concept of emancipation.[1]
However, not all forms of feminist writing occur within a clearly

demarcated political space which is ostensibly in dialogue with such concepts and such aspirations. Indeed, as we saw in the first chapter, Cixous herself has often been subjected to criticism for her apparent failure to engage with what are considered by many to be the pressing political issues facing feminism. Cixous, it is argued, is too poetic, perhaps too romantic or avant-garde. An obvious example is Moi's famous critique which argues that Cixous's poetics lacks a responsible recognition of historical and cultural issues and instead celebrates an aesthetics of femininity which is incapable of dealing with the political. In this context, Cixous's understanding of the liberation of female subjectivity through writing is read as a symptom of an elitist Romantic ideology which endows the poetic with the ability to transcend or overcome the mundane materialities of everyday oppressions. Critiques of aesthetics such as Moi's are common to Marxist readings. For example, in the classic text *The Romantic Ideology: A Critical Investigation*, Jerome McGann states that 'the idea that poetry, or even consciousness, can set one free of the ruins of history and culture is the grand illusion of every Romantic poet' (1983: 91). For McGann, such an illusion is one of the most enduring shibboleths of high culture and is, as such, an elitist retreat from the more difficult, because more material, issues of social inequality. In effect, critics such as McGann, and feminist critics of Cixous who share affinities with his basic premise, argue that Romantic subjectivism is a reaction against the egalitarian Enlightenment project, and thus an instrument of inequality.

It would clearly be a mistake, however, to argue that Cixous is suffering from Romantic illusions of aesthetic grandeur, or that her writing is in opposition to the classic democratic emancipatory ideal. It is important to recognize that her writing describes an approach to thinking or a strategy for subjectivity and not a magisterial political imperative. Like many post-structuralist thinkers, she writes within the discourse of the Enlightenment in order to open up discursive possibilities. If the concept of freedom or emancipation circulates within her writing (which it most certainly does), such a concept of freedom is not a simple refusal of Enlightenment principles but rather a careful interrogation of particular hierarchical orderings of freedom which she argues result in undemocratic exclusions. What do we mean by this? Quite simply, the marking of a body as inferior or other often corresponds to a reduction of that body's rights and access to freedom. This exclusion, argues Cixous, is not a biologically determined process but rather is something which occurs within the space of writing. By writing, she does not only mean signs on a surface, but the whole process of signification or meaning-making in general. We might say then that for Cixous, writing is language but it is also more than simply language – writing is thought in general, or the *process* of consciousness.

The type of writing in which Cixous recognizes the process of the liberation of consciousness is writing which moves beyond the already written or thought by opening up paths towards new thought. Such a process is blocked when the other is negated and excluded. In other words, free thinking/writing depends upon an open relationship to the difference of the other. In this context, an exploration of sexual difference opens up not only the issue of political emancipation but also the process of thinking. Questions to do with freedom, the other, sexual difference and thought are therefore inseparable. However, Cixous does not argue that sexual difference is biological or essential, rather sexual difference is an effect of writing or thinking and as such can be rethought or rewritten. Such a rethinking must, warns Cixous, guard against the logics of destruction, the desire to consume, colonize, and appropriate difference, because such a destructive appropriation results in the reduction of freedom and of the rights of the other. For feminism, this means we have to guard against a certain oppositional violence while keeping in mind that a politics of position is inevitably founded upon a series of exclusions. Thinking through the exclusions, as Butler argues, is a vital democratic practice. For Cixous that practice occurs in the space of writing such that writing is the thinking of democracy. In this way we can understand writing the feminine as the writing or thinking of democracy. She describes an approach to thinking democratically .

The principal and most dominant mode of thought which blocks democratic thinking is described by Cixous as the phallocentric Logic of Destruction because such a thinking rests upon the cannibalization and appropriation of the body of the other. Cixous does not simply equate phallocentrism with Enlightenment reason and argues that this thinking pollutes the entire edifice of modernity and that we must, therefore, fight against the Enlightenment, reason and modernity. Nor does she locate such a thinking in the materiality of the male body. Rather, she argues that the thinking which blocks democratic thought is grounded on the exclusion of thc other and this exclusion is articulated through a metaphorics of sexual difference. While any political position inevitably rests upon a series of exclusions or excluded bodies – and for feminism to have a material impact such positions have to be taken and indeed the taking of them is often of pressing ethical urgency – a thinking which disavows its dependence on the exclusion of the other or, worse still, claims such exclusions as eternal truths, is for Cixous a form of injustice. It is precisely this type of thinking which, Cixous argues, writing must pass through if it is to offer a vital engagement with the question of freedom. Phallocentric writing and thinking is therefore another name for fundamentalism, reactivism, negativity, all forms of signification which are based on the violent exclusion of the other and the restriction of the other's freedom.

It is important to recognize that the other is not merely a theoretical shibboleth and that a writing of difference is not simply a ludic ethics. Rather, the writing of an ethical obligation towards the other, which is inseparable with an ethics of difference, is the expression of a democratic passion for justice. In this context, the other is not simply any other, but those subjects who are forced to submit to oppression, violence, injustice. Caputo offers the following succinct point:

> Respect for the Other does not mean a pacifist submission to wanton violence; it does not mean respecting people who produce victims, i.e., respecting people who do not respect others, which would amount to letting disrespect reign. People who produce victims are not the 'Other' to whom we owe everything. The Other, as Levinas says, is always 'the widow, the orphan, the stranger,' that is, emblematically, the victim – not the victimisers.   (1993: 119)

An open, and for Caputo a respectful, relationship to the other is not then a form of pacifism or an indiscriminate obligation towards everybody. The other is not literally the not-self, or who I am not, in the sense that the other is therefore potentially everyone else. When Cixous writes about the need to embrace difference she is not advocating that we adopt a position of universal acceptance. Although Cixous doesn't spell out their exact characteristics and identities, she is clearly against subjectivities which are based on violence and oppression. Mandela is among her heroes.[2] Rather,

Cixous's approach is a rigorous and courageous confrontation with the thinking which subjects and oppresses, by way of an unflinching recognition that we inhabit that very same thinking. Cixous does not mean that we are all despots but rather that we must continually guard against despotic thinking and be critically aware of our desires. Self-reflective writing and thinking entails a strenuous commitment to an ethics of difference – *strenuous*, because to think through exclusions is so often to think beyond socially weighted truths.

Cixous's approach to the other should be distinguished from the reification of the other as an Absolute. As Gail Weiss argues, 'it is a bourgeois luxury to view the "other" as mysterious, as beyond our comprehension. And, for those all-too-numerous others whose various "excesses" or "lacks" or both are constructed as mysterious, as monstrous, the price of this "heuristic fiction" may be far too high' (1999: 174). It might seem that in some ways Cixous's writing performs just such a view of the other, for she writes about the importance of keeping alive a sense of incomprehension before the other. However, her approach is more subtle. In 'What Hour is It?' she states: 'I'm speaking in favour of non-recognition, not of mistaken cognition. I'm speaking in favour of closeness, *without any familiarity*' (1998a: 81). To view the other as simply the site of an excess or lack which is monstrous in some way would be for Cixous a form of mistaken cognition and a neglect of ethical obligation. An understanding of what constitutes the mysterious, for example, precedes our confrontation with the other as mysterious and is not the product of an intimate connection to the other. A closeness to the other without any familiarity would create a critical distance between the writing of the other as mysterious and our assumption that we know who the other really is. This distance is a form of closeness because it makes room for the singularity of the other's materiality and allows the possibility of an intimacy with the other without that intimacy being determined by what has already been written.

Cixous's understanding of non-recognition is related to her strategy of innocence as a form of knowing when not to know. Non-recognition is favoured as a strategy by Cixous because it allows critical distance between the knower and the object of knowledge, and within this distance writing is able to open up the process of thinking. Knowledge of the other can only ever be provisional, it is never complete, and that is why non-recognition is important. The Lispectorian approach Cixous advocates is about distance and knowledge, about being careful with our points of recognition because such points are the product of the already written and so potentially leave no space for the writing of the other. In *Rootprints* Cixous discusses this in terms of making sure

> the question [of what it means to be human] is constantly moving; it's that one cannot define, finish, close human definition – not more than sexual definition. On all sides there are vanishing points, points of communication, points of more and of less. It is we, with our language, who operate the closure. I remember having heard the following sentence: a Down's syndrome patient is a vegetable, at best an animal. One can ask oneself what that means. That sentence was the expression of a doctor.   (Cixous and Calle-Gruber 1977: 51)

This type of 'recognition' or 'comprehension' of a human being as a vegetable or an animal is precisely the sort of knowledge of the other which Cixous seeks to challenge. To use a rather crude example of what Cixous means here, one of the dangers of recognition or comprehension might be when white, middle-class, heterosexual feminism constructs a socio-political definition of female subjectivity which neglects to listen to the difference of black, working-class, lesbian women. Cixous is not arguing against the possibility of a politics of affiliation, or kinds of solidarity, but rather that the grounds of affiliation or solidarity should be continually opened up to thinking so that these grounds don't bury the other. In this sense I read her in accord with Butler.

In many ways, Cixous's writing is about descending into the grounds of thought, into the grounds of writing which for her are always already embodied or located in materiality. Her understanding of freedom is always already contingent upon the place of the other and not in a flight away from materiality. In effect, she describes an approach to freedom which subverts the eschatological phallocentrism of a Western metaphysical tradition which looks and moves upwards, beyond the earth and the flesh, towards the horizon of pure Being. For Cixous the horizon of freedom which writing moves towards descends into the *imund*, the impure, the space of exile.

While for Marxist critics such as McGann the ideology of Romanticism can be argued to idealize a subjectivism which is

endowed with the elite gifts of poetic insight, capable of a
Promethean bound over the crass ruins of history and culture, it
might be well to recall that some of the Romantics were subjected
to the pull of gravity. We only have to go as far as Rimbaud to find
that within Romanticism this apparent flight from materiality falls
back to earth. After experimenting with numerous ways of altering
his consciousness and transcending himself, Rimbaud falls down
to a ground he has disavowed and despised, echoing Nietzsche's
famous warning to 'stay loyal to the earth' and not let knowledge
'fly away from the things of the earth and beat with its wings
against the eternal wall' (1969: 102). Transcendence reaches a limit
where the gravity of the earth pulls the body back down: 'I called
myself an angel, free from all moral constraint. I am sent back to
the soil to seek some obligation, to wrap gnarled reality in my
arms!' (1984: 213). As Rimbaud discovered, a soaring rebellious
freedom falls back into a search for earthly obligation. Icarus's
wings melt because he has forgotten an elemental truth, an earth-
bound reality, a limit which the body cannot transcend. For
Cixous, writing is about this descent, she follows the path that
leads downwards, the fall into an obligation to the other, to difference. Hers is not, then, a poetics of Romantic transcendentalism
but rather a subversive grounding of the desire for freedom in
materiality.

And it is perhaps here, in these movements of freedom, of soaring transcendence and descent, that we discover a certain theological metaphorics of emancipation which inform the way we
imagine the path of freedom within the Western metaphysical
tradition. As David Farrell Krell writes so elegantly: 'Is there
anything more characteristic of the philosopher than his or her
desire to go up? To radiate outward to the outermost spheres,
where gods and goddesses dwell, dining on rare essences, far from
everything fallen, remote from muck, offal, the corpse, impervious
to all waste and ruin?' (1996: 77). To move down, to descend, to
stay in Plato's cave and find a passage that leads into further
depths, which burrows into the body of the earth and meets her
outlawed children, is to move against the upward pull of the
Western phallocentric metaphysical tradition which Krell calls
'ascensional reflection' (1996: 78).[3]

This narrative of linear, vertical progress, this transcendental
soaring away from, is read by Cixous as a disembodied flight of

negation. The Cixousian passage of difference *descends* into materiality not away from it, and there is no single path into these
depths, no correct, lawful and proper way but rather many open-
ings within writing down into difference. The paths of Cixous's
freedom are trodden by the impure, not angels but exiles, subjects
who are capable of risking exclusion, of connecting with outlawed
others. In 'The School of Roots' Cixous tells us that this descent:

> is much more difficult to achieve, much more tiring, much more
> physically exacting (*physically* because soul is body), than climbing
> up. It is a climb, but it requires the whole strength of everything that
> is you – which I don't want to call 'body' since it is more complex
> than the body – to go through the various doors, obstacles, walls,
> and distances we have forged to make a life.   (1993b: 118)

The descent is difficult because it requires a careful thinking
through the boundaries which have described (and limited) identity; it is a subversive thinking down into subjectivity. Cixous's
understanding of the descent shares an uncanny affiliation with
Heidegger, for in 'Letter on Humanism' he writes:

> Thinking does not overcome metaphysics by climbing still higher,
> surmounting it, transcending it somehow or other; thinking over-
> comes metaphysics by climbing back down into the nearness of the
> nearest. The descent, particularly where man has strayed into
> subjectivity, is more arduous and more dangerous than the ascent.
> (1977a: 231)

Heidegger's 'climbing back down into the nearness of the nearest'
also echoes with Cixous's call for a thinking which descends into a
proximity with the materiality of the other, towards an 'ultrasensitive intelligence of proximities'. Recalling her work on Lispector's
approach, we can also argue that this 'intelligence' entails a careful
opening towards the other that resists the many seductions to
appropriate and consume, which drive the desire to know. It is not
an indulgent subjectivism that Heidegger and Cixous are writing
about here, but rather an archaeological digging down into the
depths of the subject (of thinking), into the messy nether realms of
the impure, of difference, which is the passage of thinking.

   Cixous's descensional reflection, her writing down through the
passage of difference, can be understood within the context of a

subversion of Western transcendentalism of which philosophers such as Heidegger and Derrida are a part. The subversion is not so much an overcoming of foundations as a tunnelling through, an underground writing *within* the grounds of reason. For Kant, the Enlightenment philosopher of the autonomous will, the grounds of reason must be firm enough to build a secure morality. In the *Critique of Pure Reason*, Kant argues that 'we must level the ground and make it firm enough for those majestic edifices of ethicality. For in this ground we find all kinds of mole tunnels, which reason has dug in its confident but futile search for treasure, and which make such constructions precarious' (1965: 375–6). For Kant then, and we might also generalize, for a Western metaphysical tradition that requires a firm ground on which to build a ladder to transcendence, these mole tunnels, these passages beneath the ground that erupt onto the surface, creating pits that might if fallen through leading to an abyss, are to be erased, stopped up, dealt with as symptoms of reason gone astray. In 'Sorties' Cixous writes that the foundations of phallocentrism is in the process of being reshaped: 'We are living in an age where the conceptual foundations of an ancient culture is in the process of becoming undermined by millions of a species of mole (*topoi*, ground mines) never known before (Cixous and Clement 1989: 65).

For Cixous, and for Heidegger as we have seen, these passages down are precisely where thinking leads us. And if these breaks in the ground lead to the abyss, for Cixous this abyss is where writing leads – 'the appalling yet intoxicating excursion towards the never-yet-said'. The descent is also a courageous movement towards those others who inhabit the abyss, those who are marked as lacking, who inhabit the regions of devalued materialities. Cixous's writing moves down to that which has been devalued by this phallocentric verticalization in search of a justice and an ethics which is not built upon the silencing and stopping up of those tunnels of difference and the materialities who inhabit them. To think against values is not to devalue everything which is valued. That type of thinking would be driven by a reactionary logic and create the sort of inversion which Cixous argues limits Genet's subversive libidinal economy. Rather, to think against values is to rethink the way our values objectify the materiality of the other; to think against the objectification of the other through the economy of phallocentric lack. In 'The School of Roots' Cixous writes that these devalued others include women, foreigners, the 'abominable', the 'excluded and exiled' (1993b: 120).

In 'The Force of Law: The "Mystical Foundations of Authority" ', Derrida writes that it is important to interrogate our concepts of justice because, quite simply, much violence has been committed, and continues to be committed, in the name of justice (and freedom). For Derrida, deconstruction aims 'constantly to maintain an interrogation of the origin, grounds and limits of our conceptual, theoretical or normative apparatus surrounding justice' (1992: 20). Such an interrogation of the grounds entails moving down to a focus on the undecidable: the passage of difference is also the path of the undecidable, or that which cannot be rapidly captured by thought: 'A decision that didn't go through the ordeal of the undecidable would not be a free decision, it would only be the programmable application or unfolding of a calculable process. It might be legal; it would not be just' (32). In effect, Derrida, and Cixous too, is writing about an ethics that is able to think through the undecidable, which is, basically, capable of thinking; a critical ethics then, which is able to reflect on its foundations, or grounds, and not simply apply an already thought justice, a universal idea of justice.

In this sense Cixousian freedom is akin to deconstruction, because it describes a justice which affirms difference without demanding a calculated return for services rendered in the name of the Law. 'The "idea of justice" ', writes Derrida, 'seems to be irreducible in its affirmative character, in its demand of gift without exchange, without circulation, without recognition or gratitude, without economic circularity, without calculation and without rules, without reason and without rationality' (25). Derrida's idea of justice shares an affinity with Cixous's understanding of the feminine libidinal economy in which the gift is given without a self-serving demand for recognition or gratitude from the other. How to give to the other without calculating a return is difficult. We follow the democratic emancipatory ideal and attempt to liberate the other, we go down into those exiled depths and hold out our hand, but too often the very act of holding out our hand, the sense that we are offering something from above, blinds and deafens us to the other we are attempting to connect with. Seeing only the hand of our benevolence we are blind to the violent effects of our charity. A hand held out in the name of justice, emancipation and freedom becomes a grasping after the other. Our justice becomes dependent on our ability to grasp, know and calculate who it is that we are offering justice to. And yet, as both Cixous and Derrida argue, we must keep trying to find an approach to difference which avoids such ethical calculations because an attempt to find such an approach is the very heart of democracy.

The idea that the descending path to the becoming of freedom is entered from the ground, through an abyss in Reason perhaps, assumes that we are on the ground already and that we have a choice about whether or not we want to stay there or enter into the nether realms of difference. For Cixous, however, we have already fallen. The ground has already given way and indeed it gave way a long time ago. Difference did not suddenly come into being because someone (perhaps Heidegger and then Derrida) did some underground work. The ground was never secure and we have always been creatures of the abyss. This does not mean that reason does not exist, that everything that was has fallen, that pessimism reigns, or that the subject is entombed in the depths of non-being. For Cixous it means that we have to take stock of the situation without being seduced by the temptation not to think about it which is offered by transcendentalism, the already thought path of an eschatological, ascensional phallocentrism.

Foundations, roots, writing

Post-structuralist theorization of foundations and grounds often carries with it a certain metaphorics of penetration, where once the sky was penetrated with the edifices of metaphysical transcendentalism it is now the ground which is penetrated with the tunnelling of descensional deconstruction. While Cixous's understanding of writing derives from this context it also offers another way of thinking of the ground, which does not simply view it as a resource for re-signification. Butler, for example, argues convincingly that foundations are cultural resources which are open to subversive appropriations and re-significations, and cites an example in which a foundationalist view of the subject was taken from the French Revolution and used to liberate the Haitians (1995: 140–1). Butler's attention to the strategic possibilities of re-signifying and shifting foundations is important and her position certainly offers a positive model for emancipatory politics. Cixous, I would argue, is fundamentally in accord with Butler's position (which is basically deconstructive) but she differs in her approach to foundations.

For Cixous, as for Heidegger, the descent into thinking through the foundations of metaphysics is also a descent into subjectivity. It is the proximity between subjectivity and the foundation which Cixous argues writing moves into or through. Cixous's writing is highly subjective, autobiographical, self-conscious, self-reflexive, and yet, ironically, this hypersubjectivism undoes the subject precisely because it calls attention to the textual nature of subjectivity. The subject is read as an effect of textuality or writing, or as a product of a particular style of writing and thinking. In this respect her subjectivism is closer to a Nietzschian overcoming of the subject than it is to a confessional feminist writing which seeks to uncover the grounds of the truth of female subjectivity. And this, as I shall go on to argue, opens up the possibility of a more flexible approach to the question of writing and sexual difference precisely because it foregrounds subjectivity as a *strategy* and not as the grounds of final truth.

In 'The School of Roots' Cixous argues for a deconstructional descending into subjectivity, through 'our own marshes, our own mud', into the 'hell' or 'inferno' of the 'other country', the country of our own outlawed subjectivity (1993b: 119). Lispector describes writing as a growing down: 'I follow the tortuous path of roots breaking through the earth' (1989: 14–15). However, this following of the path of the root of writing is also a becoming root, a becoming performed through writing. The root becomes a metaphor for the relationship between foundations and subjectivity which writing creates:

> The root is twisted, doubled up, entangled, it digs with all its force into the ground, evil and good happily mingled, before the tree which separates halves, it is humble (*humilis*) for it knows that nothing is simple, that it itself is not simple, thought is a struggle with itself, one cannot reach, but one can stretch, from the two forces together springs the *moment*. And this energy is joy.
>
> Now, it is joy that is prohibited – the thing that escapes all economies. It is with joy that I am beside myself. In the non-self of the earth, down in the depths.   (Cixous 1998b: 132–3)

If the thinking/writing subject is the root which grows down into

the depths of foundations, this foundation also nurtures that growing down. Here Cixous describes a non-reactive relationship to
foundations, a writing which is potentially free of reactivism and
negativity. The joy Cixous writes of is the joy of thinking into
subjectivity down into the unthought, down through the 'accumu-
lation of mental, emotional, and biographical clichés' (119). Joy is
the *jouissance* of thinking, the pleasure of free thinking. This root-
ing down into the grounds of thought through writing is also
described as a boundary crossing, a transgression which is productive rather than reactive, which is free of *ressentiment* and radiant
with affirmation. The moment which she describes here is born of
the struggle of thought with itself, of a subjectivity which is becoming otherwise through the process of thinking through (not
against) foundations.

Writing down into subjectivity is also for Cixous the
quest(ioning) of thinking. As Heidegger puts it: 'questioning is the
piety of thought' (1977: 317). Writing, for her, is the opening up of
the question of the subject (of sexual difference): 'The immersed
author necessarily comes to the point of questioning his/her limits,
his/her frontiers, his/her passages, his/her alterations: wondering
not only which sex but towards which sex, in which relation to the
other, which other? What is the other's sex?' (1993b: 136). Here
sexual difference is destabilized and put into play, capable of a
growing down into the difference of the unthought. In 'The School
of Roots' Cixous talks about the metamorphosis of the subject, or a
becoming which is activated through intimate proximity with the
ground of thinking. For Cixous, we are always already within the
realm of a materiality which is radiant with agency and this materiality is itself the ground or foundation of thinking. Profoundly
then, we are already inside the foundations of thinking, inside
language, inhabiting an intimacy with the other/self, and this intimacy is also a form of materiality. Throughout her writing Cixous
calls attention to the corporeal roots of language and argues that
thinking is itself a corporeal process.

Within post-structuralist feminist theory, how to think through
the corporeal grounds of consciousness has emerged as a central
theoretical and political issue. While numerous articles and books
have been dedicated to exploring the question of the body, and the
term 'corporeal feminism' now circulates as an umbrella term for
this broad investigation, Cixous's work is rarely mentioned.

References to Cixous's work are usually limited to her concept of *écriture féminine* or writing the body, which might be explained by the way her work was processed in the debates about essentialism, a suspicion about her affiliation with Derrida, and her occasional misunderstood comments about feminism. However, Cixous's theorization of matter in her writing on Lispector, along with her subtle analysis of the relationship between subjectivity, foundations and writing, provide a significant contribution to the theorization of corporeality. Before we consider Cixous's particular understanding of the corporeal it is worth considering some of the central issues at stake in a feminist theorization of matter. The question of the corporeal is central to feminism for the following reasons:

1. If the violence of the phallocentric Western metaphysical tradition is built upon the repression of corporeality, undoing this repression will undermine the machinery of this violence. Phallic power depends on the subjection of the body.
2. Avowing a disavowed debt to matter is an ethical task which aims at liberating the body from the chains of phallocentric thought. Embodied knowledge is subversive.
3. More broadly, the violent repression and disavowal of matter is symptomatic of the exploitation of nature, the non-human and the bodies of Others. Disembodiment is a form of death-bound transcendentalism.
4. The importance of creating embodied thought comes with a recognition of the ethical necessity of grounding language in the specificity of the speaker's body. Foucault's 'What matter who's speaking?' becomes 'Which matter is speaking?' An archeology of the subject becomes inseparable from an archeology of matter. Unmasking power entails enfleshing the subject.
5. If feminism is to have a theoretically sound politics of position it must adequately theorize a non-essential material base for that position. How to approach the matter of the female body (and matter in general and bodies in general) becomes a vital political and theoretical issue.

In her recent book *Metamorphoses*, Braidotti uses terms such as 'radical immanence', 'enfleshed or embodied materialism' and 'sensible transcendental' to describe this broad theorization of the body within corporeal feminism and more widely within some aspects of post-structuralist theory (2002: 63). 'Radical immanence' is described as 'a deeply embedded vision of the embodied subject (ibid.) which is able to process the connections between culture and nature outside a classical mind/body division.' [Here ibid. is Braidotti 2002: 63.] Within this context, 'knowledge claims rest on the immanent structure of subjectivity and must resist the gravitational pull towards abstract transcendentality. . . . It is a path of transcendence via and through the body, not away from it' (2002: 62).

There appear to be two forms of transcendentalism operating here: abstract phallocentric transcendentalism and sensible transcendentalism or an embodied material transcendentalism. If we were to apply such terms to Cixous, we might describe her descensional writing/thinking as a form of sensible transcendentalism. But does Cixous offer something subtly different here? Is her writing more than an embodied knowledge of the subject?

If the transcendental is an outside of the subject, which is awaiting representation, the not-yet-represented or the coming into representation, to code this transcendental as sensible (or as matter) is to argue for a materialism (or a corporeality) outside the subject, which has not yet been represented. This is understood to be a productive position because it recognizes that matter is in the process of becoming and so truth claims about the body or matter are not fixed, but undergoing a process of representation. It is potentially reactive because it is a form of transcendentalism and separates the subject from the body. The subject is undergoing a process of embodied becoming but the body becomes *idealized* as the outside of the subject. Cixous, on the other hand, argues for a thinking which inhabits the nowness of matter, not a thinking which is leaping ahead towards what matter might become. For Cixous attempting to predict what matter will become is caught up in the desire to know what matter is: the transcendental trajectory is shaped by the desire to appropriate. How to think outside the grounds of thinking, how to think matter outside the grounds of matter, is for Cixous about thinking inside the grounds of thinking, inside the ground of matter. To paraphrase Derrida's famous assertion, there is no outside the ground. Or, there is no outside the body. Which does not mean that there is no ground outside the subject or that there is no body outside the subject. She is not advocating nihilism or narcissism.

What am I? is still, for Cixous, a radical question and her subjectivism a radical questioning of the grounds of the subject which
emerges from within those very grounds. Indeed, the question
constitutes the grounds of thinking. Cixous calls for a writing and a
thinking which has the strength and the courage to dwell within
the grounds of thought without taking flight. Such a dwelling is also
a growing, an immersion into the corporeal subject. Cixous's
corporeal subjectivism folds back into an anti-subjectivism
through an intense questioning of the grounds of the subject so
that what constitutes the subject is opened up to thought. It is
perhaps in her writing on Lispector that her approach to corporeal
thinking becomes focused.

As we have seen in a previous chapter, Lispector's writing
provides Cixous with a way of thinking through an ethical
approach to matter. Commenting on Cixous, Braidotti writes that
here 'The term "approach" defines for Cixous the basis of her ethical system: it designates the way in which self and other can be
connected in a new world-view where all living matter is a sensitive
web of mutually receptive entities. The key terms are affinity and
receptivity' (2002: 164–5). Braidotti claims Cixous's description of
the approach as an example of sensible transcendentalism
because such a receptivity is argued to be a description of the feminine divine. However, such sensible transcendentalism (and such
a feminine divine) is more Irigarayian than Cixousian, for it is
Irigaray who actually uses the word and who explicitly describes
the divine in many of her writings.[4] In 'Clarice Lispector: The
Approach', Cixous writes:

> And through her writing-window we enter the awesome beauty of
> learning to read: going, by way of the body, to the other side of the
> self. Loving the true of the living, what seems *ungrateful* to narcissus
> eyes, the nonprestigious, the nonimmediate, loving the origin, inter-
> esting oneself personally with the impersonal, with the animal, with
> the thing.   (1991b: 59)

The other side of the self is still within the realm of the self even
while it might be the non-self. This subjectivism, is an opening up
to that which is not-self ('what seems *ungrateful* to narcissus eyes')
and especially that which is devalued. Learning to read is also an
ethical approach to the devalued 'origin' which is matter itself.

Cixous's frequent invocation of the 'source' of thought can be understood not as an abstract transcendental idea (or an idealized thought), but rather matter. The source, origin or ground is an embodied thought which is teeming with difference just as matter in general contains a multitude of different bodies.

We might read Cixous's approach to materiality, to the question of the corporeal, through phenomenology. In his working notes for his unfinished *The Visible and the Invisible*, Merleau-Ponty writes 'It is already the flesh of things that speak to us of our own flesh, and that speaks to us of the flesh of the other' (1992: 193). Such a speaking about and between flesh is what constitutes the in-between or what Merleau-Ponty calls the 'intertwining – the chiasm', which, as I argued in the chapter on Woolf's *The Waves*, can be understood through Cixous's concept of the 'third body'. The third body is the product of a mutual receptivity, a loving proximity with the other, it is virtual but anchored in the body, a representation of the body which is not determined by the two bodies which have given rise to the representation. It is born of sexual identity but exceeds sexual identity.

The (un)decidable foundation of sexual difference

How do we inhabit an undecidable foundation, how do we inhabit 'an extremely inappropriable, unmasterable country or ground'? (1997: 52). In 'Building, Dwelling, Thinking', Heidegger writes, '*Only if we are capable of dwelling, only then can we build*' (1977b: 338). How we dwell within the undecidable foundation of language is an ethical issue. How we dwell within the undecidability of sexual difference, which is also part of this foundation, is also an ethical issue. Is it possible to build a feminist ethics on such shaky ground? Does the undecidable foundation of sexual difference make a feminist politics impossible? If feminism is grounded in the female body, isn't there something mad, even destructive, in arguing that this ground is undecidable? How can we build a materialist feminist ethics and politics if materiality is itself undecidable?

Perhaps it is a question of an approach to values. To recognize that we dwell inside the undecidable grounds of sexual difference does not mean that we are beating the drums of nihilism, of the valuelessness and nullity of sexual difference, that the long history of violence against women is meaningless, that woman is erased, like a face drawn on the sand at the edge of the sea. To recognize that a foundation is undecidable does not mean that history is erased, that all that is valued is valueless, that everything is a text and that materiality does not exist, that everything is negated. Rather it means, for Cixous, that we have not yet finished thinking through the question of sexual difference and that the horizon of the unthought question of sexual difference will be before us for as long as we think. Dwelling within the undecidable question of sexual difference means practising a careful tolerance for difference for such a tolerance is also the opening up of thinking, of a growing down with the roots of thought. It is only through a tolerance of the materiality of difference and a recognition that difference is materiality perhaps, that the task of building a world in which the devalued materiality of women is transformed can begin.

The idea of the 'post-foundational' suggests that the foundation has been left behind, transcended. For Cixous though, it is a matter of growing down into the foundations. Maybe it would be more accurate to describe her position as an ethical engagement with the undecidable foundations of sexual difference. Her theorization of writing as a growing down into thought articulates an approach to subjectivity which we can also call a strategy, and a strategic ethics of sexual difference. For example, the subjectivity of the 'newly born woman' (and the feminine subject in general within Cixous's writing) describes neither a falling back into the pre-human abundance of some essential organic unity or ground, nor a polymorphous, prelapsarian becoming, and nor does it describe a post-human liberation into the space of pure difference. Rather, the subjectivity of the 'newly born woman' describes a particular style of subjectivity which performs a *strategic* engagement with the undecidable foundation of sexual difference. Instead of avoiding the challenge of a critical engagement with the foundation through a reactivism which takes the form of a nostalgic Romantic retreat to a prelapsarian ground, or a post-modern flight into the white noise of pure difference, Cixous's writing descends into the foundations through a recognition that the foundation is undecidable. In other words, the passage of Cixous's writing into the foundations is the passage of the undecidable.

To argue that her writing 'follows' the passage of the undecidable assumes that the passage is already there, that the passage itself is a type of ground. For Cixous though, the passage opens up through a particular style of writing, which is inseparable from a particular style of thinking. This style of writing/thinking is also a style of subjectivity and this subjectivity recognizes itself as a strategy. Commenting on the concept of strategy, Claire Colebrook writes that 'strategy is the positivity of a certain position – a self, an enunciation, a style – but it is, *as strategy*, never adequate to itself, never fully at one with the forces that enable and take hold of it (1999: 139). In other words, the position taken by the subject is a provisional strategy, or the subject is a strategic position. Understanding itself as strategy, a Cixousian subjectivism avoids submission to an already given transcendent ground such as truth or identity and instead performs a positive writing/thinking of sexual difference.

In this context, the undecidability grounds of sexual difference allows the possibility of a strategic engagement with the subject of sexual difference which avoids a collapse between identity and sexuality. To say 'I am a white, heterosexual middle-class woman', for example, is not so much to articulate the truth of a sexual identity but to outline a subjectivity which contains a number of strategic possibilities. How those strategies are articulated will depend on how the elements of that subjectivity are questioned and opened up to thought. What 'white', 'heterosexual', 'middle'-class' 'woman' is has not been decided in advance, each element of that subjectivity is undoing the process of signification within thought, or writing in general. Similarly, any other element of subjectivity is also continually undergoing the process of signification. An ethical, challenging, life-affirming engagement with the process of signification (or writing) entails an opening up of the strategic possibility of emancipatory strategies. More subtly, this entails a continual questioning and expansion of the grounds of the classic emancipatory ideal so that this ground does not limit how we imagine the liberation of the subject. Such a questioning of the grounds is a vital activity for it prevents the ground from becoming infertile, non-productive, barren, something which can only breed negativity and reactivism. When the grounds of thought become sterile through lack of thinking, fundamentalism is born, intolerance reigns, and materiality is subjected to the violence of hierarchies – some bodies will be subjected, other bodies glorified. That thought is continually getting stuck, that forms of fundamentalist violence are always with us, means that we have to remain vigilant about our ethical obligation to writing a style of thinking which opens up a critical thinking through of foundations.

Even more subtly perhaps, this also means that we have to avoid thinking of fundamentalism, or forces of domination, as an impermeable ground. Or to put it this way, for feminism to assume that patriarchy is the grounds of women's oppression risks simplifying the grounds and reducing the strategic re-articulation of those grounds through a fixed definition of patriarchy. How we write the ground informs how we write liberatory strategies. If the strategic possibilities of women's liberation are to be opened up, then the grounds of patriarchy have to be re-thought. To argue, for example, that the grounds of women's oppression is the internalization of a phallocentric ideal of feminine lack is to risk assuming, among other things, that women have no agency and are passive, that all men contribute to this brainwashing, that all men benefit from women's oppression, or that men do not experience a sense of lack.

If the ethics of the undecidable foundations of sexual difference are understood as a strategic engagement with the grounds of the subject, such an ethics will be a product of the questions asked of that ground. Here questions are understood not as attempts to reveal some hidden ground, to unmask the grounds of phallocentrism and replace it with the oppositional purity of a new feminist ground: the question is not a form of reactivism or a negation of the ground, but rather a practice, the creation of a strategy, and the description of a subjectivity. For example, what grounds do we have for thinking that women internalize feminine lack? What are the grounds of feminine lack? What is feminine positivity? What is masculine negativity? What does phallocentrism lack? These are all questions which would open up the assumption that women internalize a phallocentric ideal of lack to a thinking otherwise (or an otherwise thinking). Moreover, a question such as 'what is feminine positivity?' also invites the creation of a subjectivity which is strategic in so far as it re-signifies or rewrites, rethinks, the grounds of feminine negativity. Such questions, such subjectivities, are the practising of strategies.

A recognition that the foundations of sexual difference are undecidable does not mean that decisions cannot be made, or that feminism does not have a speaking position. Rather, it means that when a decision is made or a speaking position is adopted such a decision or such a voice is understood as a strategy and not as the mapping out of a transcendental ground. Importantly this position is not driven by an oppositional piety, which would remain blind to its own foundations. It is a position situated within the discourses of the Enlightenment, which does not assume the garbs of an oppositional purity, which is able to critically reflect upon the grounds of resistance to power. In effect, it is a position which recognizes that every position is contaminated by an investment in power, but one which struggles towards a more ethical dis-invest-ment.

In the introduction to the collection of essays in *Becoming*, Elizabeth Grosz asks: 'What would an ethics be like that, instead of seeking a mode of equivalence, a mode of reciprocity or calcula-tion, sought to base itself on absolute generosity, absolute gift, expenditure without return, a pure propulsion into a future that does not rebound with echoes of an exchange dictated by the past?' (1999: 11). Such an imagined ethics, we might argue, is a post-foundational ethics of sexual difference, the ethics of a feminine libidinal economy which gives freely to the other without expecting a return. However, a 'rooted' Cixousian materialism might find within the idea of '*absolute* generosity' and '*absolute* gift' a move-ment towards transcendence which is avoiding the question of the 'roots' of writing, of the depths, of the underground places of cont-amination. A Cixousian post-foundational ethics of sexual differ-ence recognizes that the absolute is caught up in an idealist flight away from materiality. While an ethics which is based on the absolute gift is impossible, the idea of this possibility is precisely what opens up thinking to the question of the undecidable. Although we may never arrive at the point of absolute liberation, or a moment when the classical ideal of emancipation is complete, to refuse the challenge of moving thought towards that ideal is to risk letting the grounds of thinking stagnate, become sterile, and open to reactive negativity. While we will perhaps never arrive at a point in our culture (or our metaphysics) where violence does not exist, we can at least work towards such an imaginary point with the recognition that we might never fully arrive but that we have a democratic obligation to the materiality of others to patiently and rigorously work towards freedom.

For Cixous, writing the passage of sexual difference does not describe a subjectivity which can walk the path of an oppositional purity – the path is not a new ground – rather it is a rooted, tangled, sometimes tortured proximity with a materiality which is *imund*, contaminated, reactive, positive, deathly, radiant, murky, uncanny. This is what she means by inhabiting the present, not a thoughtless fusion with a moment of *jouissance*, but a recognition that we are now within the passage of writing and that there is a certain ethical obligation which comes with that recognition. The joy of the present which Cixous writes about is tied up with her celebration of positivity: once we understand our own subjectivity as a strategy and not as the submission to some transcendent ground, dwelling within the passage of (sexual) difference is understood as a positive practice for within this passage we can open up the possibility of a more mobile and strategic thinking. The strategy of Cixous's writing, then, is a profoundly creative practice for it calls on us to become thinkers. Cixous's contribution to a feminist theorization of sexual difference is, at the very least, the mapping out of an approach to a liberatory thinking which remains faithful to the heart of the classic emancipatory ideal.

Joy

Ultimately Cixous encourages us to think critically and creatively. We are, as she reminds us, thinkers, writers, creators. Her gift, then, is a recognition that we do not lack, that the fear of lack is what binds us to reactivism, negativity, and supports oppression. Her gentle writing contains the force of a Nietzschian call to become a creator, to live within and through the body dynamically, productively, with force and passion. Her insistence that we are never simply lacking, that negativity, death, the Law, phallocentrism, has no final dominion over us, is not rhetorical or the product of a lofty philosophical optimism. It is, rather, a necessary and strategic recognition that we are capable of changing the way subjectivity is constructed, that we *can* rewrite the oppressive fictions that imprison us and others and that, moreover, we have an ethical obligation to do so. We do not lack. We matter. Our actions and words have effects on others and so we must remain ever vigilant about our responsibilities. The last words of 'The Laugh of the Medusa' are, 'In one another we will never be lacking' (1980a: 264).

Thinking requires strength, courage, a fearless confrontation with the abyss. Bodies can rewrite and rethink their positions. In 1955, Rosa Parks, a 43-year-old black seamstress, refused to give up her bus seat to a white man and instigated a chain of events that led to the creation of the American Civil Rights Movement. She refused to be inscribed by racist lack and affirmed the positivity of her own body, her right to be equal, and ultimately her right to joy. As I write, millions of people all over the world have joined together and marched for peace, against death, against the wicked obscenity of the arms trade. In 'The Last Painting, or the Portrait of God', Cixous writes:

> And the kind of courage?' . . . First we have to have the courage to be afraid of being hurt. We have to not defend ourselves. The world has to be suffered. . . . And there is also the other fear, the least dazzling, the most burning: the fear of reaching joy, acute joy, the fear of allowing oneself to be carried away by exultation, the fear of adoring. We must not be afraid of feeling this fear scalding the blood in our veins.   (1991d: 121)

Why do we fear joy? To experience joy is to affirm a creative life force we have been taught is limited, restricted, measured in only so many parts to so many people. With joy comes the opening up of new possibilities for life, the affirmation of new subjectivities, movements of being that pass through the spectres of negation that block the paths to freedom. Joy is revolutionary. Joy is alien to structures, it dissolves identities, subverts hierarchies. Medusa's laugh is not a tittering at the fallacies of phallic myths of feminine lack, hers is a larger triumphant roar of life over death. Such a roar, such a laughter, is a thinking, a writing, and a practice.

Notes

Notes to Chapter 1: Poetry and Politics

1. Many post-structuralist theorists work through the implications of this loss of faith in the Cartesian cogito and Enlightenment reason. Foucault explores this in *The Order of Things* (1991a), the implications for this crisis being that 'man is in the process of disappearing' (385), 'like a face drawn in sand at the edge of the sea'. The Cartesian subject who claims 'I think' will be replaced with an interrogation into the ways in which thinking or language articulate subjectivity, or rather the ways in which 'I' (man, woman, the subject) is thought through by discourse.

2. The dawning realization that the French Left was dominated by patriarchs led to feminist resistance and autonomy. In 1968, François Parturier published *Lettre ouverte aux hommes* [An open letter to men]. During this year the 'Psychanalyse et Politique' group was formed, which controlled the influential publishing house Éditions des Femmes. Like other avant-garde intellectual groups, such as the journal *Tel Quel*, 'Psych et Po', as it was often called, argued that there would be no revolution without a massive and transgressive disruption of the Symbolic. Cixous epitomized this assumption in much of her early work, especially her Medusa manifesto. See Elizabeth Grosz, *Sexual Subversions: Three French Feminists* (1989).

3. The most prominent post-structuralist feminist theorists of difference include Julia Kristeva, Luce Irigaray, Moira Gatens, Rosi Braidotti, Elizabeth Grosz, Drucilla Cornell and Judith Butler. However, it would be a mistake to assume this group is free of internal debate. Moira Gatens and Judith Butler, for example, have been critical of the reliance on psychoanalysis. *Feminist Contentions: A Philosophical Exchange* by Seyla Benhabib, Judith Butler, Drucilla Cornell and Nancy Fraser (1995) offers a number of insights into some of the core debates. See also, 'The Future of Sexual Difference: An Interview with Judith Butler and Drucilla Cornell', with Phen Cheah and Elizabeth Grosz in *Diacritics* (1998).

4. Jane Gallop's *Reading Lacan* (1985) and Elizabeth Grosz's *Jacques Lacan: A Feminist Introduction* (1990) provide a good introduction to

the many ways Lacan's theorization of *jouissance* has been appropriated by feminist theory. See also the edited collection of Lacan's essays
on the subject, *Feminine Sexuality*, edited by Juliet Mitchell and
Jacqueline Rose (1982). In 'God and the *Jouissance* of ~~The~~ Woman'
Lacan writes of a supplementary *jouissance* which is beyond the phallus. 'What was tried at the end of the last century, at the time of Freud,
by all kinds of worthy people in the circle of Charcot and the rest, was
an attempt to reduce the mystical to questions of fucking' (1982: 147).
For Lacan, the excesses of feminine pleasure might seem to be a kind
of mysticism. But perhaps that is because he can't embody it?

Notes to Chapter 2: The Major Concepts

1. For a creative explication of Deleuze and Guattari see Brian Massumi's
   *A User's Guide to Capitalism and Schizophrenia: Deviations from
   Deleuze and Guattari* (1992). The collection of essays in Boundas and
   Olkowaski (eds), *Gilles Deleuze and the Theatre of Philosophy* (1994), is
   also a useful place to start.
2. Elaine Showalter, in particular, has taken issue with Woolf's valorization of androgyny. See her chapter 'Virginia Woolf and the Flight into
   Androgyny', from *A Literature of their Own* (1977).
3. See *Libidinal Education* (1993) by Lyotard, where he argues that desire
   is structured not like a language, as Freud had it, but as an economy.
4. See Bataille's *Visions of Excess: Selected Writings, 1927–1939* (1991),
   especially the essays 'The Critique of the Foundations of the Hegelian
   Dialectic' and 'The Notion of Expenditure'.
5. The idea that femininity is in itself a form of alienation informs many
   Marxist feminist critiques as well as more accessible and influential
   texts such as Betty Friedan's *The Feminine Mystique* (1972).
6. In her essay on Clarice Lispector (p. 61) Cixous writes: 'Clarice looks:
   and the world comes into presence. Born things are reborn, gathered
   back. For in a certain way Lispector is synonymous with *legere*, in other
   words "reading", in other words "gathering". Heidegger would say:
   "We normally understand by reading only this, that we grasp and
   follow a script and written matter. But that is done by gathering the
   letters. Without this gathering, without a gleaning [*die lese*] in the sense
   in which wheat or grapes are gleaned, we should not be able to read
   [*lesen*] a single word, however keenly we observe the written signs".'
   This quotation is taken from Heidegger's lecture 'What Calls for
   Thinking?'
7. I am referring to Irigaray's essay in *An Ethics of Sexual Difference*,
   'Wonder: A Reading of Descartes' *The Passions of the Soul*', p. 73 and
   p. 77.

8. For a discussion of the 'Body without Organs' (BwO) see the sixth chapter of Deleuze and Guattari, *A Thousand Plateaus* (1991). See also Dorothea Olkowski's 'Nietzsche's Dice Throw: Tragedy, Nihilism, and the Body Without Organs' (1994). She writes: 'the Body Without Organs is the field of desire as a process of production distributed intensively, consistently, without interruption: in short, a field of becomings' (138).
9. See, in particular, John Lechte's *Julia Kristeva* (1990), especially pp. 166–7 on apocalyptic laughter. Kristeva's ground-breaking work *Powers of Horror: An Essay on Abjection* (1982) discusses the laughter of the apocalypse.

Notes to Chapter 3: Feminine Writing and Sexual Difference

1. As T. S. Eliot said of Joyce's use of myth, it was 'a way of controlling, of ordering, of giving a shape and a significance to the immense paradox of futility and anarchy which is contemporary history' ('Ulysses, Order and Myth', *Dial*, 75, New York (1923), pp. 480–3. William Butler Yeats's chilling poem 'The Second Coming' (1921) communicates the terror of a world gone mad:

> Turning and turning in the widening gyre
> The falcon cannot hear the falconer;
> Things fall apart; the centre cannot hold;
> Mere anarchy is loosed upon the world,
> The blood-dimmed tide is loosed, and everywhere
> The ceremony of innocence is drowned;
> The best lack all conviction, while the worst
> Are full of passionate intensity

2. That Joyce was influenced by Blake is obvious in his 1912 lecture on the poet-painter 'William Blake'. See *The Critical Writings of James Joyce*, ed. Ellsworth Mason and Richard Ellmann (1959).
3. Somer Brodribb's *Nothing Mat(t)ers: A Feminist Critique of Postmodernism* (1992) uses the radical feminist theologian Mary Daly to criticize male theory for colonizing the feminine and evacuating the body of political and ethical content in a perverse quest for death. Male theory, she argues, is thanotocentric, propelled by the death instinct. A more sophisticated and less paranoid critique of a contemporary mobilization of the feminine in male theory is Alice Jardine's *Gynesis: Configurations of Woman and Modernity* (1985). She argues that 'We might say that what is generally referred to as modernity is precisely the acutely interior, unabashedly incestuous exploration of these new

female spaces: the perhaps historically unprecedented exploration of the female, differently maternal body' (33–4).

4. Butler's important *Gender Trouble: Feminism and the Subversion of Identity* (1990, 10th edition) is a key text here.

5. D. H. Lawrence engages with feminism in his twin novels *The Rainbow* (1915) and *Women in Love* (1921), which explore the developing consciousness and sensual intelligence of the two Brangwen sisters. In the former, Ursula engages in a discussion of feminism with her woman lover Winifred. In the latter, Gudrun often laments the many obstacles placed in front of women and criticizes the values of patriarchal culture.

6. Laura Mulvey's ground-breaking psychoanalytic essay 'Visual Pleasure and Narrative Cinema' (1975) argues that the male gaze fixes a passive female body. Other instances of a feminist understanding of the male gaze would include the more accessible and popular *The Beauty Myth* by Naomi Wolf (1990), Susan Brownmiller's *Femininity* (1984), and Rosalind Coward's *Female Desire* (1985).

Notes to Chapter 4: The Moment of the Third Body

1. In 'The Mind of Modernism', James McFarlane comments that within the moment of high modernism 'Obsessive attempts to say "the unspeakable" made extreme demands on the mind's elasticity. Not only literature but all art of the period seemed to be intent on stretching the mind beyond the very limits of human understanding' (1986: 72). Post-structuralism is also preoccupied with an interrogation of the unspeakable. Both high modernism and post-structuralism focus on the limits of language. In Barthes's *The Pleasure of the Text* (1975) *jouissance* is described as an explosive opening into the pleasure of a multiple subject. Woolf speaks of the 'ecstasy of the privileged moment'.

2. In *Biographia Literaria* (1817) Coleridge describes the imagination as 'Esemplastic' or 'esendoplastic', capable of synthesizing opposites (1975: 91).

3. See C. M. Bowra, *The Romantic Imagination* (1950), and Mario Praz, *The Romantic Agony* (1970).

4. Cixous has written extensively and poetically about the maternal as the source of a feminine thought. See Marilyn Manners, 'Hélène Cixous Names Woman, Mother, Other: 'a feminine plural like me', in *Hélène Cixous: Critical Impressions*, ed. Lee. A. Jacobus and Regina Barreca (1999). A significant point to remember is that for Cixous the mother, as a concept, describes a space of possibility which is not

tied to biology or to stultifying myths of the maternal. In a sense she reinvents the morphology of the maternal body and also uses the maternal as a philosophical metaphor for the opening up of feminine thought.

5. Many feminist theorists of sexual difference draw upon psychoanalytic narratives to discuss the position of the female body within culture. In *Speculum of the Other Woman* (1992), Irigaray argues that phallocentrism betrays an unacknowledged debt to the maternal body which functions as the silent sub-stratum of language. The mother's body is the caryatid which supports the edifices of phallocentric thought. Kristeva also investigates this hidden debt to the maternal body. In 'Stabat Mater' (1986b), she argues for a feminist re-evaluation of maternity as the source of a new ethics, a 'herethics'. See also, other works such as Adrienne Rich's *Of Woman Born* (1976).

6. For an explication of Deleuze and Guattari's 'nomadic thought', see chapter 12 of the second volume of *Capitalism and Schizophrenia, A Thousand Plateaus* (1991). Rosi Braidotti has appropriated nomadic thought in her *Nomadic Subjects: Embodiment and Sexual Difference in Contemporary Feminist Theory* (1994): '*Nomadism*: sexual difference as providing shifting locations for multiple female feminist embodied voices' (172). Nomadic thought is galvanized by difference and moves through multiple spaces, never remaining still enough to colonize or reduce to sameness.

7. Chapter 4 of Merleau-Ponty's *The Visible and the Invisible* [1968] (1992) discusses the Chiasm, the space of the 'intertwining' of the visible and the invisible which I have called, following Cixous, the 'third body'. It is worth quoting from his rich prose: 'When Husserl spoke of the horizon of the things – of their exterior horizon, which everybody knows, and of their "interior horizon," that darkness stuffed with visibility of which their surface is but the limit – it is necessary to take the term seriously. No more than are the sky or the earth is the horizon a collection of things held together, or a class name, or a logical possibility or conception, or a system of "potentiality of consciousness": it is a new type of being, a being by porosity, pregnancy, or generality, and he before whom the horizon opens is caught up, included within it. His body and the distance participates in one same corporeity or visibility in general, which reigns between them and it, and even beyond the horizon, beneath his skin, unto the depths of being' (148–9). The limitless horizon of this 'new type of being', this 'third body' is also gestured to by Cixous at the very end of her philosophical meditation on the poetry of the in-between in *The Third Body*: 'We go out through the top, without using force, at noon and vertically. Between the opaque pillar and the luminous pillar which commemorates the dancers who

are gone, the sky stretches out eternally and lawlessly' (1999: 161). In between these two pillars, which are presence and absence, visible and invisible, experience and memory, soars the third body into the horizonless space of that which exceeds the law.

8. We can say that this position is a form of anti-representationalism, which could be argued to carry with it a Romantic nostalgia for truth. Certainly Heidegger can be read as part of a tradition of German Romanticism and his influence on Cixous can be said to carry with it this Romantic solution to alienation and the disconnectedness of modernity. But for Cixous and Woolf, connection, the very touching upon materiality, does not necessarily signify a static arrival at truth for as they point out again and again, materiality is breathing, fluid, shifting, composed of waves of becoming. The revealing is thus continuous – there is never a moment in which the truth of matter is finally and forever captured.

Notes to Chapter 5: Libidinal Education

1. Kristeva's *Powers of Horror: An Essay on Abjection* (New York: Columbia University Press, 1982) is a psychoanalytic exploration of the theological and phenomenological aspects of the profane. Kristeva argues that the literature of abjection, and she includes Joyce, Kafka, Artaud, Dostoevsky, Bataille and Celine here, 'represents the ultimate coding of our crises, of our most intimate and most serious apocalypses' (208).

2. Mary Douglas's *Purity and Danger: An Analysis of the Concepts of Pollution and Taboo* (London and New York: Routledge, 1992, [1966]) argues that dirt and pollution are surrounded by numerous taboos which attempt to contain threats to social and physical boundaries. She links taboos about physical waste to taboos about social transgression, arguing that 'danger lies in transitional states, simply because transition is neither one state nor the next, it is undefinable' (96). Her ground-breaking work paved the way for Kristeva's analysis.

3. In one of Heidegger's most famous essays, 'What Calls for Thinking?' (1951–2), Holderlin's poem 'Memory' opens up Heidegger to a rich contemplation of the question and the poetry of thinking. Holderlin also provides Heidegger with inspiration in 'The Question Concerning Technology' [1954], to name just one other example. See Heiddeger, *Basic Writings*, ed. David Farrell Krell (New York: Harper and Row, 1977). The German poet Friederich Holderlin (1770–1843) writes in a prophetic, neo-classical style.

4. F. R. Leavis's *The Great Tradition* [1948] (London: Penguin, 1977) iden-

tifies George Eliot, Henry James, Jane Austen, D. H. Lawrence and Joseph Conrad as 'distinguished by a vital capacity for experience, a kind of reverent openness before life, and a marked moral intensity' (p. 18). Harold Bloom's *The Western Canon: The Books and Schools of the Ages* (New York: Harcourt Brace, 1994) resurrects a Leavisite concept of great literature and in doing so manages to dismiss, rather bitterly, a wide range of contemporary theory and criticism. The not so latent cultural elitism of such readings should be distinguished from Cixous's philosophical and poetical exploration of Lispector. In contrast to this position, Deleuze argues that profound literature is 'minor, existing outside of and refusing common critical standards and appealing to who we might become not who we already are'. See his *Kafka: Towards a Minor Literature*, trans. Dana Polan (Minneapolis: University of Minnesota Press, 1986). Lispector would be understood as a 'minor' writer.

5. For an analysis of Romanticism see Mario Praz, *The Romantic Agony*, trans. Angus Davidson (London: Oxford University Press, 1970); Frank Kermode, *The Romantic Image* (London: Routledge and Kegan Paul, 1966); Lillian R. Furst, *European Romanticism: Self-Definition* (London: Methuen, 1980).

6. See Martin Buber, *I and Thou* (1970). The 1998 edited collection *Ecofeminist Literary Criticism*, ed. Greta Gaard and Patrick D. Murphy (Albana and Chicago: University of Illinois Press, 1998), provides some interesting readings on the genre.

7. See Foucault, *The Order of Things: An Archaeology of the Human Sciences* (London and New York: Routledge, 1991), where he writes: 'man is in the process of disappearing' (385). Representation, he argues, has reached the limits of the human. 'From within language experienced and traversed as language, in the play of its possibilities extended to their furthest point, what emerges is that man has 'come to an end', and that, by reaching the summit of all possible speech, he arrives not at the very heart of himself but at the brink of that which limits him; in that region where death prowls, where thought is extinguished, where the promise of the origin interminably recedes' (383). For Cixous the region where death prowls is not an absence but a form of abundance, an unknowable materiality, and the space of new thought. His lack would be her positivity. See also Nietzsche, *Human, All Too Human* [1878], trans. Marion Faber and Stephen Lehmann (Harmondsworth: Penguin, 1984), which is central to the critical history of the concept of the human. Explorations of post-human subjectivities are informing an increasingly large number of critical works.

8. For a neat introduction to Spinoza see Karl Jaspers' *Spinoza*, trans.

Ralph Manheim (London and New York: Harcourt Brace, 1966); also Gilles Deleuze, *Expressionism in Philosophy: Spinoza*, trans. Martin Joughin (New York: Zone Books, 1992); and Moira Gatens and Genevieve Lloyd, *Collective Imaginings: Spinoza, Past and Present* (London and New York: Routledge, 1999). For Spinoza, God is Substance which manifests through mutually receptive bodies. His concept of Substance grounds disembodied concepts of mind in the flesh, for all flesh is part of the great collective, ever transforming Substance of the imagination, or expressive creative thinking. See Spinoza, *Ethics*, trans. William Hale White (New York: Hafner, 1949).

9. In her chapter 'Arguing with the Real' in *Bodies that Matter*, Judith Butler explores the political possibilities which open up when one recognizes that identity is a spectre produced by power. The impossibility of representation opens up the possibility of democracy. 'No signifier can be radically representative, for every signifier is the site of a perpetual méconnaisance, it produces the expectation of a unity, a full and final recognition that can never be achieved. Paradoxically, the failure of such signifiers – "woman" is the one that comes to mind – fully to describe the constituency they name is precisely what constitutes these signifiers as sites of phantasmatic investment and discursive rearticulations. It is what opens the signifier to new meanings and new possibilities for political resignifications. It is this open-ended and performative function of the signifier that seems to me to be crucial to a radical democratic notion of futurity' (191). Cixous, I would argue, is in accord with Butler's position here.

10. In *Three Steps*, Cixous writes: 'I am interested in a chain of associations and signifiers composed of birds, women, and writing. This may sound funny, it may sound gratuitous, but it is not. We only have to read the chapter in Leviticus in the Bible to realize that it is deadly serious. The chapter gives Moses and humanity in general laws on eating: dictating what is edible and what is not' (111). She goes on to write, 'it is *they* who tell us what is unclean and abominable. Clarice Lispector is a writer who has dealt throughout her work, among other questions, with this notion of the abominable in our lives, in all its forms' (113). Our relation to the abominable is political because it is at the point of contact with the unclean that the moment of exclusion occurs.

11. See, for example, Julia Kristeva, 'Word, Dialogue and Novel' [1969], in *The Kristeva Reader*, ed. Toril Moi (London: Basil Blackwell, 1986), pp. 34–61, where she explores Bakhtin's carnivalesque discourse. 'The laughter of the carnival is not simply parodic; it is no more comic than tragic; it is both at once, one might say that it is *serious*. This is the only way that it can avoid becoming either the scene of the law or the scene of its parody, in order to become the scene of its *other*' (50). Subversive,

carnivalseque laughter is therefore an expression of the possibility of thinking otherwise. It is a touching upon alterity.

Notes to Chapter 6: The Question of Transgression

1. For an analysis of the so-called crisis and its impact on feminist thought, see Alice Jardine's *Gynesis* (1985), especially chapter 3, 'Crises in Legitimation: Crossing the Great Voids'. Somer Brodribb's negative appraisal of the crisis, in *Nothing Mat(t)ers: A Feminist Critique of Postmodernism* (1992), can be contrasted with Judith Butler's *Bodies that Matter* (1993).

2. Niall Lucy's *Postmodern Literary Theory: An Introduction* (London: Basil Blackwell, 1997) offers an intelligent overview of the major debates. See also Christopher Norris, *What's Wrong with Postmodernism: Critical Theory and the Ends of Philosophy* (New York and London: Harvester Wheatsheaf, 1990).

3. See Joan Cocks, *The Oppositional Imagination: Feminism, Critique and Political Theory* (London: Routledge, 1989); Peter Stallybrass and Allon White, *The Politics and Poetics of Transgression* (London: Methuen, 1989); and Marion Tapper, 'Ressentiment and Power: Some Reflections of Feminist Practices', in *Nietzsche, Feminism and Political Theory*, ed. Paul Patton (New York: Routledge, 1993), pp. 130–43.

4. As Suleiman writes in *Subversive Intent* (1990): 'The fundamental aggressiveness of what Renato Poggioli calls the "avant-garde posture" is inscribed in the military connotations of the term: the avant-garde is the most daring, most fearless group within a fighting force. The early European avant-gardes, starting with Futurism, exploited to the hilt, the antagonistic potential inherent in the concept of the avant-garde, directing the aggression both against the (bourgeois) public and against what they perceived as the dominant tradition, in art as in ethics or politics' (33).

5. For a critical reading of Carter, see *Flesh and the Mirror: Essays on the Art of Angela Carter*, ed. Lorna Sage (London: Virago, 1994).

6. Love is central to the Cixousian universe; love pervades all of her writing in the sense that we can understand her work as a movement towards loving, towards the opening up of an ethics of love. In 'La – "The" (Feminine)' [1976] in *The Hélène Cixous Reader*, ed. Susan Sellers (London and New York: Routledge, 1994), Cixous writes about a feminine writing which sings love into and through the abyss of negation. Love is understood as the source of an affirmative creative expression, as a gentle force which is capable of transforming death, negativity and loss into the production of new energies, new thinking. Here 'she' is the feminine and also the feminine writer:

Her art of living her abysses, of loving them, of making them sing, change, resounding their air with the rhythms of her earth tongues, regardless of the littoral and acoustic deliminations of their syllables.

Her art of crossing the whole of history and its little histories and the contests of the sexes, and of crossing unscathed the foul economies, in a spirited stroke,
from her inexhaustible source of humour
To vanquish the impossible each day and have always a yes in advance on chance.
To liberate love and affirm it (59)

7. For a discussion of some of the major debates about contemporary theories of subjectivity, see *Feminist Contentions: A Philosophical Exchange*, by Seyla Benhabib, Judith Butler, Drucilla Cornell, Nancy Fraser, introduction by Linda Nicholson (New York and London: Routledge, 1995).

Notes to Chapter 7: Where Do We Go From Here (Moving towards Freedom)

1. For a discussion of the debt to Wollstonecraft and the consequences of an equality versus difference binary within feminist thought, see Moira Gatens *Feminism and Philosophy: Perspectives on Difference and Equality* (Cambridge: Polity, 1993); Drucilla Cornell, *At the Heart of Freedom: Feminism, Sex, and Equality*, Princeton, NJ: Princeton University Press, 1998); Abigail Bray, 'Not Woman Enough: Irigaray's Culture of Difference', *Feminist Theory*, 2: 3 (2001), pp. 311–27.
2. Cixous writes about Mandela in 'Manna to the Mandelstams to the Mandelas', which is her attempt to offer a compassionate understanding of the physical and emotional consequences of apartheid. 'This book is an attempt at compassion. Only an attempt, for I am capable of going to the foot of the olive trees, but I will never manage to feel in my feet the nails Sergeant Visser drove into the feet of old Willie Smit, in spite of the supplications and tears. Only the supplications pass through my heart. I hear and do not feel, I weep and do not bleed. The next day my tears come no more. I have spent all I had' (Sellers, *The Hélène Cixous Reader*, 1997: 165).
3. For a significant feminist philosophical subversion of Plato's cave, see Irigaray's *Speculum of the Other Woman*, trans. Gillian C. Gill (Ithaca, NY: Cornell University Press, 1985b), especially the section 'Plato's

Hysteria' and the chapter 'The "Way Out" of the Cave'. She reads the cave as the womb.
4. See, for example, Irigaray's *Divine Women*, trans. Stephen Muecke (Sydney: Local Consumption Papers, no. 8, April 1986).

Annotated Bibliography

The texts mentioned here are some of the more important of Cixous's *oeuvre* which have been translated into English. Reading them will provide you with further insights into her work. This annotated bibliography is not exhaustive and readers are urged to explore further afield if they want to pursue the challenge of Cixous's thought.

Cixous, Hélène and Jacques Derrida, *Veils*, translated by Geoffrey Bennington, with drawings by Ernest Pignon-Ernest. Stanford, CA: Stanford University Press, 2001.

The first section of this text is an essay by Cixous called 'Savoir', which is followed by a much longer meditative essay by Derrida called 'A Silkworm of One's Own: Points of View Stitched on the Other Veil'. Cixous's essay explores metaphors and tropes about the visible and the invisible, blindness and insight, through a dense and poetic meditation on her own myopia. The text draws on the rhetoric of revelation, often using religious connotations, to focus on the delicate but passionate art of (un)seeing the other. Derrida's lengthier essay weaves threads from various secular and non-secular myths in this complex and often difficult, almost mystical meditation on sight, veils and the process of revelation. *Veils* demands careful and slow reading but offers the reader many news ways of thinking through the process of perception and knowing.

Cixous, Hélène, *The Third Body*, translated by Keith Cohen. Evanston, IL: Northwestern University Press, 1999.

Originally published in 1970 in French, this text is a lengthy prose-poem about the relationship between two lovers, which meanders into speculative meditations on familiar Cixous themes such as writing the Other, feminine thinking and writing, and the impossibility of capturing the Other. Interspersed with autobiographical musings, philosophical reflections, passionate descriptions of the tender relationship between the lovers, and descriptions of the body and subjectivity as an endlessly permeable and metamorphosing post-human entity, the book is written in the style of *écriture féminine*. *The Third Body* is a complex, surrealistic text which demands patience and careful, slow attention to detail.

Cixous, Hélène, *Stigmata: Escaping Texts.* New York and London: Routledge, 1998.

This is an excellent broad selection of most of the more provocative and important of Cixous's writing until 1998. The overarching theme is texts which escape capture by the already known, the already written and, as such, all of the essays in this collection urge the reader to speculate and think beyond the boundaries. Essays on Stendhal, Joyce, Derrida, Lispector, the Russian poet Tsvetaeva, Rembrant, Leonardo da Vinci and Picasso, explore a range of poetical and philosophical questions about loss, death, autobiography, representation, the non-human, and embodiment. A useful starting point for readers who want to dive into the complex range of Cixous's writing, the range of writing demonstrates how Cixous's thinking is versatile enough to engage with a variety of genres and issues. *Stigmata* also offers a very useful bibliography of Cixous's book-length publications from 1967 to 1998.

Cixous, Hélène, *The Hélène Cixous Reader*, edited by Susan Sellers, with a preface by Hélène Cixous and a foreword by Jacques Derrida. New York and London: Routledge, 1997.

The following selection of Cixous's work can be found in this most comprehensive of readers on Cixous: 'Neutral', 'Inside', 'First Names of No One', 'The Newly Born Woman', 'Breathes',

'La – "The" (Feminine)', 'Angst', 'To Live the Orange', '(With) Or the Art of Innocence', 'The Book of Promethea', 'Extreme Fidelity', 'The Terrible but Unfinished Story of Norodom Sihanouk, King of Cambodia', 'The Place of Crime, the Place of Forgiveness', 'Indiada or the India of their Dreams', 'First Days of the Year', 'Deluge', 'Three Steps on the Ladder of Writing'. A Foreword by Derrida explores the relationship between love and the scene of (Cixous's) writing and reading. A Preface by Cixous situates her writing in relation to the specificity of her own life and also offers some personal insights into why she writes within particular genres. An Afterword by Calle-Gruber mediates key Cixousian concerns through Calle-Gruber's sensitive intelligence of the text. A lengthy bibliography of all of Cixous's work provides the reader with plenty of references. Each one of the sections from Cixous's work also comes with a very useful introduction by Sellers which provides not only a short history of the piece but also a succinct summary. Sellers' *Reader* is one of the more important introductory books on Cixous in English.

Cixous, Hélène and Mireille Calle-Gruber, *Hélène Cixous Rootprints: Memory and Life Writing*, translated by Eric Prenowitz. London and New York: Routledge, 1997. First published in French as *Photos de Racine*, Paris: Éditions des Femmes, 1994.

The text is divided into several sections, each one of which provides intimate readings of Cixous and her life/work. The first section is a compelling exchange between Calle-Gruber and Cixous which is usefully divided by subheadings so that the reader can sift through the various philosophical topics meditated on with some direction. Many of Cixous's more recent concerns are examined here and the reader will find it an inspiring voyage into the rich complexity of her writing. The second section is a shorter essay by Derrida on Cixous and the question of sexual difference, which demonstrates the deep affinity between these two philosophers. The third section, 'Portrait of the Writing', is by Calle-Gruber and is a creative exposition and meditation on Cixous's poetics. Calle-Gruber emerges as a significant theorist in her own right in this book and readers are encouraged to pursue her work on Cixous and in general. The following section, 'Albums and Legends', is Cixous at her auto-biographical best, revealing the ways her personal history, and her cultural heritage, suffuse and situate her major preoccupa-tions. This section includes many photos of her and her family along with commentary by Cixous herself. There follows a short chronology of Cixous's life up until 1998 by Calle-Gruber, which usefully plots the main events in Cixous's life and work. An extensive bibliography of Cixous's work then provides the reader with a comprehensive list of the international and intel-lectual reach of Cixous's impressive contributions. The last section is an exceptional essay by Eric Prenowitz which explores the concepts of difference, love, the undecidable and subjectiv-ity.

Cixous, Hélène, *Three Steps on the Ladder of Writing*, translated by Sarah Cornell and Susan Sellers. New York: Columbia University Press, 1993.

This is one of the more important of Cixous's writings and should be read by anyone who is interested in understanding her thinking. Poetic, philosophical, erudite, passionate, the text guides the reader through various stages of quasi-mystical initi-ation into the secrets of writing. Divided into three section ('The School of the Dead', 'The School of Dreams', 'The School of Roots'), the texts focuses on Cixous's theorization of the writing process as lessons in thinking. The first section explores the inti-mate connection between death and writing, arguing that a birth into and through writing is also a process of mourning. The second section explores the role of dreams and the unconscious as essential inspiration for writing. The last section explores the importance of thinking down into the profane, the forbidden, with humility and passion in order for writing to achieve a wise depth and a profound celebration of *jouissance*. Cixous draws heavily on Lispector, Dostoevsky, Tsvetaeva, Genet, and espe-cially Kafka throughout the text. Each section or 'school' is divided into several sections, representing various stages of the lesson. This is a necessary starting point for anyone interested in understanding Cixous's theorization of writing.

Cixous, Hélène, *The Book of Promethea*, translated by Betsy Wing. Lincoln, NE: University of Nebraska Press, 1991.

Here Cixous performs a radical subversion of one of the central myths of Western culture, that of Prometheus, the culture builder and hero. The original archetype for countless myths of male creativity, romantic anti-heroes, and self-destructive male passion, here Prometheus is finally unbound and recomposed as a myth of feminine *jouissance*. The text is a poetic search for feminine positivity, creativity, passion, and a language which loves without appropriating and possessing. A moving meditation on the generative, life-affirming qualities of the feminine which arose after Cixous's transformative encounter with Ariane Mnouchkine, the director of the experimental Théâtre du Soleil. The text brings down the epic dimensions of the myth by grounding passion and creativity in the quotidian, a minimalist vision, and a humble openness to the Other.

Cixous, Hélène, *Readings: The Poetics of Blanchot, Joyce, Kafka, Kleist, Lispector, and Tsvetayeva*, translated by Verena Andermatt Conley. Hemel Hempstead: Harvester Wheatsheaf, 1991.

This is a useful guide to a range of Cixous's writings on the above writers. Central to all the readings is an investigation of feminine textuality. The text provides readers with a way to understand Cixous's approach to literary criticism, at once poetic and rigorously philosophical, which opens up the texts to creative rewritings.

Cixous, Hélène, *'Coming to Writing' and Other Essays*, edited by Deborah Jenson, with an introductory essay by Susan Rubin Suleiman, translated by Sarah Cornell, Deborah Jenson, Ann Liddle and Susan Sellers. Cambridge, MA and London: Harvard University Press, 1991.

This is a selection of six essays by Cixous originally published in French between 1979 and 1989 and reproduced here as 'Coming to Writing', 'Clarice Lispector: the Approach', 'Tancredi

Continues', 'The Last Painting, or the Portrait of God', 'By the Light of an Apple', and 'The Author in Truth'. Lispector features quite strongly in the selection and overall the reader is provided with a comprehensive overview of Cixous's theorization of feminine writing and thinking. The final essay, by Deborah Jenson, provides an engaging and inspirational guide to reading Cixous. The opening essay, by Susan Rubin Suleiman, 'Writing Past the Wall, or The Passion According to H.C.', introduces the reader to Cixous and the major themes of the collected essays. This is an indispensable guide to her thinking and to her major essays.

Cixous, Hélène and Catherine Clement, *The Newly Born Woman*, translated by Betsy Wing, with an introduction by Sandra M. Gilbert. Minneapolis, MN: University of Minnesota Press, 1991. Originally published as *La Jeune Née*, Paris: Union Générale d'Éditions, 1975.

This is a key text in the development of French feminist thought and one of the more important feminist classics of our time. A passionate demolition of the many sexual and textual repressions of the feminine and an exploration of the untapped resources of women's power, this text introduces the concept of *écriture féminine* as a way of escaping phallocentric capture. This first section of this book, by the Marxist psychoanalyst and structuralist thinker Catherine Clement, interrogates a range of psychoanalytic, cultural, literary and mythic representations of women's madness, energetically and intelligently breaking apart the self-serving posture of phallocentric rationality which governs the economies of women's 'hysteria'. Clement's 'The Guilty One' and 'Seduction and Guilt' are followed by Cixous's lengthy and ground-breaking essay 'Sorties: Out and Out: Attacks/Ways Out/Forays'. Here Cixous describes the potentials of *écriture féminine*, performing a passionate deconstruction of various representations of feminine lack and madness, while opening up a range of sexual/textual spaces through which women and the feminine can subvert and recompose the libidinal body politic. The last section, 'Exchanges', is a frank discussion by both thinkers about the political and philosophical differences between their positions, and offers a useful way of identifying some of the tensions between the political and poetico-philosophical aims of feminist thinking. A glossary at the end provides readers with a comprehensive yet accessible description of some of the key concepts used in the book.

Cixous, Hélène, *Reading with Clarice Lispector*, edited, translated and introduced by Verena Andermatt Conley. Minneapolis, MN: University of Minnesota Press; London: Harvester Wheatsheaf, 1990.

This collection is from a series of lectures delivered in Paris between 1980 and 1985 on Lispector. The lectures include '"Sunday, before falling asleep": A Primal Scene'; '*Auga viva*: How to Follow a Trinket of Water'; '*The Apple in the Dark*: The Temptation of Understanding'; ' "The Egg and the Chicken": Love is Not Having'; ' "Felicidade clandestina": The Promise of Having What One Will Have'; '*The Hour of the Star*: How Does One Desire Wealth or Poverty?'. The issues covered are reading, writing, difference, the gift, love, passion, the feminine libidinal economy, exchange, and the mysteries of embodiment. The selection calls attention to the profound impact of Lipsector's writing on Cixous's philosophy and poetics and all of the essays here are deep investigations into Lipsectorian thought, which Cixous connects to and develops with a range of other writers and philosophers. The brilliant introduction by Verena Andermatt Conley situates the importance of the collection both to Cixous's work in general but also in relation to the history of ideas. This is a rare, passionate and deeply intelligent collection which provides unsurpassed insights into Cixous's major ideas.

Cixous, Hélène, *The Exile of James Joyce*, translated by Sally A. J. Purcell. London: John Calder, 1979.

This is Cixous's doctoral dissertation on Joyce and while it is very different from her more recent work, it is significant because it provides the reader with a background on the development of her thinking. A massive 765 pages long, the thesis is formidable, exhaustive and at times exhausting to read. The theme of exile, creativity, the limits of language, and subversion are all explored in Joyce's work.

References

Adorno, Theodor and Max Horkheimer (1979), *Dialectic of Enlightenment*, trans. John Cumming (London: Verso).

Alpert, Michael (1969), 'Introduction', in *Two Spanish Picaresque Novels: Lazarillo de Tormes, Anon, and The Swindler, Francisco de Quevedo* (London: Penguin), pp. 7–16.

Bachelard, Gaston (1971), *The Poetics of Reverie: Childhood, Language, and Cosmos*, trans. Daniel Russell (Boston, MA: Beacon Press).

Banting, Pamela (1992), 'The Body as Pictogram: Rethinking Hélène Cixous's *Écriture Féminine*', *Textual Practice*, 6:2 (1992): 225–46.

Barthes, Roland (1975), *The Pleasure of the Text*, trans. Richard Miller (London: Jonathan Cape).

Barthes, Roland (1976), *Sollers écrivain* (Paris: Éditions du Seuil).

Bataille, Georges (1979), *The Story of the Eye, By Lord Auch*, trans. Joachim Neurgroschal (Harmondsworth: Penguin).

Bataille, Georges (1991a), 'The Deviations of Nature', in *Visions of Excess: Selected Writings, 1927–1939*, ed. and intro. Allan Stoekl, trans. Allan Stoekl, Carl R. Lovitt and Donald M. Leslie, Jr (Minneapolis, MN: University of Minnesota Press), pp. 53–6.

Bataille, Georges (1991b), 'The Critique of the Foundations of the Hegelian Dialectic', *Visions of Excess: Selected Writings, 1927–1939*, ed. and intro. Allan Stoekl, trans. Allan Stoekl, Carl R. Lovitt and Donald M. Leslie, Jr (Minneapolis, MN: University of Minnesota Press), pp. 105–15.

Benhabib, Seyla, Judith Butler, Drucilla Cornell and Nancy Fraser (1995), *Feminist Contentions: A Philosophical Exchange* (New York and London: Routledge).

Bergson, Henri (1911), *Matter and Memory*, trans. Nancy Margaret Paul and W. Scott Palmer (London: George Allen and Unwin).

Bloom, Harold (1994), *The Western Canon: The Books and Schools of the Ages* (New York: Harcourt Brace).

Boone, Joseph Allen (1998), *Libidinal Currents: Sexuality and the Shaping of Modernism* (Chicago, IL, and London: University of Chicago Press).

Boundas, Constantin V. and Dorothea Olkowski (eds) (1994), *Gilles Deleuze and the Theatre of Philosophy* (New York and London: Routledge).

Bowra, C. M. (1950), *The Romantic Imagination* (London: Oxford University Press).

Braidotti, Rosi (1950), *Nomadic Subjects: Embodiment and Sexual Difference in Contemporary Feminist Theory* (New York: Columbia University Press).

Braidotti, Rosi (2002), *Metamorphoses: Towards a Materialist Theory of Becoming* (Cambridge: Polity Press).

Bray, Abigail (2001), 'Not Woman Enough: Irigaray's Culture of Difference', *Feminist Theory*, 2: 3 (2001): 282–327.

Brodribb, Somer (1992), *Nothing Mat(t)ers: A Feminist Critique of Postmodernism* (Melbourne: Spinifex Press).

Brown, Norman O. (1985), *Life against Death: The Psychoanalytic Meaning of History*, 2nd edn (Hanover: Wesleyan University Press).

Brownmiller, Susan (1984), *Femininity* (London: Paladin Books).

Brunsdon, Charlotte (1999), 'Pedagogies of the Feminine: Feminist Teaching and Women's Genres', in *Feminism and Cultural Studies*, ed. Morag Shiach (Oxford: Oxford University Press), pp. 343–67.

Buber, Martin (1970), *I and Thou*, trans. Walter Kofman (New York: Scribus).

Bullfinch, Thomas (1985), *The Golden Age of Myth and Legend* (London: Bracken Books).

Butler, Judith (1990), *Gender Trouble: Feminism and the Subversion of Identity* (New York: Routledge).

Butler, Judith (1993), *Bodies that Matter: On the Discursive Limits of 'Sex"* (New York: Routledge).

Butler, Judith (1995), 'Contingent Foundations', in *Feminist Contentions: A Philosophical Exchange*, with Seyla Benhabib, Judith Butler, Drucilla Cornell and Nancy Fraser (New York and London: Routledge), 35–58.

Califia, P. (1993), 'Power Exchange' in T. Woodward (ed.), *The Best of Skin Two* (New York: Masquerade Books).

Calle-Gruber, Mireille (1997), 'Afterword', in *The Hélène Cixous Reader*, ed. Susan Sellers (London and New York: Routledge), pp. 207–20.

Calle-Gruber, Mireille (1999), 'Hélène Cixous: Music Forever, or Short Treatise on a Poetics for a Story to be Sung' in *Hélène Cixous: Critical Impressions*, ed. Lee A. Jacobus and Regina Barreca (London: Routledge, 1999), pp. 52–88.

Caputo, John D. (1993), *Against Ethics: Contributions to a Poetics of Obligation with Constant Reference to Deconstruction* (Indianapolis, IN: Indiana University Press).

Carter, Angela (1972), *The War of Dreams* (New York and London: Harcourt Brace Jovanovich).

Carter, Angela (1992), *The Sadeian Woman: An Exercise in Cultural History* (London: Virago).

222   References

Carter, Angela (1993), 'The Alchemy of the Word', in *Expletives Deleted: Selected Writings* (London: Vintage), pp. 67–74.

Chanter, Tina (1995), *Ethics of Eros: Irigaray's Rewriting of the Philosophers* (New York and London: Routledge).

Cheah, P. and Elizabeth Grosz (1998), 'The Future of Sexual Difference: an Interview with Judith Butler and Drucilla Cornell', *Diacritics*, 28:1 (1998): 19–42.

Cixous, Hélène (1976), 'The Exile of James Joyce', PhD dissertation, translated from the French by Sally A. J. Purcell (London: John Calder).

Cixous, Hélène (1980a), 'The Laugh of the Medusa', trans. Keith Cohen and Paula Cohen, in *New French Feminisms: An Anthology*, ed. Elaine Marks and Isabelle de Courtivron (Amherst, MA: University of Massachusetts Press; New York: Schoken Books), pp. 245–64.

Cixous, Hélène (1980b), *Illa* (Paris: Des Femmes).

Cixous, Hélène (1981), 'Castration or Decapitation?', trans. Anette Kuhn, *Signs*, 7: 1 (1981), 41–55.

Cixous, Hélène (1986), 'Sorties: Out and Out: Attacks/Ways Out/Forays', in Hélène Cixous and Catherine Clement (1991), *The Newly Born Woman*, trans. Betsy Wing (Minneapolis, MN: University of Minnesota Press), pp. 63–129.

Cixous, Hélène (1988), 'Conversations' with Susan Sellers, in *Writing Differences: Readings from the Seminar of Hélène Cixous*, ed. Susan Sellers (Milton Keynes: Open University Press; New York: St Martin's Press), pp. 141–54.

Cixous, Hélène (1990), *Reading with Clarice Lispector (Seminar 1980–1985)*, ed. and trans. Verena Conley (London: Harvester Wheatsheaf Press; Minneapolis, MN: Minnesota University Press).

Cixous, Hélène (1991), *'Coming to Writing' and Other Essays*, ed. Deborah Jenson and intro. Susan Rubin Suleiman, trans. Sarah Cornell, Deborah Jenson, Ann Liddle and Susan Sellers (Cambridge, MA and London: Harvard University Press).

Cixous, Hélène (1991a), 'Coming to Writing', in *'Coming to Writing' and Other Essays*, ed. Deborah Jenson and intro. Susan Rubin Suleiman, trans. Sarah Cornell, Deborah Jenson, Ann Liddle and Susan Sellers (Cambridge, MA and London: Harvard University Press), pp. 1–59.

Cixous, Hélène (1991b), 'Clarice Lispector: the Approach', in *'Coming to Writing' and Other Essays*, ed. Deborah Jenson and intro. Susan Rubin Suleiman, trans. Sarah Cornell, Deborah Jenson, Ann Liddle and Susan Sellers (Cambridge, MA and London: Harvard University Press), pp. 59–77.

Cixous, Hélène (1991c), 'Tancredi Continues', in *'Coming to Writing' and Other Essays*, ed. Deborah Jenson and intro. Susan Rubin Suleiman, trans. Sarah Cornell, Deborah Jenson, Ann Liddle and Susan Sellers (Cambridge, MA and London: Harvard University Press), pp. 78–103.

Cixous, Hélène (1991d), 'The Last Painting, or the Portrait of God', in *'Coming to Writing' and Other Essays*, ed. Deborah Jenson and intro. Susan Rubin Suleiman, trans. Sarah Cornell, Deborah Jenson, Ann Liddle and Susan Sellers (Cambridge MA and London: Harvard University Press), pp. 104–31.

Cixous, Hélène (1991e), 'By the Light of an Apple', in *'Coming to Writing' and Other Essays*, ed. Deborah Jenson and intro. Susan Rubin Suleiman, trans. Sarah Cornell, Deborah Jenson, Ann Liddle and Susan Sellers (Cambridge, MA and London: Harvard University Press), pp. 132–5.

Cixous, Hélène (1991f), 'The Author in Truth', in *'Coming to Writing' and Other Essays*, ed. Deborah Jenson and intro. by Susan Rubin Suleiman, trans. Sarah Cornell, Deborah Jenson, Ann Liddle and Susan Sellers (Cambridge, MA and London: Harvard University Press), pp. 136–82.

Cixous, Hélène (1991g), *The Book of Promethea*, trans. Betsy Wing (Lincoln, NE: University of Nebraska Press).

Cixous, Hélène (1993a), *Beethoven à jamais, ou, L'existence de Dieu* (Paris: Des Femmes, Antoinette Fouque).

Cixous, Hélène (1993b), *Three Steps on the Ladder of Writing*, trans. Sarah Cornell and Susan Sellers (New York: Columbia University Press).

Cixous, Hélène (1998a), 'What is it O'clock? or The Door (We Never Enter)', trans. Catherine A. F. MacGillivray, in *Stigmata: Escaping Texts* (London and New York: Routledge), pp. 57–83.

Cixous, Hélène (1998b), 'Unmasked!', trans. Keith Cohen, in *Stigmata: Escaping Texts* (London and New York: Routledge), pp. 131–8.

Cixous, Hélène (1998c), 'Writing Blind: Conversation with a Donkey', trans. Eric Prenowitz, in *Stigmata: Escaping Texts* (London and New York: Routledge), pp. 139–52.

Cixous, Hélène (1999), *The Third Body*, trans. Keith Cohen (Evanston, IL: Northwestern University Press).

Cixous, Hélène and Catherine Clement (1991), *The Newly Born Woman*, trans. Betsy Wing, intro. Sandra M. Gilbert (Minneapolis, MN: University of Minnesota Press).

Cixous, Hélène and Mireille Calle-Gruber (1997), *Hélène Cixous Rootprints: Memory and Life Writing*, trans. Eric Prenowitz (London and New York: Routledge).

Cocks, Joan (1989), *The Oppositional Imagination: Feminism, Critique and Political Theory* (London: Routledge).

Cohn, Dorrit (1978), *Transparent Minds: Narrative Modes for Representing Consciousness in Fiction* (Princeton, NJ: Princeton University Press).

Colebrook, Claire (1999), 'A Grammar of Becoming: Strategy, Subjectivism, and Style', in *Becomings: Explorations in Time, Memory, and Futures*, ed. Elizabeth Grosz (Ithaca, NY and London: Cornell University Press).

Coleridge, Samuel Taylor (1975), *Biographia Literaria: Or, Biographical Sketches of My Literary Life and Opinions*, ed. George Watson (London: J. M. Dent).

Conley, Verena Andermatt (1984), 'An Exchange with Hélène Cixous', in *Hélène Cixous: Writing the Feminine* (Lincoln, NE and London: University of Nebraska Press), pp. 129–61.

Cornell, Drucilla (1998), *At the Heart of Freedom: Feminism, Sex and Equality* (Princeton, NJ: Princeton University Press).

Coward, Rosalind (1985), *Female Desire: Women's Sexuality Today* (London: Granada).

De Beauvoir, Simone (1962) *The Second Sex*, trans. H. M. Parshley (London: Four Square).

De Lauretis, Teresa (1984), *Alice Doesn't: Feminism, Semiotics, Cinema* (Bloomington, IN: Indiana University Press).

De Quevedo, Francisco (1969), *The Swindler, Two Spanish Picaresque Novels*, trans. Michael Alpert (Harmondsworth: Penguin).

Deleuze, Gilles (1986), *Kafka: Toward a Minor Literature*, trans. Dana Polan (Minneapolis, MN: University of Minnesota Press).

Deleuze, Gilles (1988), *Bergsonism*, trans. Hugh Tomlinson and Barbara Habberiam (New York: Zone Books).

Deleuze, Gilles (1992), *Expressionism in Philosophy: Spinoza*, trans. Martin Joughin (New York: Zone Books).

Deleuze, Gilles and Félix Guattari (1991), *A Thousand Plateaus*, trans. and foreword by Brian Massumi (Minneapolis, MN: University of Minnesota Press). This forms the second of the two parts of *Capitalism and Schizophrenia*.

Deleuze, Gilles and Félix Guattari (1992), *Anti-Oedipus*, trans. Robert Hurley, Mark Seem and Helen R. Lane (Minneapolis, MN: University of Minnesota Press). This forms the first of the two parts of *Capitalism and Schizophrenia*.

Deleuze, Gilles and Félix Guattari (1994), *What is Philosophy?*, trans. Hugh Tomlinson and Grahamn Burchill (London and New York: Verso).

Derrida, Jacques (1979), *Of Grammatology*, trans. G. C. Spivak (Baltimore, MD: Johns Hopkins University Press).

Derrida, Jacques (1985), 'On College and Philosophy', *ICA Documents 4 and 5*, ed. Lisa Appignanesi (London: ICA).

Derrida, Jacques (1988), *Limited Inc.*, ed. Gerald Graff (Evanston, IL: Northwestern University Press).

Derrida, Jacques (1992), 'The Force of Law: The "Mystical Foundations of Authority"', trans. M. Quaintance, in *Deconstruction and the Possibility of Justice*, ed. D. G. Carlson, D. Cornell and M. Rosenfeld (New York and London: Routledge), pp. 3–67.

Derrida, Jacques (1997), 'Foreword', in *The Hélène Cixous Reader*, ed.

Susan Sellers (London and New York: Routledge), pp. vi–xiii. [Excerpts from 'Fourmis', trans. Eric Prenowitz, in *Lectures de la différence sexuelle*, ed. Mara Negron (Paris: Des Femmes, Antoinette Fouque).]

Devlin, Kimberley J. (1994), 'Pretending in "Penelope": Masquerade, Mimicry, and Molly Bloom', in Richard Pearce Madison (ed.), *Molly Blooms: A Polyogue on 'Penelope' and Cultural Studies* (Madison: University of Wisconsin Press).

Donavon, Josephine (1998), 'Ecofeminist Literary Criticism: Reading the Orange', in *Ecofeminist Literary Criticism: Theory, Interpretation, Pedagogy*, ed. Greta Gaard and Patrick D. Murphy (Chicago, IL: University of Illinois Press), pp. 74–96.

Douglas, Mary (1992), *Purity and Danger: An Analysis of the Concepts of Pollution and Taboo* (London: Routledge).

Ebert, Teresa (1996), *Ludic Feminism and After: Postmodernism, Desire, and Labour in Late Capitalism* (Ann Arbor, MI: University of Michigan Press).

Editorial Collective (1990), 'Variations on Common Themes', *Questions Féministes*, trans. Yvonne Rochette-Ozzello, in *New French Feminisms: An Anthology*, ed. and intro. Elaine Marks and Isabelle de Courtivron (New York: Schoken Books; Amherst, MA: University of Massachusetts Press), pp. 212–30.

Eliot, T. S. (1932), 'Ulysses, Order and Myth', *Dial*, 75 (New York): 480–3.

Ellesworth, Mason and Richard Ellmann (1959), *The Critical Writings of James Joyce* (New York: Viking Press).

Felski, Rita (1989), *Beyond Feminist Aesthetics: Feminist Literature and Social Change* (London: Hutchinson Radius).

Felski, Rita (1995), *The Gender of Modernity* (Cambridge, MA: Harvard University Press).

Foucault, Michel (1991a), *The Order of Things: An Archaeology of the Human Sciences* (London: Routledge).

Foucault, Michel (1991b), 'What is Enlightenment?', trans. Catherine Porter, in *The Foucault Reader*, ed. Paul Rabinow (Harmondsworth: Penguin), pp. 32–50.

Friedan, Betty (1972), *The Feminine Mystique* (Harmondsworth: Penguin).

Furst, Lillian R. (1980), *European Romanticism: Self-Definition* (London: Methuen).

Gallop, Jane (1985), *Reading Lacan* (Ithaca, NY: Cornell University Press).

Gatens, Moira (1993), *Feminism and Philosophy: Perspectives on Difference and Equality* (Cambridge: Polity Press).

Gatens, Moira and Genevieve Lloyd (1999), *Collective Imaginings: Spinoza, Past and Present* (London and New York: Routledge).

Gilbert, Stuart (1952), *James Joyce's 'Ulysses': A Study* (London: Faber and Faber).

Gilman, Charlotte Perkins (1992), 'An Obstacle', in *The Captive Imagination: A Casebook on The Yellow Wallpaper*, ed. Catherine Golden (New York: Feminist Press).

Grosz, Elizabeth (1989), *Sexual Subversions: Three French Feminists* (Sydney: Allen and Unwin).

Grosz, Elizabeth (1994), *Volatile Bodies: Towards a Corporeal Feminism* (St Leonards, Sydney: Allen and Unwin).

Grosz, Elizabeth (1990), *Jacques Lacan: A Feminist Introduction* (Sydney: Allen and Unwin).

Grosz, Elizabeth (1999), ed. *Becoming: Explorations in Time, Memory, and Futures* (Ithaca, NY: Cornell University Press).

Heidegger, Martin (1977a), 'Letter on Humanism', in *Basic Writings*, ed. David Krell (New York: Harper and Row), pp. 189–242.

Heidegger, Martin (1977b), 'Building Dwelling Thinking', in *Basic Writings*, ed. David Krell (New York: Harper and Row), pp. 319–39.

Heidegger, Martin (1977c), 'What Calls for Thinking?', in *Basic Writings*, ed. David Krell (New York: Harper and Row), pp. 341–67.

Heidegger, Martin (1977d), 'The End of Philosophy and the Task of Thinking', in *Basic Writings*, ed. David Krell (New York: Harper and Row), pp. 373–92.

Heidegger, Martin (1991), *Nietzsche*, vol. 1: *The Will to Power as Art* and vol. II: *The Eternal Recurrence of the Same*, trans. David Farrell Krell (New York: Harper and Row).

Huyssen, Andreas (1986), *After the Great Divide: Modernism, Mass Culture, Postmodernism* (Bloomington, IN: Indiana University Press).

Irigaray, Luce (1985), *This Sex which is Not One*, trans. Gillian C. Gill (Ithaca, NY: Cornell University Press).

Irigaray, Luce (1986), 'Divine Women'. trans. Stephen Muecke (Sydney, Local Consumption Publications, Occasional Paper 8, April 1986).

Irigaray, Luce (1991), *The Marine Lover of Friedrich Nietzsche*, trans. Gillian C. Gill (New York: Columbia University Press).

Irigaray, Luce (1992), *Speculum of the Other Woman*, trans. Gillian C. Gill (Ithaca, NY: Cornell University Press).

Irigaray, Luce (1993a), 'Wonder: A Reading of Descartes' *The Passions of the Soul*', in *An Ethics of Sexual Difference*, trans. Carolyn Burke and Gillian C. Gill (Ithaca, NY: Cornell University Press), pp. 72–82.

Irigaray, Luce (1993b), 'The Fecundity of the Caress: a Reading of Levinas, Totality and Infinity, "Phenomenology of Eros"', in *An Ethics of Sexual Difference*, trans. Carolyn Burke and Gillian C. Gill (Ithaca, NY: Cornell University Press), pp. 185–217.

Irigaray, Luce (1993c), *Je, Tu, Nous: Towards a Culture of Difference*, trans. Alison Martin (New York and London: Routledge).

Jacobus, Lee A. and Regine Barreca (eds) (1999), *Hélène Cixous: Critical Impressions* (London: Routledge).

Jacobus, Mary (1986), *Reading Woman: Essays in Feminist Criticism* (London: Methuen).

James, William (1890), *Principles of Psychology*, vol. 1 (New York: Henry Holt).

Jameson, Fredric (1979), *Fables of Aggression: Wyndham Lewis, the Modernist as Fascist* (Berkley, CA, Los Angeles, London: University of California Press).

Jardine, Alice (1985), *Gynesis: Configurations of Woman and Modernity* (Ithaca, NY: Cornell University Press).

Jaspers, Karl (1966), *Spinoza*, ed. Hannah Arendt, trans. Ralph Manheim (New York and London: Harcourt Brace).

Jenson, Deborah (1991), 'Coming to Reading Hélène Cixous', in *'Coming to Writing' and Other Essays*, ed. Deborah Jenson and intro. Susan Rubin Suleiman, trans. Sarah Cornell, Deborah Jenson, Ann Liddle and Susan Sellers (Cambridge, MA: Harvard University Press), pp. 183–96.

Johnson, Jeri (1993), 'Introduction', in James Joyce, *Ulysses* (Oxford: Oxford University Press), pp. ix–xxxvii.

Johnson, Pauline (1994), *Feminism as Radical Humanism* (Sydney: Allen & Unwin).

Jones, Ann Rosalind (1981), 'Writing the Body: Towards an Understanding of *écriture féminine*', *Feminist Studies*, 7:2 (Summer 1981), 247–63.

Joyce, James (1993), *Ulysses*, ed. and intro. Jeri Johnson (Oxford: Oxford University Press).

Kant, Immanuel (1965), *Critique of Pure Reason*, trans. Norman Kemp Smith (New York: St Martin's Press).

Kermode, Frank (1966), *The Romantic Image* (London: Routledge and Kegan Paul).

Krell, David Farrell (1996), *Infectious Nietzsche* (Indianapolis, NY: Indiana University Press).

Kristeva, Julia (1980), *Desire in Language*, trans. Leon Roudiez (New York: Columbia University Press).

Kristeva, Julia (1982), *Powers of Horror: An Essay on Abjection*, trans. Leon S. Roudiez (New York: Columbia University Press).

Kristeva, Julia (1984), *The Revolution in Poetic Language*, trans. Margaret Waller (New York: Columbia University Press).

Kristeva, Julia (1986a), 'Word, Dialogue and Novel', in *The Kristeva Reader*, ed. Toril Moi (New York: Columbia University Press), 34–61.

Kristeva, Julia (1986b), 'Stabat Mater', trans. Leon S. Roudiez, in *The Kristeva Reader*, ed. Toril Moi (New York: Columbia University Press), pp. 160–86.

Kristeva, Julia (1986c), 'A New Type of Intellectual: the Dissident', trans. Sean Hand, in *The Kristeva Reader*, ed. Toril Moi (New York: Columbia University Press), pp. 292–300.

Lacan, Jacques (1982), 'God and the Jouissance of Woman', in *Feminine Sexuality: Jacques Lacan and the école freudienne*, ed. Juliet Mitchell and Jacqueline Rose, trans. Jacqueline Rose (London: Macmillan), pp. 137–48.

Lacan, Jacques (1975), *Encore: Les séminaires*, xx, 1972–3 (Paris: Seuil).

Lawrence, D. H. [1915] (1978), *The Rainbow* (Harmondsworth: Penguin).

Lawrence, D. H. [1921] (1973), *Women in Love* (Harmondsworth: Penguin).

Leavis, F. R. (1977), *The Great Tradition* (Harmondsworth: Penguin).

Lechte, John (1990), *Julia Kristeva* (New York and London: Routledge).

Levi, Albert William (1967), 'Existentialism and the Alienation of Man', in *Phenomenology and Existentialism*, ed. Edward N. Lee and Maurice Mandelbaum (Baltimore, MD: Johns Hopkins University Press), pp. 243–66.

Lispector, Clarice (1989), *The Stream of Life*, trans. Elizabeth Lowe and Earl Fitz (Minneapolis, MN: University of Minnesota Press).

Lispector, Clarice (2000), *The Passion According to G.H.*, trans. Ronald W. Sousa (Minneapolis, MN: Minnesota Press).

Lucy, Niall (1995), *Debating Derrida* (Melbourne: Melbourne University Press).

Lucy, Niall (1997), *Postmodern Literary Theory: An Introduction* (Oxford: Blackwell).

Lyotard, Jean-François (1993), *Libidinal Economy*, trans Iain Hamilton Grant (Indianapolis, IN: Indiana University Press).

Manners, Marilyn (1999), 'Hélène Cixous Names Woman, Mother, Other: "a feminine plural like me", in *Hélène Cixous: Critical Impressions*, ed. Lee A. Jacobus and Regina Barreca (1999).

Marcuse, Herbert (1972), *Eros and Civilization: A Philosophical Inquiry into Freud* (London: Sphere).

McCollum, Pamela (1985), 'New Feminist Readings: Woman as Écriture or Woman as Other?' *Canadian Journal of Political and Social Theory*, 9:1/2, pp. 127–32.

McFarlane, James (1986), 'The Mind of Modernism', in *Modernism 1890–1930*, ed. Malcolm Bradbury and James McFarlane (Harmondsworth: Penguin), pp. 71–93.

McGann, Jerome (1983), *The Romantic Ideology: A Critical Investigation* (Chicago, IL: University of Chicago Press).

Mason, Ellsworth and Richard Ellmann (eds) (1959), *The Critical Writings of James Joyce* (New York: Viking Press).

Massumi, Brian (1992), *A User's Guide to Capitalism and Schizophrenia: Deviations from Deleuze and Guattari* (Cambridge, MA: Massachusetts Institute of Technology Press).

Merleau-Ponty, Maurice (1992), *The Visible and the Invisible*, trans. Alphonso Lingis (Evanston, IL: Northwestern University Press).

Moi, Toril (1985), *Sexual/Textual Politics: Feminist Literary Theory* (London: Methuen).

Mulvey, Laura (1975), 'Visual Pleasure and Narrative Cinema', *Screen*, 16:3 (Autumn).

Nadeau, Maurice (1973), *The History of Surrealism*, trans. Richard Howard (Harmondsworth: Penguin).

Nietzsche, Friedrich (1969), *Thus Spake Zarathustra*, trans. R. J. Hollingdale (Harmondsworth: London).

Nietzsche, Friedrich (1973), *Beyond Good and Evil: Prelude to a Philosophy of the Future*, trans. R. J. Hollingdale (Harmondsworth: Penguin).

Nietzsche, Friedrich (1984), *Human, All Too Human*, trans. Marion Faber and Stephen Lehmann (Harmondsworth: Penguin).

Norris, Christopher (1990), *What's Wrong with Postmodernism: Critical Theory and the End of Philosophy* (New York and London: Harvester Wheatsheaf).

Nye, Andrea (1988), *Feminist Theory and the Philosophies of Man* (London: Routledge).

O'Brien, Darcy (1968), *The Conscience of James Joyce* (Princeton, NJ: Princeton University Press).

Olkowski, Dorothea (1994), 'Nietzsche's Dice Throw: Tragedy, Nihilism, and the Body without Organs', in *Gilles Deleuze and the Theatre of Philosophy*, ed. Constantin V. Boundas and Dorothea Olkowski (New York and London: Routledge), pp. 119–40.

Paturier, François (1968), *Lettre Ouverte aux Hommes* (Paris: Albin Michel).

Plant, Sadie (2000), 'Coming Across the Future', in *The Cybercultures Reader*, ed. David Bell and Barbara M. Kennedy (London and New York: Routledge), pp. 460–7.

Praz, Mario (1970), *The Romantic Agony*, trans. Angus Davidson (London: Oxford University Press).

Prenowitz, Eric (1997), 'Aftermaths', in Hélène Cixous and Mireille Calle-Gruber, *Hélène Cixous Rootprints: Memory and Life Writing*, trans. Eric Prenowitz (London and New York: Routledge), pp. 243–54.

Proust, Marcel (1970), *Remembrance of Things Past: Swann's Way*, trans. C. K. Scott Moncrieff (New York: Random House).

Reich, Wilheim (1970), *The Mass Psychology of Fascism*, trans. Vincent R. Carfagno (London: Souvenir Press).

Rich, Adrienne (1976), *Of Woman Born: Motherhood as Experience and Institution* (New York: W. W. Norton).

Rimbaud, Arthur (1976), *Arthur Rimbaud: Complete Works*, trans. Paul Schmidt (New York: Harper and Row).

Robbins, Ruth (2000), *Literary Feminisms* (Basingstoke: Palgrave Macmillan).

Rousseau, J. J. [1762] (1992), *Emile*, trans. Barbara Foxley (London: J. M. Dent).

Sage, Lorna (ed.) (1994), *Flesh and the Mirror: Essays on the Art of Angela Carter* (London: Virago).

Sartre, Jean-Paul (1975), *Nausea*, trans. Robert Baldick (Harmondsworth: Penguin).

Scott, Bonnie Kime (1984), *Joyce and Feminism* (Bloomington, IN: Indiana University Press).

Sellers, Susan (1996), *Hélène Cixous: Authorship, Autobiography and Love* (Cambridge: Polity Press).

Sellers, Susan (ed.) (1997), *The Hélène Cixous Reader* (London and New York: Routledge).

Schiach, Morag (1991), *Hélène Cixous: A Politics of Writing* (London and New York: Routledge).

Shelley, Percy Bysshe (1977), 'A Defence of Poetry' [1821], in *The Romantic Reader*, ed. and intro. by Howard E. Hugo (Harmondsworth: Penguin), pp. 533–41.

Showalter, Elaine (1977), *A Literature of their Own: British Women Novelists from Brontë to Lessing* (Princeton, NJ: Princeton University Press).

Showalter, Elaine (1992), 'Towards a Feminist Poetics', in *The New Feminist Criticism: Essays on Women, Literature and Theory*, ed. Elaine Showalter (London: Virago), pp. 125–43.

Sollers, Philippe (1968), *L'Ecriture et l'expérience des limites* (Paris: Éditions du Seuil).

Spinoza, Benedictus de (1949), *Ethics*, trans. William Hale White (New York: Hafner).

Spivak, Gayatri (1987), 'French Feminism in an International Frame', in *Other Worlds: Essays in Cultural Politics* (New York: Methuen).

Stallybrass, Peter and Allon White (1989), *The Politics and Poetics of Transgression* (London: Methuen).

Suleiman, Susan Rubin (1990), *Subversive Intent: Gender, Politics and the Avant-Garde* (Cambridge, MA: Harvard University Press).

Suleiman, Susan Rubin (1994), *Risking Who One Is: Encounters with Contemporary Art and Literature* (Cambridge, MA, and London: Harvard University Pres).

Tapper, Marion (1993), 'Ressentiment and Power: Some Reflections on Feminist Practices', in Paul Patton (ed.), *Nietzsche, Feminism and Political Theory* (New York: Routledge), pp. 130–43.

Unkeless, Elaine and Suzette Henke (eds) (1982), *Women in Joyce* (Urbana, IL: University of Illinois Press).

Weiss, Gail (1999), 'The Durée of the Techno-Body', in *Becomings: Explorations in Time, Memory, and Futures*, ed. Elizabeth Grosz (Ithaca, NY: Cornell University Press), pp. 161–75.

Wolf, Naomi (1990), *The Beauty Myth* (London: Chatto and Windus).

Wolff, Janet (1990), *Feminine Sentences: Essays on Women and Culture* (Cambridge: Polity Press).

Wollstonecraft, Mary (1992), *A Vindication of the Rights of Woman*, ed. Miriam Brody (Harmondsworth: Penguin).

Woolf, Virginia (1987), *A Room of One's Own* (London: Grafton Books).

Woolf, Virginia (1989), *The Waves* (London: Grafton Books).

Woolf, Virginia (1992), *To the Lighthouse*, ed. and intro. Margaret Drabble (Oxford: Oxford University Press).

Yeats, William Butler (1974a), 'Easter 1916', in *Poems of W. B. Yeats*, ed. A. Norman Jeffares (London: Macmillan), 91–3.

Yeats, William Butler (1974b), 'The Second Coming', in *Poems of W. B. Yeats*, ed. A. Norman Jeffares (London: Macmillan), pp. 97–8.

Index